RECONCILING
CATHOLICISM
AND FEMINISM?

RECONCILING CATHOLICISM AND FEMINISM?

PERSONAL REFLECTIONS

ON TRADITION AND CHANGE

Foreword by Sandra M. Gilbert

Edited by
SALLY BARR EBEST
and
RON EBEST

UNIVERSITY OF NOTRE DAME PRESS

Notre Dame, Indiana

Copyright © 2003 by University of Notre Dame
Notre Dame, Indiana 46556
www.undpress.nd.edu
All Rights Reserved

Manufactured in the United States of America

Library of Congress Cataloging-in-Publication Data
Reconciling Catholicism and feminism? : personal reflections on
tradition and change / edited by Sally Barr Ebest and Ron Ebest;
foreword by Sandra M. Gilbert.
p. cm.
Includes index.
ISBN 0-268-04014-1 (cloth : alk. paper)
ISBN 0-268-04020-6 (pbk. : alk. paper)
1. Women in the Catholic Church.   2. Feminism—Religious
aspects—Catholic Church.   3. Catholic Church—Doctrines.
I. Ebest, Sally Barr.   II. Ebest, Ron, 1956–
BX2347.8.W6 R42   2003
282'.082—dc21
  2003009071

∞*This book is printed on acid-free paper.*

For Ron Ebest, Sr.

CONTENTS

PART II   Looking Ahead: Feminism and Catholicism
in the Next Generation

FOREWORD
In the Stone Forests of Yearning

Sandra M. Gilbert

This fascinating collection of essays—rich in the range of Catholic attitudes it represents, complex in the variety of feminist strategies it offers—reminds me that I am and am not a Catholic.

Am a Catholic because I was raised as one: despite some ambivalence on my parents' part, I was baptized, sent to "religious instruction," guided into a First Communion, confirmed, and even, for a while in high school, deeply engaged in an exhilarating, "born again" Catholic dialogue with a favorite local priest. Am *not* a Catholic because that "born again" feeling didn't last very long, my faith collapsed (as did my bond to the mentoring priest), and I ceased the ongoing "practice" of *any* religion, despite nostalgic longings to return to what often feels like the safety of the Church's mystical community.

Am a Catholic because I continue to admire the power and beauty of the institutional structures and achievements that surrounded me as I was growing up: the solemn liturgy of the mass, the brilliant argumentation of the Church fathers. Am *not* a Catholic precisely because those structures for so long and so nakedly embodied—and perpetuated—the assumptions and oppressions of a patriarchal culture that defines those of us who are women as secondary and inferior, indeed as basically vessels for the transmission of physical life.

Am a Catholic because I almost never enter a church without light-ing a candle for the souls of those I love who are dead, often cross myself before the altar, frequently even want to take Communion when the mass reaches its crisis of transformation. *Am* a Catholic or would-be Catholic because as I wander through the great cathedrals of Europe with their immense columns and arches reaching ceaselessly upward, those spaces seem to me to be stone forests of yearning, emblems of our human desire for something we don't have here and now in the flesh. Am *not* a Catholic because I'm not sure we can ever have the transfigu-ration for which we yearn. Am *not* a Catholic because in subordinating me as a woman the hierarchical theology of the Church essentially dis-allows those very yearnings that might have otherwise brought me to the altar.

Most of the deeply thoughtful women whose writings are assembled in this rewarding volume start from a position of faith, a stance I envy them. Victoria Kill, one of the contributors represented here, summarizes the central problem these writers address when she defines herself as part of a "large community" of feminists "who contest the boundaries of Catholic identity as defined by the Vatican, not in spite of but precisely because we passionately embrace participation in the Catholic commu-nity." Thus, as the book's editors note, quoting another contributor, "Most Catholic feminists, embracing faith but 'full of pain, anger and frustration with the Church,' live in a state of resistance"—resistance not so much to the theological tenets of their religion as to the institutional structures and strictures that have arisen from those tenets. In other words, to the extent that one can separate faith in certain theological doctrines from acquiescence in what many proponents of those doctrines claim as necessary consequences of that belief, these women feel able to reconcile their (spiritual) Catholicism with their (political) feminism.

As I read through their essays, I realize that my own ambivalence toward the Church may be even deeper and more recalcitrant than most of the misgivings I encounter on these pages. My problems with the faith—the rock—on which the Church is founded are probably as deep-seated as my worries about the culture that faith has shaped.

At the moment, I'm working on a book about what the great twentieth-century American poet Wallace Stevens called "the mythology of modern death," so I've spent a lot of time thinking about our representations of God and the soul, about our notions of the afterlife, about faith and doubt, heaven and hell. There's a story (perhaps apocryphal) that Stevens, among the most famously skeptical of thinkers, was converted to Catholicism not long before he died, and I often wonder whether this poet, who had a "day job" as an insurance executive, was buying himself a kind of insurance. Perhaps he was accepting the well-known wager proposed by the seventeenth-century mathematician-philosopher Blaise Pascal: "Let us weigh the gain and the loss in wagering that God is. . . . If you gain, you gain all; if you lose, you lose nothing. Wager, then, without hesitation that He is."

Though I was oblivious of probability theory, my earliest education in theology must have in some sense been shaped by that wager—a wager on which Pascal himself acted with deep fervor in his last years, just as Stevens may have, along with many other twentieth-century writers I revere. T. S. Eliot, for instance, accepted in principle the Credo of the Roman Catholic Church, although as a devout, lifelong Anglophile he chose instead to be baptized into the Church of England. But when I was a teenage "born-again" Catholic myself, the struggle for redemption and salvation dramatized in Eliot's long, intricate poem "Ash Wednesday" fascinated me.

"Teach us to care and not to care/Teach us to sit still," implored Eliot, adding—from the Hail Mary—"Pray for us sinners now and at the hour of our death." And then, even more explicitly celebrating the "Lady of silences," he offered,

> Grace to the Mother
> For the Garden
> Where all love ends.

Although Eliot's philosophical and theological expertise was way beyond me, I intuited that, perhaps even more than Christmas and Easter Sunday, this day of which he was writing—this day of monitory warning, contrition, and repentance—was at the heart of the human problem the Church seeks to address.

Ashes to ashes, dust to dust. Dust thou art, and unto dust thou shalt return.

Even as a child studying the catechism every Wednesday afternoon during what the New York City school system rather curiously defined as "released time"—time "released" from regular studies, I suppose, but not, surely, from the hardship of education—I was frightened and vaguely sickened by Ash Wednesday. Since those of us who were "released" to learn more about the faith into which we had been born were in any case spending each Wednesday afternoon at the parochial school associated with our local church, St. Joan of Arc, it was easy and efficient to lead us in a solemn if straggly line from the classroom, where we'd been taught that God was infinite, omnipotent, and immortal, to the altar, where we were to be reminded that we ourselves were finite, powerless, and mortal.

Still in winter coats or jackets, breath still marking the cold not-yet-spring air with little clouds of our own warmth, we stumbled from the brightness outside into the dark of the church, which seemed especially gloomy on this especially scary day. The priest, in liturgical purple signifying death and grief, loomed mysteriously behind the railing that surrounded the sanctuary. I remember the ferocity, so it seemed to me, with which his thumb dug into my forehead, marking it with a cross of ashes. I remember the grim satisfaction, so it seemed to me, with which he muttered his sacred Latin phrases more *at* me than *to* me, words in an indecipherable undertone that were said to mean "Ashes to ashes, dust to dust," or "Dust thou art and unto dust thou shalt return," or both, I was never sure which.

"On this day," the *Catholic Encyclopedia* tells us, "all the faithful according to ancient custom are exhorted to approach the altar . . . and there the priest, dipping his thumb into ashes previously blessed, marks the forehead—or in case [*sic*] of clerics upon the place of the tonsure—of each with the sign of the cross, saying the words 'Remember man that thou art dust and unto dust thou shalt return.'"

On these occasions, as I recall, I brooded a good deal on my relationship to "dust," which I visualized as the little gray balls of fluff that my mother's mop would retrieve from under my bed. Was *I* originally made of such dust? Was I destined, then, to drift off or down (under a bed, for instance) as mere fluff?

At the same time, there was the question of ashes. These I imagined, the way any city child of the time probably would have, as the smelly gray-white leavings of cigarettes and cigars that were heaped in ashtrays after the grownups had finished smoking their Old Golds or Pall Malls or Havana Specials.

As for the mark the priest made on my forehead, it often elicited gales of laughter from Jewish or Protestant school friends whom I encountered on the street as I made my nervous way home from St. Joan's. "Your face is dirty, face is dirty, dirty, dirty," they'd taunt. Why did the priest, a holy man, want to put *dirt* on my skin?

Comical as my puzzlement may seem now, though, I don't remember finding it funny *then*. Though I may have misunderstood the symbolism of dust and ashes, I knew from the hollow feeling I got as I stood before the altar, as the hand of the priest descended toward my head, as he said his strangely indecipherable words, just what the occasion meant.

You started out as next to nothing, you came *from nothingness, and you'll end up as next to nothing again on your way* back *to nothingness.*

"The ashes used in this ceremony," adds the *Catholic Encyclopedia,* "are made by burning the remains of the palms blessed on the Palm Sunday of the previous year."

The palms of victory will inexorably become the ashes of defeat. Entering Jerusalem in triumph, Christ himself, son and body of God, exited bearing the cross on which He himself was destined to journey toward the gray pall of death.

Not even the great stone forests of the cathedrals that the Church built in response to human yearnings could conceal the terror of extinction toward which the priest's ashen finger, his sepulchral words, pointed us annually. *Timor mortis conturbat me,* complained the medieval poets and clerics, including, often enough, the most faithful among them. "The fear of death confounds, dismays, *perturbs* me!"

And did I believe that after dwindling into a bit of fluff under the bed or a heap of ashes in a little dish some part of me would "expire" into the bosom of a transcendent Father? So, arrayed in celestially white organdy, I told the bishop, daunting in his sacerdotal costume, his tall proud miter, on the day I was confirmed. Like the priest's on Ash Wednesday, yet very differently, his holy finger came down onto my forehead, carving in the sign of the cross, this time in godly oil, to mark me as one of the saved.

To be saved, though, I had had to memorize the knotty narrative of the Apostles' Creed, with its rush of clauses, its piling on of theological pointers. And perhaps because at heart I was a "modern" child, imbued with an increasingly modern dread of an increasingly tenuous, indeed absent, "hereafter," I suffered terribly at this task, stumbled in my recitation, couldn't seem to make dramatic or rhetorical sense of what I was saying: *I believe in God, the Father Almighty, Creator of heaven and earth; and in Jesus Christ, His only Son, our Lord . . . born of the Virgin Mary . . . crucified, died, and was buried . . . arose again from the dead . . . ascended into heaven . . . shall come to judge the living and the dead . . . communion of Saints . . . resurrection of the body . . . life everlasting.*

If someone had asked me that day, as I fidgeted in the procession of children assembled before the stately bishop, did I truly *believe* in the beliefs—the Credo—I was enunciating, I'm not sure what I'd have said or thought. How did I imagine the risen Christ? What did I think, to come right down to it, about the possibility of an ultimate restoration of my own body? And did I suppose that if I died in a "state of grace" at that sacramental minute of confirmation I'd go straight to some sort of heaven?

Meditating on these questions now, so many years after the event, I can barely begin to construct answers. Good Friday always absorbed and frightened me, much as Ash Wednesday did. We children had been very specifically "instructed" that as Jesus hung on the cross, in the afternoon hours between three and five, God the Father was so displeased that the sky blackened, the earth quaked and gave up its dead. This all seemed quite real and right to me; brooding in the darkened church, I contemplated the sufferings of Our Lord with pity and anxiety and felt deep sympathy, too, for the onlookers who were flung about like straws in the wind by the divine wrath that was causing rocks and tombs to tremble. But the risen Christ? Maybe because my family wasn't truly religious, I pictured him as standing in a kind of gigantic sugar egg, the whole festooned with candy roses, for baskets and sweets, rather than spirits and miracles, signified Easter to me.

Yet in thoughts of my own resurrection I was relatively provident, as I recall, and remained so for many years, always wondering what would happen if I lost a limb or, once organ donation became common, gave up a kidney or liver: how, then, could I rise radiant and whole on the latter day? Did I truly believe, though, that at some point, soon after death but long before my bones could be reassembled and newly fleshed, I'd fly upward into a dazzling empyrean? I know I worried a lot about hell and purgatory so perhaps in some yearning part of my mind I had visions of a place not unlike the ancient Greek Isles of the Blessed, about which I read in Bulfinch's *Mythology*, where people and things were edged with hard lines of radiance and everyone strolled in a glow of satisfaction among friends and relatives. But if I did somewhere, somehow, have that vision, it wasn't very compelling.

And by the time I was old enough and at least relatively sophisticated enough to reimagine the Church's teachings less naively, new intellectual obstacles had arisen to impede any progress I might have made in my pilgrimage toward faith. For if even as a child I stumbled over the majestic narrative of the Credo, despite its powerful assertions of faith and mystical promise of spiritual transformation, as an adult woman I had to confront the place of womanhood itself in that story—and I stumbled over that too.

To be sure, as countless writers on Marian theology and on the very concept of the Great Mother have pointed out, the Virgin Mary is a figure of queenly redemptiveness. "That the 'fruit of the womb' contains the Incarnation itself is an extraordinarily powerful idea," as Mary Kenny, one of the contributors to this volume, rightly notes. God needed *woman* in order to incarnate himself as a *man*. But of course, as Kenny also says, this means that "the Hail Mary resonates with a strongly prolife message," reminding us of what for feminists must almost always be the Church's vexing views on abortion and contraception, indeed on female reproductive rights in general. In addition, however, I suspect that though I wasn't entirely conscious of just what bothered me when in my early teens I faltered at my catechism, I must have intuited the heavenly hierarchy implicit in the tale the Credo tells: God is *spirit* and *male*, his vessel, Mary, is *flesh* and *female*. And for this reason, God's Church both uses and subordinates woman, who comes—as *mater*—to represent precisely the mater-ial world that the divine spirit seeks to transcend.

By now, so much has been written about this point that it doesn't need much expansion or reiteration. But that doesn't mean that the patriarchal power structure Mary has been forced to embody ceases to oppress or distress. Hanging on one of the walls in the room where I'm writing these words is a copy of Lorenzo Lotto's astonishing 1527 *Annunciation,* a work whose scene of implacable heavenly will and worldly tumult seems to me to summarize much of what is distressing in the Church's view of female instrumentality.

In the upper right corner of Lotto's painting, a fiercely virile, bearded God the Father leans out of a whirling cloud, his hand aimed toward the Virgin, who cowers on the lower left, her gown and cape blowing in the wind of God's passion. Behind her are a large, dark-curtained bed, a book on a *prie-dieu,* a mantel, garments, some other furnishings—the things of this world, its dust and ashes. We who know the story know that she's to become a sacred intermediary, T. S. Eliot's "Lady of silences," but here, now, in this painting, she's ducking as if to avoid a bolt of lightning, and her hands are flattened in front of her as if she were pressing against the glass of the picture frame in a vain effort to escape.

Just below God, the Angel of the Annunciation has been flung into the room, one hand raised and gesturing upward, the other bearing the usual symbolic lily. Like Mary's clothing, his swirl of celestial finery is in some disarray, as if he too had been hastened into his place by the exigencies of the story in which he has to play his crucial part. And between God and the angel on the one side of the picture and Mary on the other, a small gray cat flees across the floor, its fur on end, its head turned toward the angel as it looks anxiously over its shoulder at the divine presences.

Here is one of the paradigmatic encounters that has shaped the thinking of what Kierkegaard called "Christendom"—the socialized Western world that takes its shape from unexamined assumptions based on the Christian story. God the (male) spirit utters the Word; and if even the frightened cat seems to want to get away, Mary the (female) flesh is even more desperate, in this iteration of the plot, to escape the confining definitions of the narrative. But in particular Mary seems to me desperate to escape because, as her books and prie-dieu suggest, she (unlike the cat) is a creature of spirit, language, ideation. In this particular painting, in fact, she doesn't want to be the "Lady of silences."

Figuratively speaking, have Mary's yearnings—for speech, authority, and power as well as for transcendence and transfiguration—helped shape those stone forests still ruled by the fathers of the Church? If so, how can we acknowledge *her* desire, *her* being?

And perhaps, even more to the point, how can the Catholic feminists of the present and the future reshape the theological structures of the past so that Mary and her descendants needn't be merely vessels (or vassals) of patriarchal rule? Despite my own disquieting doubts, my failures of faith, I still revere the beautiful meanings of the mass. Yet like Lotto's Mary, along with many other women, I want to get out of the picture if there's no way of reconciling my own selfhood with the adamant structures bestowed by a history that has institutionalized a forest of human yearnings. Ron Ebest and Sally Barr Ebest have put together a collection of essays that forcefully addresses these crucial issues haunting the sexual politics of theology.

ACKNOWLEDGMENTS

As with any project of this size, we owe debts of gratitude to a number of people. Special thanks to Charles Fanning, director of Irish Studies at Southern Illinois University–Carbondale. Charlie not only introduced us to Irish studies; he also strongly supported our ideas, urged us to pursue them, and suggested we contact the Chicago historian Ellen Skerrett because of her ties to Catholic feminists around the country. We are grateful for Ellen's suggestions to contact Katherine Tobin and Kate Joyce and to submit our prospectus to the University of Notre Dame Press. We also want to thank Jeff Gainey, Notre Dame's associate director, who enthusiastically endorsed the project and provided invaluable advice; Jeff's editorial assistant, Christina Catanzarite, who cheerfully and efficiently answered our many queries; and Barbara Hanrahan, the press's director, who supported our efforts.

Thanks go to Judith Wilt, who, upon seeing the call for papers, invited us to the National Association of Women and Catholic Education (NAWCHE) at Boston College to describe the project and solicit contributors. Her efforts led us to Victoria Kill, Lorraine Liscio, and Jeanne Noonan-Eckholdt. Thanks to Eamonn Wall, University of Missouri (UM)–St. Louis Jefferson Smurfit Chair of Irish Studies, and Joel Glassman, director of the Center for International Studies at UM–St. Louis, who provided funding to attend NAWCHE. Thanks also to the UM–St. Louis Institute for Women's and Gender Studies for providing us the opportunity to present our ideas and offering solid feedback.

Thanks to Maeve Binchy, who suggested we contact her friend Mary Kenny; to Elizabeth Rankin, at the University of North Dakota, who led us to Nancy Mairs; and to Clare Fischer, at the University of California–Berkeley, who recommended Jean Molesky-Poz. Thanks also to Jim Rogers, managing editor of the *New Hibernia Review* at the University of St. Thomas, for his advice regarding sites in which to solicit proposals, and to Nan Sweet, former director of the UM–St. Louis Institute for Women's and Gender Studies, who led us to Flavia Alaya and Sandra M. Gilbert.

Thanks to Robert Bliss, dean of the UM–St. Louis Honors College, for allowing us to offer a seminar on Irish American women writers; thanks also to the students in that seminar—Fawn, Stephanie, Heather, Charlotte, Julie, and Rebecca—for their ideas, insights, and evolving feminisms.

Needless to say, this collection would not have been possible without our contributors. We are grateful for their willingness to share their personal and professional experiences as feminists, Catholics, and teachers of future generations of Catholics, feminists, and feminist Catholics.

Finally, thanks to the Barr family for their interest, encouragement, and support. And thanks especially to the Ebest family for teaching us, by example, what it means to be a good Catholic.

Sally Barr Ebest and Ron Ebest

INTRODUCTION

This book represents the collective contemplation, observation, and argumentation of an important group of scholars, theologians, essayists, teachers, and writers about the most pressing question facing the Roman Catholic Church at the turn of the twenty-first century: Is it possible to be both a faithful Catholic and a progressive, independent, even feminist, thinker?

For some people, like those friends of scholar Janet Kalven who have "been ordained priests in the Episcopal Church or have joined other denominations," who "refuse to have a daughter baptized—'too damaging for her self-esteem,'" or who have moved "away from Christianity altogether," the question is moot. Indeed, they have satisfactorily answered it. Others follow the example of the nineteenth-century American Catholic novelist Mary Anne Madden Sadlier, who, according to historian Mary Jo T. Marcellus, opposed feminism because it appeared to involve a break from tradition. For these women the question is equally moot; they have arrived at a much different, though for them, at least, equally satisfying, conclusion. But for women like the essayist Nancy Mairs, committed simultaneously to a progressive feminist ideology and to the Eucharist, or like the historian Linda McMillin, who rejects "the patriarchal god of [my] childhood" while still finding "meaning in the rhythm of a weekly liturgy celebrated in a community of faith," the question gnaws. It is for such women (and men) that these essays, representing a spectrum of opinions, philosophies, and stories, in a score of voices, have been compiled.

Reconciling Catholicism and feminism is no easy task. The most glaring problem, of course, is the Church's historical maltreatment of women, a fault Pope John Paul II has himself acknowledged. This problem has manifested itself in various ways. The memoirist Flavia Alaya, for example, has traced a connection between the twelfth-century proclamation by Pope Innocent III forbidding priests to marry and the "pudency, if not outright disgust," with which some early prelates associated sexuality and women. Effectively, she argues, misogyny in part accounts for the "principle of (male) asexual political superiority" with which an exclusively male Church hierarchy has exercised power for some eight centuries. The issue is especially poignant for Alaya, whose own long-term relationship with the late Father Harry Browne has provoked her to contemplate the human impact of a celibate priesthood.

But even sacramentalized Catholic marriage has proven troubling to some women. As Nancy Mairs observes, the Church "takes its very identity from a marital model based on domination and subordination: Christ is the Bridegroom; the Church, the Bride; and there's no mistaking who's in charge of whom." That the Church, in identifying itself with the Bride, has made "the feminine element . . . a symbol of all that is 'human'" is cold comfort. "Listen, guys," Mairs observes, "you can take it from me, being a woman in our society, even a purely symbolic one, is not all that hot." Equally troubling is the Church's prohibition against divorce. "To the extent that the Church intends to support and strengthen me in fulfilling that [marriage] vow, I'm grateful," observes Mairs, whose essay "Dis/Re/Com/Union" is a meditation on the perils and pleasures of lifelong fidelity. ". . . But in effect, the Church's stand seems more coercive and punitive than supportive." The scholar Victoria Kill, whose essay "After Sufficient Reflection: Catholic, Feminist, and Divorced" is a painstaking (and painful) recounting of her own divorce, agrees. "There is a large community of us," she asserts, "who contest the boundaries of Catholic identity as defined by the Vatican, not in spite of but precisely because we passionately embrace participation in Catholic community."

Examples of even more overt Church-sanctioned discrimination against women surface. Janet Kalven, a former leader of the women's theological movement called the Grail, recalls in "Feminism and Catholicism" the roadblocks presented by prelates whose intransigence ultimately caused her break with Catholicism. "My problems with the Church increased as I saw the great gap between the gospel values and the behavior of too many churchmen," she recalls. "When I talked to contemporary women working in Church structures, I heard . . . stories of gross injustice and contempt for women and their contributions." The problem is obviously exacerbated in countries whose governments are bound more closely to the Church. "My experience as a Catholic woman has been full of traditions that view women as objects," writes former Catholic Nilsa Lasso-von Lang of her youth in Panama. ". . . As a Hispanic, I know very well that in Latin American society a woman's mission and reason for being is still 'reproduction.'"

Of course, "reproduction" occupies the center of this debate; the moral dilemma posed by abortion rights may well be the most difficult one Catholic feminists face. "Even as I continue to defend the legal right to abortion," ruminates Kathleen Joyce, "I find myself moved by the Church's compelling defense and embrace of life. By asserting that all lives are of equal value, the Catholic Church dignifies the lives of all people, from the socially privileged to those marginalized by, among other things, poverty, race, or disability. The power of the Catholic faith for me lies in this celebration of life as an incontestable good." Adds the Irish journalist Mary Kenny:

> There are too many hidden agendas within the Irish collective consciousness to regard abortion as a simple issue of personal choice or to imagine that there can be an easy reconciliation between the issue of feminism and Catholicism. . . . Fertility is even intertwined in traditional Irish drinking toasts. "Health and long life to you; land without rent to you; a child every year to you; and death in Ireland."

Historically, of course, American feminism and Catholicism have often found themselves at odds. Mary Anne Sadlier, as Mary Jo T. Marcellus points out, rejected feminism in part because anti-Irishness and anti-Catholicism were staples of the nineteenth-century women's rights campaign. Suffrage newspapers, she notes, stereotyped Irish women and men as ignorant, lacking common sense, possessed of violent tempers, and supine before a foreign ecclesiastical authority. As the historian Rosemary Radford Ruether notes, "The women's suffrage movement itself was led by middle-class Protestant women and shared an American reform culture that was implicitly anti-Catholic. When feminism became linked with temperance at the turn of the century the anti-Catholic bias sometimes became explicit, vilifying the growing Catholic working-class political leadership of cities, such as Boston and Chicago, as the epitome of 'rum, Romanism, and rebellion.'" And as the historian Kathleen A. Tobin observes, the early birth control movement proved even more troubling. By taking a series of contradictory and even incoherent stands on the issue of artificial contraception, the American Church hierarchy earned the vilification heaped upon it by activists like Margaret Sanger. But not all Catholic antipathy to the movement was unjustified. Emerging from the same Progressive-era ideology that spawned eugenics theory, the birth control movement tried to persuade the middle classes that contraception would prevent the proliferation of the "feeble-minded," inferior, and predominately Catholic urban working class.

Yet not every encounter between women and the Church has been agonistic. When the scholar Jane Zeni filed for divorce, her parish "loved and supported me through the process. . . . After the divorce, I found that joint custody was beyond the grasp of our city and public school officials (when my younger son was suspended, the school notified his father, who happened to be out of town), but the secretary at church routinely sent notices to my children at both households. Amusing, I thought: the institution that didn't recognize divorce in theory dealt with it best in practice." Similarly, journalist Madeleine Blais's memoir *"Serviam"* recalls an intervention by an Ursuline nun that "in a way" helped the young Blais and her sisters come to grips with what was certainly the most traumatic collective event of the postwar era for American Catholics—the Kennedy assassination.

Given this tangled and combative history, one must ask: Is it even possible to reconcile feminists and Catholics? "*Reconciliation* might be too kindly and too inert a term for feminism's reaction with Catholicism," observes writer Jean McGarry. ". . . The action of one on the other is volatile and doesn't bring about a clean, easy, or permanent resolution. *Dialectic* or *struggle* might be a better term—I seem to have favored the word *correction,* which carries with it the mortifying but bracing lash of a long-lasting Catholic education." Janet Kalven agrees. "By far the largest number of feminists I am acquainted with," she observes, "would answer the question with 'conflictual but possible.'" What this means is that most Catholic feminists, embracing faith but "full of pain, anger, and frustration with the Church," live in a state of resistance.

This resistance is expressed in many ways. Some women negotiate a separate peace with their consciences by rejecting outright those Church teachings they cannot abide. "Many people do not go along with every-thing the Church says, with 'Church rules,'" observes one of Theresa Delgadillo's students, when Delgadillo asks whether it is possible to be both a lesbian and a Catholic. "But that doesn't mean that they don't have faith. For example, the Church says that we're not supposed to have sex before marriage, but most people don't follow that. Because I wear a cross around my neck doesn't mean that I do what the Church tells me. And because I do not follow 'all the rules' does not make me less of a Catholic."

For others, resistance implies a programmatic response. In "American Catholic Feminism: A History," Rosemary Radford Ruether charts the development of the major feminist movements within the Church, movements whose collective goal has been to expose and eliminate the Church's "institutionalized injustice." Among those movements are the Leadership Conference of Women Religious, the Grail, the Catholic Family Movement, the Women's Ordination Conference, the Women-Church Conference, and Catholics for a Free Choice, whose board includes Radford Ruether herself, and whose goals are the preservation of reproductive choice and the articulation of "a counterview on sexu-ality" to that promoted by the hierarchy. "Although the official Church [seems] more determined than ever to deny the feminist critique on issues of sexuality and ministry," Rosemary Radford Ruether observes, "the vehemence with which the Vatican seeks to silence such questions itself points to the actual success of Catholic feminism in gaining a wide and sympathetic audience for its issues among American Catholics." Theologian Jean Molesky-Poz agrees that Catholic feminists have an obligation to engage in "an insistent, determined movement to be visible, articulate, and public in the Church" and argues that "women have lived too long in a Church where the authority has been male, where men have been deferred to, where Father knows best.' We, as women, some as mothers of daughters and sons, have too much at stake for ourselves and for future generations."

For still others, programmatic resistance means the education of those future generations. "Over the course of a single semester," writes Sally Barr Ebest, "my undergraduate honors students moved beyond stereotypes to an understanding that feminism, like Catholicism, is not a monolithic structure. Through our readings and discussions, they began to perceive that beneath the rubric of feminism, numerous factions, theories, and theorists exist within a system that tends to sway with, if not reflect, sociocultural, economic, and political trends." But educators of the next generation are apt to find challenges to reconciliation that defy the interventions even of the feminist classroom. "For a majority of students coming from strong Catholic backgrounds," asserts Lorraine Liscio, "a room of their own where they might imagine themselves as autonomous agents who can go beyond the father produces great anxiety."

Overcoming the impact of this entrenched conservative ideology may pose the greatest challenge to Catholic feminist educators. One emerging strategy is to help young Catholic feminists understand the issues in the debate by studying the lives and works of past Catholic women. Henrik Borgstrom's juxtaposition of the fifteenth-century French writer Christine de Pizan against the work of the twentieth-century Canadian dramatist Denise Boucher permits his students to "consider a traditionally male-dominated faith system through a feminist lens." The result is encouraging: "[F]or several weeks in an academic and literary setting, a small group of women had the opportunity to engage in open discussions about the choices and questions they often face when imagining their identity in the context of the Church. . . . [I]t is quite revealing to hear young people debating fundamental questions of their belief systems." Similarly, Brad Peters's students, having read the work of the fourteenth-century mystic Julian of Norwich, discover "a model of prayer" that "opens up discursive spaces where women's voices and spiritual experiences can feminize collective memory, thereby transforming public dialogue in the Church." Such engagements, suggests Sally Barr Ebest, help students understand that "neither feminism nor

Catholicism is a perfect entity. Although one was designed by women and the other by men, both bear traces of the times in which they were conceived."

This volume, then, is an attempt to offer answers to an increasingly pressing question: Can progressivism and feminism be reconciled with Catholicism? Despite papal intransigence, there is some reason to feel sanguine about the possibilities of reform. For one thing, in the United States, at least, surveys consistently demonstrate that lay Catholics are considerably more sympathetic to progressivism than is the Vatican. Further, the Church's own history endorses reform. It is a cherished belief among many Catholics that the Church is "timeless." In fact, nothing could be further from the truth. As a number of studies have demonstrated,[1] the Church is a "survival organization" par excellence, its continued growth through the ages reflecting not "changelessness" but on the contrary an aptitude for evolution. Since the reign of Constantine, the Church's practical policy has been to adapt itself at least partially to surrounding power structures in order to preserve a handful of core doctrines. Indeed, as the sociologists John Seidler and Katherine Meyer have argued, many of the aspects of contemporary Catholicism that most concern progressives—its patriarchal mentality, hierarchical structure, and bureaucratic methodologies—are not Catholic products but examples of outside structures annexed over the ages by the Church to facilitate its interactions with the surrounding world. This is not to underestimate the Church's facility for entrenchment: the period between the Reformation and the Second Vatican Council is rather a remarkable span of inertia. Still, Vatican II *has* presented contemporary Catholics with the tools for change. And despite his conservatism, John Paul II's various overtures to women, to Jews, to Muslims, to Greek Orthodox Catholics, and to other groups, as well as his famous "apology," his denunciation of the gap between the world's richest and poorest nations, and his willingness to intervene in political situations such as the Israeli-Palestinian conflict in the Middle East, demonstrate a sophisticated awareness of the relationship between the Church's ability to accommodate itself to the contemporary world and its ability to thrive. How far-reaching such accommodations might prove to be— and whether in a succeeding papacy they will include the incorporation of a more democratic, power-sharing structure upon which reform depends—remains to be seen. In the meantime, discussions like those contained in, and, one hopes, prompted by, these essays are one valuable means for keeping progressivism in the forefront of the Catholic debate.

NOTE

1. See John Seidler and Katherine Meyer, *Conflict and Change in the Catholic Church* (New Brunswick, N.J.: Rutgers University Press, 1989).

PART ONE

Looking Back:
Feminism and Catholicism
in the Twentieth Century

ONE

American Catholic Feminism: A History

Rosemary Radford Ruether

There was virtually no organized Catholic participation in the first wave of American feminism that extended from the First Women's Rights Convention in Seneca Falls, New York, in 1848 to the winning of women's suffrage in 1920. The reasons for this lie in several factors. First, the Catholic bishops were vehemently opposed to feminism, associating it with a secular modern apostasy from Christian and "family" values, represented by child labor laws, the Equal Rights Amendment, birth control, divorce, liberalism, and socialism. Many bishops explicitly rejected women's suffrage itself, claiming that it would take women out of their proper sphere in the family.[1]

Second, the women's suffrage movement was led by middle-class Protestant women and shared an American reform culture that was implicitly anti-Catholic. When feminism became linked with temperance at the turn of the century, the anti-Catholic bias sometimes became explicit, vilifying the growing Catholic working-class political leadership of cities, such as Boston and Chicago, as the epitome of "rum, Romanism, and rebellion." This marriage of Protestant temperance, feminism, and anti-Catholicism reached its apogee in the attack on the presidential candidacy of Al E. Smith in 1928.[2]

This does not mean that Catholic women were not politically and socially active in the late nineteenth century and the first half of the twentieth century. But they were active either in defense of class and ethnic interests or as Catholics engaged in forming and founding institutions to spread Catholicism, and not as women engaged in an explicitly prowoman agenda. Thus, Catholic nuns who outnumbered priests by four to one at the turn of the century were the backbone of a pioneering Catholic evangelization of the continent, founding not only churches but hospitals, schools, orphanages, old age homes, and other social service institutions.[3]

Irish women such as Elizabeth Flynn Rogers, Mary Kenny O'Sullivan, Lonora Barry, and Mother Jones were engaged in union organizing on behalf of women as well as male workers as part of the labor movement. Although there was some support for the labor movement among a few bishops and priests, this was based on the presupposition of winning for men a "family wage" that would allow women to stay home as "full-time mothers and wives." Thus, clerical Catholic support for labor did not extend to women's labor organizing. Some Catholic women labor leaders, like Mother Jones, were vehemently anticlerical, but most did not make a public issue of their Catholicism. Women from predominantly Catholic ethnic groups were also active in forming ethnic cultural and mutual benefit societies, such as the Fenian Sisterhood and the Polish Women's Alliance, and these enjoyed good support from priests, often meeting in ethnic parishes, but again the focus was not on the promotion of a woman's agenda explicitly.[4]

From 1920 to 1950, there were several Catholic lay movements, led by women, that aimed at a combination of social reform and the deepening of one's faith. Many of these became the seedbed for the Catholic left of the 1960s, and some developed an explicitly feminist perspective. The most famous of these was the Catholic Worker, founded by Dorothy Day with the French peasant philosopher Peter Maurin in 1933. Explicitly socialist-anarchist, it was and continues to be an expression of a kind of Catholic radicalism that combines ascetic renunciation of wealth with service to the "down and out."

But Day herself was conservative in liturgical matters and unsympathetic to feminism, particularly to birth control, and this continues to be the perspective of the Catholic Worker (focusing today on the "seamless garment" argument against abortion). Another somewhat similar movement that drew scores of dedicated young Catholic women to the "slums" in the 1950s was Friendship House, which focused on both poverty and racial discrimination against blacks in urban America.[5]

Several other Catholic movements of laywomen, laymen, and women religious, however, became seedbeds of Catholic feminism. These were the Sister Formation Movement, the Catholic Family Movement (CFM), and the Grail. The Sister Formation Movement arose from efforts of Sister Madeleva Wolff, president of St. Mary's College in Notre Dame, Indiana, and other nun-educators, beginning in 1948, to remedy the poor educational opportunities of American Catholic nuns, many of whom were being pressed into parochial school teaching in their early twenties without a college education.

Ironically, Catholic nuns, who had been the pioneers since the eighteenth century in establishing schools from grade school through college to educate Catholic women and girls, found themselves educationally deprived in the first half of the twentieth century vis-à-vis a new generation of women professionals who were earning college and graduate degrees. Bishops, anxious for the cheap and abundant labor provided by Catholic women religious in schools and hospitals, often assumed that they did not need advanced education to do this work.

Madeleva Wolff and others organized a campaign to ensure that Catholic sisters would receive a college education as well as adequate religious studies before being sent off to teach or nurse. They were also concerned that sisters receive more adequate salaries.[6] Many women religious shaped by the Sister Formation Movement in the 1950s went on in the 1960s to organize groups, such as the Leadership Conference of Women Religious (LCWR), that explicitly identified a growing sense of women's identity among nuns with feminism. They began to define themselves in opposition to injustice toward women, not only in the larger society, but in the Church as well.

The study packet *Focus on Women,* prepared by the LCWR in 1975, started with a feminist call to arms, declaring not only that "human history has been one constant and accumulative oppression of women on the basis of sex" but also that "religion . . . has been a major force in its continuance, perpetuation and 'canonization.' The main stream tradition within the Catholic Church . . . is one of the most oppressive of all religious super-structures." Women, it stated, were now bonding together and refusing to accept such "institutionalized injustice."[7]

The Grail, which began as a noncanonical Catholic women's religious "order" in the Netherlands in 1921, from its beginning had a certain ideology of promoting the ministry of women as a group in the Church and in service to society. But between 1930 and 1950, this was seen as bringing "femininity" as a corrective to "harsh masculinity" in social values. In the 1960s the Grail in the United States became active with the peace and civil rights movements as well as liturgical renewal.

In the 1970s the Grail constructed an explicitly feminist agenda with the Women's Seminary Quarter, which met in its main headquarters in Loveland, Ohio. Organized by Janet Kalven, among other Grail leaders who were beginning to define themselves as feminists, these seminary quarters, which ran from 1974 to 1978, brought together Catholic, Protestant, and Jewish women who were studying theology in graduate theological schools. Many American women who were to become the leading feminist theologians between 1970 and 1990 did their first explorations of feminist theology during these seminars at the Grail.[8]

A third movement, the CFM, had its heyday from 1950 to 1968 as a network of Catholic couples that sought to use the methodology of Catholic Action, "See, judge and act," to reflect on their social responsibilities. They did not initially imagine themselves as challenging church teaching on either sexuality or women's roles in the family; rather, they defined themselves as participating as laity in the "apostolate of the hierarchy."

CFM was catapulted into conflict with the Church in 1968, ironically at the moment of its greatest recognition by the Church hierarchy. CFM founders Pat and Patty Crowley were invited in 1964 by the Papal Commission on Birth Control set up by Pope Paul VI to participate in an official reexamination of the Church's teachings on contraception. The American couple brought with them to the deliberations of the commission a study they had made of their own membership, faithful married Catholic couples all, that showed deep dissatisfaction with the one method of birth control sanctioned by the church, periodic abstinence.

Presentation of these data made a deep impression on the priests and bishops of the commission, who had never before heard such frank criticism not only of the ineffectiveness but also of the demoralizing effects of periodic abstinence on the lives of these Catholic couples. The commission voted to change Catholic teaching by an overwhelming majority, allowing any medically approved method of birth control within marriage committed to family life. A few dissident members of the commission persuaded the Pope to reject the conclusions of the commission, and the Pope then issued a reaffirmation of the traditional teachings in 1968 in the encyclical *Humanae Vitae*.

The Crowleys were stunned by these results and concluded not only that this rejection of their work was wrong but that it revealed a clerical mentality more concerned with the maintenance of its power than with the welfare of the Catholic people. Their refusal to accept the papal encyclical spelled the beginning of the decline of CFM as an active movement, but many of its former members, including Patty Crowley herself, went on to become leaders and supporters of Catholic progressive movements, including Catholic feminism. Patty Crowley recently collaborated with the journalist Robert McClory to retell the story of the Papal Birth Control Commission as she experienced it, as a betrayal of justice for Catholic laywomen and laymen, lest the facts of this story be forgotten by a new generation of Catholics.[9]

Although the 1950s saw several movements that would become seedbeds of American Catholic feminism, this became explicit only in the late 1960s in the wake of the Second Vatican Council. For Catholic women Vatican II correlated with trends in American society and culture in a way that had an explosively transformative effect. The 1960s saw a new movement of social criticism and reform in American society led by the civil rights movement. By 1965 this was also expressed in a rebirth of feminism that sought to complete the agendas of full equality for women that had been left truncated by the Depression and the Second World War.

American Catholics also were moving from ghettoized ethnic working-class communities into the mainstream, educated middle class. The presidency of John F. Kennedy set the seal on this mainstreaming of Catholics in American political and cultural life. The ecumenical movement, blessed by Vatican II, brought Catholics, Protestants, and Jews together, not only in political and social life, but also arm in arm in protest movements working to overcome racial apartheid. Thus, the new sense that one could critique one's country and still be a "good

American" came together in a dramatic way with the sense that one could also critique one's Church and still be a "good Catholic." Out of this combination Catholic women felt able to claim to be both Catholic and feminist.

Since much of American Catholic feminism is closely allied in its organization and sympathies with other social justice movements, against racism, poverty, and militarism, Catholic women who would regard themselves as working out of a feminist perspective can be found throughout such movements. Peace and justice organizations, such as the Quixote Center (Washington, D.C.) and the Eighth Day Center for Justice (Chicago), and Catholic reform movements, such as Call to Action, would all see feminism as a major part of their perspective and justice for women around gender-related problems as a major part of their work.[10] But the center of an explicitly Catholic feminism can be defined around two major arenas: sexuality and women's ministry.

Sexuality is arguably the major cause of dissent within Catholicism in general in recent decades. It involves a variety of issues—clerical celibacy, the moral status of homosexuality, remarriage after divorce, contraception, and abortion—in which those arguing for more liberal positions conflict with Church teaching. From a feminist perspective, all of these issues are related to a fundamental defect in the Church's worldview on sexuality and women.

Feminist Catholics believe that the root of this defect is the view that sexuality is sinful in itself and opposed to the higher spiritual life, allowable only within heterosexual marriage for the purpose of procreation, and the concomitant view of women as a lesser form of humanity, linked with the inferiority of the body and sexuality, whose primary destiny is motherhood. Only by remedying these views of sexuality and women can progress be made on developing more adequate teachings that will liberalize Church policies on celibacy, divorce, homosexuality, contraception, and abortion.

We have already detailed, through the story of Patty Crowley, how growing dissent on the Church's teachings on contraception sparked feminist consciousness for many Catholic women. In the 1970s, in the wake of *Humanae Vitae*, as well as the legalization of abortion by the Supreme Court in the *Roe v. Wade* decision, Catholic struggles about reproductive rights moved to a focus on abortion. Since polls as well as practical experience showed priests and bishops that American Catholic laypeople had made up their own minds to ignore the Church's teaching on contraception, bishops perhaps saw the focus on repealing legal abortion as "higher ground" on which to conduct this struggle.

The major Catholic feminist organization that has chosen to vie with the hierarchy on abortion is Catholics for a Free Choice (CFFC), which has become in the 1990s an increasingly international movement with major branches in Mexico, Brazil, and the southern cone of Latin America. CFFC, led by Frances Kissling, has several major Catholic feminists on its board (Rosemary Ruether, Sheila Briggs), as well as growing representation from Hispanic Americans. It see its agenda not only as keeping abortion legal in the United States but as articulating a coherent alternative sexual ethic, expressed particularly through its magazine *Conscience* (and its Latin American version, *Conciencia Latinoamericana*). In the 1995 UN meetings in Cairo and Beijing, CFFC was represented in international delegations to openly express a counterview on sexuality and women's rights to that being promoted by the Vatican delegation.[11]

Homosexuality is a major arena of conflict in all the American denominations, but it is complicated in the Catholic context by celibacy, which, in the view of many, allows gay men to "hide" in the ranks of the celibate clergy, often officially maintaining very traditional views on women. The Catholic gay rights movement Dignity is largely male, and women often don't feel comfortable in its meetings. As a result, Catholic lesbians have organized their own groups, which combine feminist and lesbian agendas. Several Catholic lesbian feminists have also articulated this perspective in theological writings, such as Mary Hunt in her 1991 book *Fierce Tenderness: A Feminist Theology of Friendship*.

The issue of women's ministry has become similarly multifaceted in American (and world) Catholicism. In the mid-1970s, as American Episcopal women fought for and won ordination, Catholic women organized the Women's Ordination Conference (WOC) to promote women's ordination to the priesthood in Roman Catholicism. The first major meeting of this movement was held in Detroit in November 1975, with 1,200 in attendance. This movement was broadly supported by women religious as well as a new generation of theologically educated laywomen active in parish ministry and in teaching. WOC articulated its perspective as one that not only promoted women's ordination but did so within the context of a "renewed priestly ministry"—that is, a reform of the clerical hierarchy that would bring the ordained and the laity into a more democratic and participatory relationship.[12]

This combination of goals—women's ordination and democratization of the Roman Catholic Church—has increasingly come into tension as the official hierarchy has retreated from Vatican II reform to a more intransigent authoritarianism. In 1979, at the Second WOC conference in Baltimore, some leaders articulated the view that Catholic women should shelve ordination in favor of "women-church," the formation of autonomous feminist-based communities for liturgy, spirituality, and social praxis.

In 1983, this suggestion gave birth to the first Women-Church Conference, which brought together a growing network of Catholic feminist base communities, such as Chicago Catholic Women, with other Catholic feminist groups such as CFFC.[13] Mary Hunt and Dianna Neu's organization, WATER (Women's Alliance for Theology, Ethics, and Ritual), became a kind of think tank and organizing center for the women-church movement.[14] The WOC twenty-year anniversary conference in November 1995 saw this movement almost split between the women-church and women's ordination agendas.

The conference was heavily dominated in its official agenda by the view, promoted by Mary Hunt and the Catholic feminist New Testament scholar Elisabeth Fiorenza, that Catholic women should seek communities of the "discipleship of equals" and not ordination, which inevitably signified acceptance of a hierarchical church. However, the majority of the thousand people, mostly women, who attended this conference were by no means willing to surrender the goal of ordination, even as the Vatican was tightening the screws by declaring that the ban on women's ordination was "infallible."

Many of the women at the WOC conference were already serving in parish ministry and chaplaincies, where the lack of ordination was a very practical impediment to their daily work in ministry, not a matter of abstract theory about "ideological correctness." While many women serving in such church ministries did not reject the women-church option as an additional support community, they refused to surrender the hope of reforming the existing institutional church in a way that would affirm their work in it as fully ordained. By the end of 1995, this incipient conflict was on its way to resolution with a reorganization of WOC to clearly focus on its combined historical goals of women's ordination within the context of "renewed priestly ministry," without rejecting the parallel movements of "free" feminist communities and movements under the umbrella of women-church.[15]

As of 1996, Catholic feminism in the United States can be said to be entering its second generation. It has a number of seasoned feminist theologians who are teaching at major and minor Catholic universities and colleges, as well as in Protestant and nondenominational seminaries and colleges. Organizations among black and Hispanic Catholic women have also been established, aligning the "mujerista" and "womanist" views with Catholic intellectual and social life.[16]

These Catholic feminist scholars and activists have built a solid intellectual tradition through published books and articles over a twenty-five-year period. Their views have been well represented in all the major Catholic progressive movements, as well as expressed in explicitly feminist Catholic organizations. Although the official Church has seemed more determined than ever to deny the feminist critique on issues of sexuality and ministry, the vehemence with which the Vatican seeks to silence such questions itself points to the actual success of Catholic feminism in gaining a wide and sympathetic audience for its issues among American Catholics.

NOTES

1. See James J. Kenneally, *History of American Catholic Women* (New York: Crossroad, 1990), 131–44.

2. For attitudes of women suffrage leaders to immigrants, blacks, and the working class, see Aileen S. Kraditor, *The Ideas of the Woman Suffrage Movement, 1890–1920* (Garden City, N.Y.: Doubleday, 1971), 105–37.

3. See Mary Ewens, "The Leadership of Nuns in Immigrant Catholicism," in *Women and Religion in America: The Nineteenth Century,* ed. R. Ruether and R. Keller (San Francisco: Harper and Row, 1981), 101–49.

4. See Rosemary R. Ruether, "Catholic Women," in *In Our Own Voices: Four Centuries of American Women's Religious Writings,* ed. R. Ruether and R. Keller (San Francisco: Harper-SanFrancisco, 1995), 24–26, 42–43.

5. The archives of Friendship House are in the Chicago Historical Society. See also Elizabeth Sharm, *A Strange Fire Burning: A History of the Friendship House Movement* (Ph.D. diss., Texas University, 1977).

6. See M. Patrice Noterman, S.C.C., *An Interpretative History of the Sister Formation Movement, 1954–1964* (Ph.D. diss., Loyola University, Chicago, 1988).

7. See Rosemary R. Ruether, "The Roman Catholic Story," in *Women of Spirit: Female Leadership in the Jewish and Christian Traditions*, ed. R. Ruether and E. McLaughlin (New York: Simon and Schuster, 1979), 375–78.

8. See Janet Kalven, "Women Breaking Boundaries: The Grail and Feminism," *Journal of Feminist Studies in Religion* 5 (Spring 1989): 119–42.

9. Robert McClory, *Turning Point: The Inside Story of the Papal Birth Control Commission* (New York: Crossroad, 1995).

10. See Rosemary R. Ruether, "Spirituality and Justice: Popular Church Movement," in *A Democratic Catholic Church*, ed. Rosemary Ruether and E. Bianchi (New York: Crossroad, 1992), 189–206.

11. *Conscience* can be obtained through CFFC, 1436 U Street NW, Washington, D.C., 20009-3916; *Conciencia Latinoamericana* can be obtained from the Washington CFFC office or from Catolicas por el Derecho a Decidir, C.C. Central 1326, Montevideo, Uruguay.

12. For the proceedings of the first WOC conference in 1975, see *Women and Catholic Priesthood: An Expanded Vision*, ed. Detroit Ordination Conference (New York: Paulist Press, 1976).

13. See Rosemary R. Ruether, *Women-Church: Theology and Practice of Feminist Liturgical Communities* (San Francisco: Harper and Row, 1986).

14. See Mary Hunt and Dianna Neu, *Women-Church Source Book* (Silver Spring, Md.: WATER, 1993).

15. See "Fitzpatrick Resigns as WOC Coordinator," *National Catholic Reporter* 32 (December 29, 1995/January 5, 1996): 5.

16. A major Catholic representative of womanist theology and ethics is Toinette Eugene. See her "Moral Values and Black Womanist Ethics," *Journal of Religious Thought* 44:2 (1988): 23–34. Mujerista theology and ethics come from Catholic Hispanic women in the United States. The leading representatives are Yolanda Tarango and Ada Maria Isasi-Diaz. See their *Hispanic Women: Prophetic Voice in the Church*, 2d ed. (Minneapolis: Fortress Press, 1993).

TWO

The Form Didn't Fit:
Charting New Maps,
Illuminating New Spaces

Jean Molesky-Poz

It was at age twelve that the seeds of a religious vocation took root in me. An age when a young girl's breasts begin to swell and her body's blood first flows. Her whole world waking, she is open for life and begins to think about her future. As a young woman I felt an acute desire for "something more," "a longing for the living God," coupled with an abandon, a generous giving of my life to others. The Catholic tradition of that time taught adolescent girls of our generation to interpret these qualities as a call to religious life.[1] After high school I left the San Francisco Bay Area and entered a Franciscan convent in Milwaukee, Wisconsin. By the age of nineteen, I was virgin, bride, and spouse of Christ, a sister of St. Francis.

Though at age eighteen I had entered the convent as a young woman confident, adventurous, mature, and a leader, gradually through the next ten years I grew socially to feel small, confined, bound, untrustworthy, like a damaged child. A persistent restlessness, contradictions of a comfortable religious life versus the poverty of others, struggles with the structure of obedience, and a series of dreams pursued me. One night, when I viewed Ken Kesey's *One Flew over the Cuckoo's Nest*, the words of the asylum inmate, "I can't make it out there!" shocked and jarred me into a decision. At twenty-eight, I had handed my life over; I was institutionalized and afraid I couldn't make it on my own. I fled.

Reality hit me, hard. Immersed in a secular world for which I was not prepared constantly reminded me of the debilitating convent experiences. Silenced. Restricted. Neutered. Taught to distrust my feelings, thoughts, and body. Taught to twist, warp, and bury my dreams, energies, and desires as I was reminded that I was to serve within an institution. I had spent ten valuable years of my own life for the Church!

Reconciling myself as a woman with Catholicism has been a long process, marked with starts and stops. The reconciliation is not a done deal but continues to be a cautious, determined discernment and assertion. I still find my psyche strewn with emotional land mines. But I have learned to trust my life experiences in the light of grace. In friendships with women, I continue to learn to affirm and claim my perceptions and voice; in conversations with people of diverse religious backgrounds, I have learned to validate and own my distinct faith journey shaped by Catholicism. A biracial, bicultural marriage teaches me the give and take of life. Pregnancy and the birthing of our children, growing with them, ushers me into wisdom. To contest and struggle against the inequities formed by global economic and political structures, I find the Church's teachings on prayer and mysticism, on social justice, and on prophetic individuals and communities of resistance that have sprung up throughout her history to be rich resources from which I draw to navigate my life in faith and to construct possibilities with others.

To address the question of reconciling Catholicism and feminism one must begin with a definitional common ground of the term *reconciling*. First, positioning the word *reconciling* as a gerund indicates an action "to do or carry out" as the word *gerund* is rooted in the Latin word *gerere*. It indicates an action in process, moving. More important to clarify is the theme of reconciling, as it conjures up the notion that the women have stepped out of bounds and now come to reconcile, to ask forgiveness. The notion is further aggravated in the Catholic tradition, as the activity of reconciliation is attached to the sacramental process of being "forgiven," then "healed." Webster's Dictionary defines *reconcile* as "settle a quarrel," "make friendly again," "make content, submissive, or acquiescent," and "become reconciled to one's lot," yet each of these renderings must be rejected as a working definition. Women have lived too long in a Church where the authority has been male, where men have been deferred to, where "Father knows best." We, as women, some as mothers of daughters and sons, have too much at stake for ourselves and for future generations. So I take up the question of reconciling Catholicism and feminism, utilizing the one remaining definition: "make arguments, ideas, consistent, compatible, bring into harmony."

However, this narrative is not a liberal call to harmonize and resolve difference but rather a call to articulate our difference, to uncover and engage resources anew that are part of our legacy, and to chart new relations and maps, with the intent to assert our positions and engage our lives visibly, vocally, and publicly in the Church. Two personal experiences serve as windows into this text and will guide this narrative. First, I recall my entrance into the convent landscape. Here I reflect upon ways my life was encoded and inscribed by the Catholic definition of woman. However, in this religious landscape I was also introduced to rich traditions, rituals, relationships, and resources for charting my life, for confronting life's struggles in faith. Second, I retell an experience that flashed up as a warning of danger if we as women remain publicly silent in the Church. These two recollections help us to understand differences in terms of the historical and social grounds on which they have been and are being organized. Further, this narrative proposes resources we as Catholic women can uncover, relations we can establish, and ethical positions we can take from which we will create new geographies in the Church, not only for ourselves but with others who find themselves alienated and marginalized.

Virgin, Bride, Spouse, Servant, Martyr

A courier novice scurried halfway down the choir stairs, bent over the banister, and called out, "The priest is ready! You can begin processing in."

On that cue, two sisters pushed the heavy oak ceiling-high doors open, and the fine deep-toned bell rang out loud and lively from the convent belfry. The fifteen of us, dressed in yellowed muslin bridal gowns, listened in joyful anticipation as we waited at the threshold of the chapel.

From where I stood I could see that the Gothic chapel was crowded with hundreds of sisters and our families. The priest stood in the center of the marble sanctuary, flanked by two altar boys who held tall beeswax candles. Gold candelabra and bouquets of white lilies decorated the hand-carved European altar. As the convent choir began singing the solemn "Let All Mortal Flesh Keep Silent," the congregation craned around to view the fifteen of us as, single file, we processed into the chapel.

Flushed with excitement, we were that day the brides of Christ, dressed in simple, identical gowns. Those gowns had been worn by thirty preceding generations of novices each year on the feast of St. Clare. They hung down to our ankles, where our black shoes and stockings were visible. Sheer yellowed veils each with a crown of equally antiqued artificial roses flowed over our hair. Each of us held a neatly folded black serge habit and white veil before her. We were participating in the ancient religious sacrifice of young virgins offering themselves to God at the altar.

"Please sit down while I share a few words with you," the priest directed. "I would like to address myself today principally to the parents, relatives, and friends of the young women who will be received into the community of the Sisters of St. Francis of Assisi.

"These young girls are moving into *womanhood*—which means that they are beginning to assume *responsibility for others*. They understand this—and this makes them very happy—for being Christian women—like their mothers before them—they realize that it is only by giving themselves to others that they will achieve their full stature. Let me assure you that these fifteen young women have been taken up today in a marvelous family . . . a family of a thousand women, very much like them, who are *spending their lives* loving and caring for the *Father's children*."

After his sermon, while the organist played a Bach concerto, we processed down the aisle out of the chapel and scurried into a side room. I stripped off the lovely white dress, fingering the sheer veil, thinking this would be the last time to know this sensation of beauty about myself. I donned a man's white undershirt and a long ankle-length black half-slip and pulled the serge habit over my head. As the professed sister approached me with large sharp scissors, she seemed to grow in size. I shut my eyes, bit my lips, and swallowed hard to steel myself from any tears as I heard the scissors chop off locks of hair. Then she pinned back my cropped hair and bound it under a white wimple, which she fastened with a large safety pin. I donned the white veil, which for two years would symbolize my initiation into the community.

Shortly after, we marched up the chapel aisle again. We knelt evenly spaced along the marble altar rail, awaiting bestowal of our religious names that would erase our family-given names, our baptismal names. The choir sang from the loft, their voices traveling across the Gothic chapel.

> True to my heart's promise
> I have eyes only for you.
> I long, Lord, for your Presence.

That afternoon as we processed out of the chapel, we were leaving the place of contemporary American society behind and entering an unknown region. The romantic ascent up the novitiate steps was a tumble back ten centuries into a patriarchal, medieval form. Once inside the novitiate, like Jonah in the belly of the whale, we abandoned secular time, place, and activity and entered the womb of Mother Church. In compulsory confinement for two years, we would be shaped in the way of obedience, a voluntary condition for practicing religious life.[2] At that time it all made sense to us. In our quest, as we entered the novitiate, we forfeited the real world of the twentieth century and were absorbed in an all-encompassing medieval spirituality, one that would inscribe our lives as virgin, bride, spouse, servant, and martyr.

Withdrawn from the world, our lives were enveloped, beginning and ending, at the motherhouse. Life held together and centered on the daily monastic ritual. We rose at 5:30, chanted the liturgical office—a wonderful arrangement of prayer in sequence of canonical hours—four or five times a day, celebrated the Eucharist, steeped ourselves in spiritual traditions, did manual labor, and took meals in common and in silence. We were taught how to walk "light on our feet" along the corridors and staircases of the motherhouse, greeting one another with only one phrase: "Praise be Jesus Christ." The passing sister nodded, "Forever, Amen." In the evening, we recreated together for an hour, prayed compline, then retired to our cells by 10:00 P.M. We were immersed in male images and pronouns for God. All emotions were channeled into religious ceremonies. Yet within the context of the motherhouse, our spiritual lives grew—among many, to a high level of consciousness. I remember feelings of a sustaining joy the first years. Without distraction, I could finally give myself to the irresistible attraction that drew me to the Lord. I was finally at *home*.

We were young and passionate about giving our lives to a high ideal and were bonded together by our desires to grasp it. Friendships developed that were rooted deep in multiple levels of our psyches. In that prime community, we carried out our common search. We were led to believe that the ideal worked, that others who went before us were saved.

The initial longing and yearning that drew us into religious life gradually got twisted, warped, and deformed; it turned in on itself. Trained to pay attention to an order outside ourselves, to follow rules, we internalized a distaste for our bodies, scrutinized our actions, learned to distrust our thoughts and feelings. When we questioned, spoke out, or challenged, we were accused of being "vain," "proud," and "rebellious." The formation of our lives, molded by prescribed disciplinary practices, aimed to construct and reorganize distinctive emotions toward the Christian virtue of obedience to God within institutional goals. We confessed in unison every evening at compline, "I confess to almighty God, to Mary ever Virgin, to the angels, apostles, and saints, that I have sinned exceedingly in thought, word, and deed: through my fault, through my fault, through my most grievous fault." Once a week on Friday afternoon we confessed to a priest and every third month to an "extraordinary confessor" brought in from the seminary. During our novitiate at the Chapter of Faults, we knelt in a circle, and one by one each novice lifted her bowed head and accused herself publicly—"Sisters, I accuse myself of. . . ."—and begged forgiveness. Once a year, we did an inventory of our personal needs; then, on an appointed evening, each novice knelt before the Superior, held up her worn, darned, and patched underwear, and said, "Sister, I beg for a new underwear for the next year." Sometimes, in clandestine spaces (basement tunnels, attic corners, or convent gardens) and retrieved moments, we, as young novices, attempted to salvage ourselves, to articulate, defend, and trust our own perceptions against the rules, order, and images imposed by the daily instructions and practices that inscribed our lives. Individually and collectively, many of us turned inward to survive.

Each woman was draped behind yards of black serge, her hair cropped to stubble and bound under a white wimple, her body denied. Her sacrifice and offering were sincere and heroic. It was a religious system based on the ideal of *victim*, Jesus the obedient victim: "Offer it up." Women were prepared to be victims. Molded in a Catholic patriarchal vision of women, we were neutered and fashioned to be "plain people at everyone's service," trained to become women who tried to understand everyone—even more so in our particular congregation, as we were known as the "seminary sisters." From the time of the founding of the convent in 1853, the sisters became the seminarians' housekeepers; they cooked and washed dishes, hauled water from a pump, milked the cows, and washed, folded, and ironed the seminarians' clothing. And 130 years later we were being instructed that they did this domestic work "with holy ardor," "motivated by the thought that they were sharing in the education of future priests who would eventually work for the salvation of souls."[3]

Though religious women were the paradigmatic workers of the Church's schools, hospitals, and orphanages, we were rendered silent, obedient, and faceless. A Eurocentric worldview inscribed religious life: Chinese sisters, once college professors and high school teachers in mainland China and later exiled to the United States, were relegated to the sacristy, convent laundry, or sewing room; Latina sisters were assigned as cooks in the kitchen or as housekeepers in the nearby seminary. It was a time when the Church was more interested in obedience inscribed in order and rules and more preoccupied with sexual sin than with baptismal claims or with invoking the gospel in social and political contexts. It was a time when Pope Paul VI wrote the document *Sister, the Church Loves You:* "The Church loves you, for what you are and what you do for the Church, for what you say and what you give, for your prayer, your renunciation, the gift of yourselves."[4]

It was also the time when the civil rights movement, the Native American occupation of Alcatraz, the Attica uprising, urban and national marches against poverty, protests against the U.S. involvement in Vietnam, liberation theology emerging from Latin America, and later the United Farm Workers' national boycott called critical attention to economic and political inequities and racial discrimination. It was a time when projects based on justice and peace—War on Poverty, Project Head Start, urban renewal programs, war resistance—were founded. Daily, we faced the contradictions. People were suffering, hungry, oppressed on the basis of race, denied adequate education due to social, political, and economic structures; yet we, who vowed ourselves to the gospel in poverty, chastity, and obedience, lived comfortable and safe lives. Over time, the contradictions escalated.

While there were socially damaging experiences for us as women in religious life, there were beautiful inner landscapes and friendships cultivated through solitude and silence, through living in common. The liturgical cycle of the Church year framed our lives so that we tended to cosmic as well as personal rhythms in the powers and shades of dawn, noon, dusk, and night. In silence we carved out interior space to hear, embrace, and render the Word in our daily lives. Through common recitation of the Divine Office four times a day, we immersed ourselves in the psalms and learned to pray; we read and delved into spiritual traditions from over the centuries. We walked along the shores of Lake Michigan as water lapped the smooth rocks; we hiked through the convent woods, in spring looking for trilliums, in fall crunching leaves underfoot. In the convent choir we swelled with song, our breaths and voices rendering heartful praise and thanksgiving, sometimes subtly, then building in crescendos, bursting in joy. We lived and learned to cherish simplicity, seeking to love and to serve one another. We heard, saw, felt, touched, and were touched by God's presence. We found an abiding sense of grace in the ordinary and, at other times, in Love's gentle, or sometimes awesome, breakthrough into our lives. In turn, we vowed ourselves to God. We vowed ourselves in obedience, in poverty, and in chastity.

For some of us, it was our faith and the beauty and art of it that planted dreams in us. It was the romantic myth and ritualism, coupled with the insecurity of childhood, that kept us. We learned painfully that medieval ideals did not necessarily apply to the times in which we were living and that the life of faith, as it had been laid out for women, insulated, confined, and protected us. As in the myth of Rapunzel, we found ourselves locked in a tower. Years later, wakening to ourselves, some of us escaped and fled the locked tower; others remained to disassemble the tower. Some stayed to bolster it up.

We cruelly found out that the form didn't work anywhere else. Our lives had been structured on a worldview that had no foundation in the twentieth century or in the discourse of feminism. These experiences imprinted us. For one, we didn't learn the lesson of boundaries, of defining our lives, of saying "No." In religious life, we were bound; convent life structured protective temporal and spatial boundaries both to form us in obedience and to enable our interior lives to soar. We were instructed that our lives as religious women were for unconditional love and service; we were to be subservient to authority. More important, in part because of our generous giving of our lives, and often our naïveté, we grossly underestimated the power of darkness and evil. Insulated in the cloister, we couldn't separate the form from the energy that captured us. Life was packaged. There were no questions, just answers. Years later, like a mummy once out in the open air, that reality crumbled.

Over the years, most of us have salvaged and reconstructed our lives from those disciplines of obedience. Memories recounted now often burst in good healthy laughter. Some of us have left Catholicism; some of us continue to reconcile our places in the Church. Most of us have learned resources and relationships of faith to value our lives as well as to interpret, endure, and pass through the difficulties of life. Further, we know friendships beyond the power of words, relationships we carry through life as our lives crisscross the continent and planet.

Becoming Public, Visible, and Articulate

Several years ago at a Sunday homily, the young celebrant asked us to comment to the person next to us on the gospel readings. I was somewhat irritated, somewhat embarrassed, because I was so tired I hadn't even heard the readings. I turned toward the woman next to me to explain that I had been up with a sick child during the night and was exhausted, but before I could, she said, "I am really sorry. I'm so tired. I was up until 3:30 with my two sick children." We nodded to one another in mutual support.

The celebrant then asked individuals in the congregation to share ways their faith healed them. One person after another testified on a healing, on the power of faith, on regaining health through prayer. Then

I realized all who spoke out were women! At the exchange of peace, nine of eleven who extended their hands in peace to me that morning were women! Suddenly, as if struck by lightning, I sobbed. I sobbed for the silencing of women, of young girls, for the denial of women's public voices in the Church for centuries. I wept *for the tremendous loss.* For the loss of women's voiced wisdom, leadership, and full ministry in the Church. For women's internalized compliance. And for the many women who, because they had not found places for their capacities and calls in the Church, searched for and shared their spirituality, intelligence, faith, love, and creativity elsewhere. What place did the Church offer the coming generations of women? And I had a daughter!

Several weeks later, I went to the pastor and said, "I have a daughter who is nine. She has not yet heard a woman give a homily. Where are women to speak publicly in the Church of their faith life? Where is the space for women to interpret the gospel from their experiences? I teach at a university and have the freedom to speak. But here, where I have been ushered into life through baptism, shaped my decisions, relationships, and values, and will most likely be buried, I have no place to speak my faith or to hear other women speak publicly. Until women are included in all the ministries of the Church, for the sake of this generation of women, for girls who will be the next generation of women, women must preach, must be publicly visible. Otherwise, we will lose our daughters, the next generation of women, who can find no room for themselves. They will find other open spaces to answer their questions, to give of their intelligence, creativity, and talents."

Two months later, it was decided women could preach five of the fifty-two Sundays. Four years later, we still preach five weeks of the year.

Drawing New Maps, Illuminating New Spaces

The predicament of women in the Church is one of structural, and thus personal, paradox and contradiction. In the face of this paradox, there is no single "woman's perspective"; rather, the female experience as Catholic is understood and constructed through shifting forms of consciousness, shaped as women filter their experiences through the intersection of their social, class, racial, ethnic, and sexual identities. As women reflect upon and analyze available discourses and practices, they choose diverse relations to the Church. Some women experience the hegemonic patriarchal values in the Catholic Church as so overwhelming that they no longer participate in the institution. These women seek the foundations of women's spirituality and religious experience elsewhere. Other women, despite the pervasive sexism of the Roman Catholic Church, struggle to expand critical space and activity, but now with more practice and patience than they anticipated. Still other women navigate their lives through a more fluid relationship with the institutional Church. The Church is no longer the microcosm of their moral order or spiritual identity, nor is it the only site of their religious search and practice. They may find in the Church rich resources to nourish and chart their lives, but due to the schemes of male hierarchies, narratives, and processes that omit, silence, or oppress women's experience, they seek out and develop other sites, more hospitable and generative to their lives. In these sites, they develop practices of prayer, study, discussion, encouragement, and discernment. They employ their intelligence, their leadership, and their energies in public arenas where they are esteemed as counterparts in civic, professional, or community projects.

At this historical juncture, women who choose to remain with the institutional Church may not be able to transcend the patriarchal structures of power, but we can conduct transformative work in our own lives and in solidarity with others to construct new spaces of discourse. This means taking seriously the knowledge and experiences through which we author our voices, construct our identities in faith, and give meaning to ourselves and to others. Many feminist theorists begin with the local narrative, opening the world to cultural, ethnic, and gender differences, and the positing of difference as a challenge to hegemonic power relations parading as universals. Taking this lead, we ought to take seriously our *local narratives,* that we trust our bodies, our intuitions, our minds, our hearts and experiences filtered through the *indwelling* of the Spirit with an attentive listening. Attentive listening means tending to our connectedness to the earth, to the cycles of the cosmos and the rhythms of our bodies, to our connectedness on multiple levels with others. This means honoring our need for solitude at times and our engagement with community at other times. It is honoring the intuitive as a way of knowing. This listening leads us to examine social, economic, and political structures that marginalize, racially categorize, or alienate ourselves and others, and it compels us to respond in ethical and creative ways. This is honoring the wisdom given to us. And in this, we learn to tend to how God is in us. This self-knowledge is essential to prayer.

A Discerning Mind and Heart

As Catholic women we have entered into the paschal mystery through our baptism, and this baptismal union is the very basis of our sharing in divine life, as well as the life-giving source of community. We have come to know that the Incarnation—the union of the human and the divine— is foundational to Christianity: not just God around us, before us, or behind us, but God revealed as *God in us*. We are women of the resurrection, of Pentecost; thus, like all baptized persons, we have "an anointing (interior gift; interior activity of the Holy Spirit) from the Holy One" (1 Jn 2:20) that teaches us what we need to know about God's presence in the center of our personality. In the First Letter of John, the author writes, "And by this we know that He remains in us; by the Spirit which He has given to us" (3:24). This *remaining* or *abiding* in us, this *mutual indwelling* of God in our hearts, is eternal life and is the source of our lives. The Church's rich sacramental life offers us opportunities to deepen in this mutual indwelling. Thus, I have come to understand one of the resources of Catholic mysticism to be that of *interiority*—a certain kind of awareness that emanates from a living covenant with God.

There is a wonderful line about Mary, "She treasured all these things and reflected on them in her heart" (Lk 2:19). This generative passage is one we can keep in mind as we find our way through the mazes and minefields of daily life. We know the heart is the inner resource. A discerning heart is informed, in part, by contemplative prayer. Kathleen Norris points out that the term *mysticism* came into use during the Renaissance and unfortunately continues to carry undertones of special revelations that come to a select few. Rather, she clarifies, writers of the early Church used the word *contemplation* to convey their experience of the presence of God. Mysticism in its ordinary manifestation is a means for tapping into the capacity for holiness that exists in us all.[5] "The mystical name for God," writes German theologian Dorothee Soelle, "is the silent cry," a longing many humans share across time and space.[6]

I find in the *contemplative memory* of the Church tremendous spiritual resources. Through the centuries and in diverse geographies, individuals in the Church have sought to grow in their *capacity* for God, for a relationship of love and friendship with God. These women and men have left rich legacies of faith, legacies that can be guides for us and reveal to us our capacities for knowing, for loving—some through their prophetic lives, some through their desire and long-suffering, some through generous giving of their lives, others through resisting and denouncing repressive systems. As Dorothee Soelle writes, "For the mystical consciousness, it is essential that everything internal become external and made visible."[7] Some have founded lifestyles, others have constructed religious traditions based on particular charisms or responses to needs of their times. Their narratives form our collective Catholic memory and are remaindered in oral stories, biographies, autobiographies, written texts, and rituals of remembrance, art, and architecture, as well as in spiritual practices, monasteries, and diverse alternative communities such as the Taizé movement, the Grail, the Catholic Worker, and other prophetic resistance projects. We can select, stretch out, and examine these treasures, these *filaments of light;* then, with the loom of time and space stretched before us, we can twist and braid cords that resonate as a living impulse to extend our capacity for God and remap our identities, places, and movements.

Memory is necessary for personal and communal identity. Memory is not a repository; it exists not only for the sake of preservation but for creative transformation. "The link between memory and the organism," Jonathan Boyarin writes, "is connected to the peculiar relations between life and the universe. . . . Memory is not only constantly disintegrating and disappearing but constantly being created and elaborated."[8] Memory's potential, then, lies in ways we remember our past, reassess and interpret it for our lives. "In one's remembered past and a reassessment of it," explains Mikhail Bakhtin, "one possesses the conditions for creativity and freedom."[9] As we sift through our legacies and resources, much of it the product of male transmission, it is essential that women bring feminist perspectives to our consideration of the texts and narratives: situate the social, political, and economic contexts of their production; critique silences, glaring omissions and contradictions; and engage in that which resonates life, then interpret the narratives in light of our experiences. In this reflective praxis, we are claiming our place in the past and in the present; we are working for insights that will contribute to liberatory and transformative forms. In this reflexive process, we create and elaborate meanings.

For example, in reading letters, autobiographies, or recorded words of women who set their hearts and visions on their capacity for God, we can inform and bolster our lives. Teresa of Avila's (1515–82) indomitable determination can resonate with and engender the same in her readers. She writes of those who want to practice prayer that they must journey the road of prayer and continue until they reach the end: "They must have a great and very resolute determination to persevere until reaching the end, come what may, happen what may, whatever work is involved, whatever criticism arises, whether they arrive or whether they die on the road, or even if they don't have the courage for the trials that are met, or if the whole world collapses."[10]

In Clare of Assisi's letters to young Agnes of Prague (1232–82), written over the span of nineteen years, we find valuable expressions of Clare's spiritual wisdom. They narrate the transformative activity of contemplation that can guide our spiritual practices. "Transform your whole being into the image of the Godhead through contemplation. Taste the hidden sweetness which God has reserved from the beginning for those who live in Him."[11]

Communion with these women and men saints crosses boundaries, addressing a communal participation in the mystery of God from generation to generation, writes Elizabeth Johnson in her feminist theological reading of the communion of saints. The living dead continue to belong to the living community as sustainers and guides among the living. In communion with these women and men, one uncovers models of wisdom, courage, and patient endurance.[12] We can invite them to be among our council of mentors.

Dialogic Activity

Dialogue, a communication between simultaneous differences, expands seeing and understanding. As a wife and a mother, I learn from so many experiences. I learn from my daughter. When she was four years old, one night she couldn't go to sleep. "Mom, I have rocks in my heart." We talked about forgiving. Several weeks ago, Joseph, age eleven, asked, "Mom, would Christianity be so popular if Jesus just died of old age as Grandpa will? Or does his dying on the cross make it so popular?" I figure Joseph and I will spend our lives rephrasing the question and seeking to unveil the revelation of the cross, to recognize the nature of its claims, of its spiritual and historical significance. One Sunday a missionary priest from India celebrated the liturgy. After mass, I asked Martín, my husband, how the liturgy was for him. "I couldn't understand anything he said because of his accent. But I felt a relief in my heart to see a person of color at the altar." I realized I really didn't understand how being racialized, even in the Catholic Church, feels.

In charting new maps, I have found conversations with women and men of diverse faith traditions, different memories, and different hopes clarify and confirm the richness of and valid significance of different spiritual traditions. Sharing a shabbat, a passover meal, or a daughter's bat mitzvah with Jewish friends situates and deepens understandings of the Christian Eucharist. In conversation with women of various faiths, we find points of convergence and difference, enriching our own faith itineraries. In my work with indigenous practitioners in the Guatemalan highlands or in northern California, I learn other ways of knowing, of intuitive capacities and relations we can have as humans as we are attentive to the creation; indigenous perspectives and rituals engender dynamic respect, gratitude, and a felt attunement to the natural world. As we converse, our spiritual lives resonate from inner geographies; our spiritual capacities increase and multiply. I've learned to tend toward clarity through questioning, dialogue, and contemplative reflection.

Praxis

From the Catholic Church, I have learned the importance of service, of aligning with the oppressed and the marginalized, and of constructing more just structures with others. Gospel narratives lay out the map, the preferential call to the poor. Today's structures of class, race, ethnicity, gender, and sexual preferences inscribe people's lives; global economic processes, driven by capitalism, deterritorialize people both in local communities and in the world, particularly in the Southern Hemisphere. Women's and children's lives, in particular, are at risk in these capital-building processes, which benefit from exploitation of cheap labor, whether in agricultural fields, in garment industries, or in clandestine sweatshops. Capital accumulation drives the middle class; hunger, poverty, underemployment, homelessness, and dislocation paralyze the working class and the poor. Critical at this historical juncture of materialism is resistance to these death-dealing aspects of our contemporary culture. Many women, informed by the Catholic culture of justice, resistance, and peace, initiate or participate locally, or across borders, in transnational community-building groups to construct more just alternatives. In these activities, prayer, community, and sacramental life sustain, invigorate, and transform.

To expand space within the institutional Church, we need to make ourselves visibly present. In local parishes, it may mean participating in parish councils, faith formation programs, or preaching and ministry teams. It may mean praying and discerning with other women regularly, as spiritual companions, to tend to God's presence in our lives or to support one another in life choices. In other family, work, or professional spheres, it could be encouraging another's prophetic voice as a peacemaker, an organizer, or a journalist. It may mean supporting emotionally, spiritually, and financially women who must put themselves through academic preparation to work as active ministers in the Church.

Eucharist

The heart of Catholic spiritual life is the Eucharist: the community of believers who gather at the table in thanksgiving, in memory, to proclaim our faith and share in the paschal mystery, the death and resurrection of Jesus Christ. At this table, we remember the legacy that has made us, who were once strangers to one another, now friends, even sisters and brothers. We remember that we are loved. We remember those who have gone before us in faith. In eating the bread, drinking the cup, the body and blood of Christ, we are healed, put back together. We are nourished and graced. We are bolstered in grace to continue in our lives. In turn, we are charged to become this same loving leaven in our world.

Eucharist, however, is not only that event. It is also the encounter that we have with other people. As we share words, we break our lives. The commitment to Eucharist is a love for Jesus, but it's more than that. It's also a commitment to heal, to build community, to engage our lives ethically. The Eucharist is a spiritual and affective place to unite with others, to remember them, and in some way, to build a bond with one another.

I am more than weary of seeing only males as the "official celebrants." Women had much fuller public roles in the early Church, and it's time new space is created at the table. Patience over the long haul, I tell myself. But there are moments when I've come to what I think is the end of my patience with the invisibility and subjectivity of women in the Catholic Church. Why not pack up and go elsewhere? I've considered it. But I haven't left yet.

I return to the table, to the Eucharistic table. Several Sundays ago, I stood before a lay Eucharistic minister. He held the bread before me, looked at me, and said, "Sister, the body of Christ." The address this time as "sister" was a graced moment, a felt relationship. A transformative moment! He and I, though strangers, knew the bond of love; we are in a covenanted relationship, have a life in common.

Last Sunday, I preached. It was the story the Church has called "The Widow's Mite." Through prayer, exegetical, ethnographic, and collaborative preparation with other women, I constructed a new reading on the story, playing with the progression of words: the widow's *mite,* her *site* (marginal position in society), her *sight* (perspective of her life in a conscious, graced relationship with God), and, finally unveiling, her *might.* I concluded, "That woman had no idea how her simple act of dropping two coins into the treasury would resound across continent and centuries, that two thousand years later, Christians all over the world would be revisiting her gesture."

As I sat back with my family, Joanna, our daughter, now thirteen, gave me a huge smile and a "thumbs up!"

So now, we return to our initial question: *reconciling* feminism and Catholicism. The future of women in the Catholic Church lies neither in a deferential disposition toward the Church's patriarchy nor in a complacency with our lives. Rather, the future of women in the Church is the *work we have to do,* the praxis we have to take up, to live honestly and truthfully with ourselves and with the Church to live out the passion for God in our lives. I propose that we women confirm and engage our self-knowledge and draw on multiple spiritual, intellectual, political, and cultural resources from which we can grow deep and wise in God; I propose that we create new relations and new spaces with others in an insistent, determined movement to be visible, articulate, and public in the Church. This work is not only for ourselves but for and with all to whom we are connected. Our work is to claim reverence and a hearing for women's presences and activities in the Church. As midwives, we work, pray, and eagerly await the next generations, our daughters and sons, with their longings and searching for God, in the hope that they will find landscapes in the Church open to them, spaces from which they can live the *indwelling of the Spirit* integrally, honestly, and fully.

NOTES

I'd like to acknowledge and thank Jane Clare Ishiguro, Dee Jaehrling, and Sr. Diana Tergerson, O.S.F., for insights, clarity, laughter, and wisdom sifting over many years of a shared legacy; Fr. Tom West, O.F.M., for conversations that have illuminated the rich resources of my experience; and Diana Wear, M.Div., whose attention to theological, personal, and editorial details influenced the completeness of this chapter.

1. In 1965, there were two hundred thousand women in religious orders in the Catholic Church. Today there are eighty thousand; more than half are over seventy, and a quarter are over eighty.

2. Talal Asad, *Genealogies of Religion: Discipline and Reasons of Power in Christianity and Islam* (Baltimore, Md.: Johns Hopkins University Press, 1993).

3. Sr. Mary Eunice Hanousek, O.S.F., *A New Assisi: The First Hundred Years of the Sisters of St. Francis of Assisi, Milwaukee, Wisconsin, 1849–1949* (Milwaukee, Wisc.: Bruce, 1948).

4. "Pope Paul VI to Participants in the 14th General Assembly of the Union of Major Superiors of Italy, May 16, 1966," *The Pope Speaks,* vol. 11 (1966): 109–13.

5. Kathleen Norris, *Amazing Grace: A Vocabulary of Faith* (New York: Riverhead Press, 1998), 285.

6. Dorothee Soelle, *The Silent Cry: Mysticism and Resistance* (Minneapolis: Fortress Press, 2001), 6.

7. Ibid., 13.

8. Jonathan Boyarin, "Space, Time and the Politics of Memory," in *Remapping Memory: The Politics of TimeSpace* (Minneapolis: University of Minnesota Press, 1994), 22.

9. Quoted in Gary Saul Morson and Caryl Emerson, *Mikhail Bakhtin: Creation of a Prosaics* (Stanford: Stanford University Press, 1990), 229.

10. Teresa of Avila, *The Collected Works of St. Teresa of Avila*, vol. 2 (Washington, D.C.: Institute of Carmelite Studies, 1980), 117.

11. Clare of Assisi, "The Letters of Saint Clare to Blessed Agnes of Prague," in *The Complete Works of Francis and Clare*, ed. and trans. Regis J. Armstrong, O.F.M., and Ignatius C. Brady, O.F.M. (New York: Paulist Press, 1982), 196–97.

12. Elizabeth A. Johnson, *Friends of God and Prophets: A Feminist Theological Reading of the Community of Saints* (New York: Continuum Press, 1999).

THREE

Feminism and Catholicism

Janet Kalven

Feminism and Catholicism: Can they be reconciled? I have lived with this question since November 1969, when I took part in a seminar in Holland, organized by the Grail, an international women's movement, entitled "The Co-operation of Men and Women in Church and Society." There, French philosopher Yvonne Pellé-Douël presented with compelling clarity the existentialist position: women are self-defining human beings, subjects who transcend any attempt to limit them to a set of roles, a God-given vocation, or a fixed nature. For me that lecture was the beginning of developing a feminist consciousness and facing openly the conflicts between feminism and Catholicism.

I am a Jewish Catholic crone from an upper-middle-class Reform Jewish family, born in 1913, baptized into the Catholic Church in 1937, after a long, serious search for meaning and direction in my life. I was looking for absolutes, for an all-encompassing goal to which to dedicate myself. The certitudes offered by the time-honored traditions of the Roman Catholic Church met my need, and I eagerly embraced them. Looking for ways to live my new-found faith as fully as possible, I became actively involved in the Calvert Club, the Catholic center at the University of Chicago, where I was working as the teaching assistant in the Great Books program. At the Calvert Club I met the Grail in the persons of Lydwine van Kersbergen and Joan Overboss, who had just arrived in Chicago to begin the American branch of this movement of Catholic laywomen. For me, it was love at first sight. I was immediately attracted by their vitality, their spiritual insight, their ability to draw young women together in a rich and vibrant community, and most of all, their vision of women's potential for changing the world. Women count—that was their message. Women should lead women, and women together can make a difference in the world. In 1942 I left my job at the university to become a full-time member of the core group of the Grail.

As members of the Grail, we were deeply committed to living a radical Christian life ourselves and bringing that spirit into the world. Now when I look back on my first twenty-seven years in the Grail (1942–69), I am amazed at how blind I was to the tensions between the patriarchal Church and the autonomy we aspired to in our own group. We certainly defined ourselves as 100 percent loyal Catholics, accepting the doctrines and the authority of the Church and working closely with the bishops. In the history of the Grail there was a notable example of our ethos of obedience. The group, begun in 1921, had set their hearts on starting a women's university in Java, based not on Western traditions but on Javanese culture. The bishop of Haarlem, under whose auspices they had been established, asked them to abandon this project in favor of working with young women in the chocolate factories in Haarlem. They made strenuous efforts to change his mind. However, when he persisted, they accepted his directive as the will of God. Margaret van Gilse, the Grail's international president from 1921 to 1949, in our training often compared the sacrifice of these cherished plans to Abraham's sacrifice of Isaac. She commented that God moves in mysterious ways, that the group's obedience to the bishop led to the development of the Grail as a youth movement, which in turn facilitated its expansion to Britain, Germany, Australia, and the United States.

We combined the spirit of obedience with an equally strong spirit of initiative. We saw ourselves as an autonomous group of women, defining our own goals, earning our own way, creating our own women's space, and empowering young women for leadership through our programs and projects. We jealously guarded our autonomy. In the 1940s, no group could call itself Catholic without the approval of a bishop. But when Bishop Sheil in Chicago made running a summer camp for boys a condition of using Doddridge Farm as our home and center, we simply refused. "That is not our work," Lydwine told the bishop. Our refusal meant that we had to move out immediately and were literally homeless from May 1943 to February 1944.

We were resourceful refugees. We managed to give our summer courses in borrowed facilities. We managed to stay together as a group thanks to the hospitality of the Sisters of the Holy Ghost, who gave us shelter for several months, during which time we managed to find a bishop, John T. McNicholas in Cincinnati, who was in sympathy with our ideas. Once established in the Cincinnati Archdiocese, we blithely undertook all kinds of initiatives on our own responsibility. We bought a 380-acre dairy and beef farm to use as our main center, named it Grailville, and ran it successfully, doing all the work ourselves. We designed and conducted a yearlong program of alternative education for young women; organized lecture tours; promoted lay participation in the liturgy; and produced and distributed publications, recordings, and works of contemporary religious art. We wrote and produced original dramas on religious themes. We pioneered in ecumenism, modern catechetics, work with international students, and an overseas service program for laywomen, a real innovation for Catholics. In a highly clericalized Church, we did all these things as a lay group under lay—and female—leadership.

There were seeds of feminism in the original vision of the Grail as formulated by the founder, a Dutch Jesuit, Jacques van Ginneken. Among the key ideas that we held firmly were the following: women had never had a fair chance to develop their full potential either in society or in the Church; women had wonderful gifts and talents; women should lead women; women could trust their own perceptions and experience; and women in solidarity with each other could do great things for the Church and society. In the first twenty-five years of our existence, we identified with most of the liberal trends in the Church: lay leadership in the burgeoning Catholic lay movements; active participation of the laity in the liturgy; ecumenical outreach to non-Catholic Christians; Jewish-Christian dialogue; antiracism work; a view of marriage that put the relationship of the couple on a par with procreation as equally important purposes of their union; and a developmental approach in catechetics, using insights from modern psychology, emphasizing affective as well as cognitive elements and making ample use of the arts. We were fast women in a slow Church, pushing these novel ideas, which were quite suspect to the Catholic mainstream. In effect, we were claiming a large measure of religious agency for women.

In the light of Gerda Lerner's *The Creation of Feminist Consciousness,* I would now say that we were prefeminist: that is, we undertook feminist actions but without a feminist consciousness.[1] We met two of the criteria in Lerner's definition: we set our own goals and methods, and we were strongly bonded with each other. But we lacked the other three elements: (1) we did not regard ourselves as belonging to an inferior, oppressed group; (2) we did not have an analysis of the social construction of oppressions; and (3) we had not developed an alternative vision of society and Church beyond a few vague generalities. I was certainly blind to the sexist, patriarchal, and misogynist aspects of the Scriptures and Catholic tradition. Moreover, while I was in favor of women entering the public sphere, I thought of the nineteenth-century feminist movement as a misguided attempt to make the woman "a slavish imitation of the man." Had someone at that time asked me how I reconciled my feminism with Catholicism, I would have indignantly rejected the label *feminist* and insisted that my group enjoyed autonomy within the Church. I saw myself as a loyal Catholic who fully accepted the divine mission of the Church and trusted that the Holy Spirit was guiding Church authorities, even though some priests and bishops were not quite au courant with the latest trends.

As I look back on this period, I can identify a number of factors that made my blissful state of unawareness possible. First of all, the Church authorities were not quite as intransigent as they have become in recent years. The climate was not one of litmus tests for orthodoxy and demands for mandates and loyalty oaths. I think the climate began to change in 1968 with Pope Paul VI's statement on birth control, which provoked the first widespread public dissent from official Church teaching in the United States. With each succeeding statement on sexuality issues—contraception, divorce, abortion, homosexuality, use of condoms for prevention of HIV/AIDS, ordination of women—both dissent and Church efforts to control it have increased. At present, every few weeks there is another incident in which some individual or group is censured or refused the use of Catholic facilities because of failing the litmus tests. This was not the climate of the 1940s.

Moreover, I lived and worked in a women's space, where women were clearly in charge and made all the decisions. We designed our courses, chose our speakers, wrote our pamphlets and books as we saw fit. We made careful choice of the speakers we invited—we wanted only the leading writers and thinkers from the Catholic world. They were mostly priests, but there was the occasional layman and even rarer laywoman. We were the hosts, they were the guests; the relationship was a collaborative one. Even when it came to the official liturgy, I did not feel restricted. I was often part of the team that did the planning, chose the hymns, and arranged the processions, and in the paraliturgies (i.e. unofficial celebrations), we not only designed our own prayer hours, using contemporary texts and songs, but also created new ceremonies like the solemn engagement and the blessing of the bride before marriage.

Occasionally we would run into one of the Church regulations that would remind us that our free space existed within a controlling structure. For instance, our first publication was a fifty-page mimeographed pamphlet of practical suggestions for bringing the spirit of Advent into the home, the school, and the apostolic group. We received a reprimand, in the form of a letter from the chancery, reminding us that all publications dealing with religious topics required an imprimatur, a license to publish, from the bishop. Lydwine wrote a dignified apology, promising to submit future manuscripts for review by the diocesan censor. As our publications multiplied, the chancellor apologized to the censor: "Those Grail girls are at it again—sorry they are making so much work for you."[2]

Of course, in the back of my mind I knew that our free space depended on the goodwill of the bishop. The burden of keeping that goodwill rested heavily on our president, Lydwine van Kersbergen. She was a reassuring presence, a tall, dignified woman, mature, balanced, clearly a deeply spiritual person, with a doctorate in philology. People trusted her. Many priests and some bishops turned to her for advice. Under her leadership, we nurtured the episcopal goodwill, making frequent use of the traditional female method of tactful manipulation. We were especially attentive to Archbishop McNicholas and his successors in Cincinnati, our home base. We never asked permission, but we always kept the bishop well informed about our new initiatives and asked his blessing on whatever we had decided to do. We maintained a close, friendly relationship, remembering his feast day and ordination and consecration anniversaries, sending special homemade gifts from the Grailville farm on Christmas and Easter. Every year, we invited him to open our busy summer season by celebrating mass at Grailville. In sacramental theology, the celebrant represents Christ, and we could not have given Jesus himself a warmer or more enthusiastic reception.

Another factor contributing to our freedom was our lay character. We were not nuns; we were not a secular institute; we were a lay movement. We were friendly with the Glenmary Sisters, a religious community established in the archdiocese at about the same time as the Grail. We shared many interests and values with them. In the bishop's mind, certain activities were not appropriate for religious sisters—for instance, traveling alone or being out late at night, even to take advantage of opportunities for professional development through evening lectures or courses. He laid down a number of restrictive rules for the Glenmarys. He did not dream of applying such rules to the Grail—after all, we were lay.

In short, in this period, from 1942 to 1969, I was able to reconcile our autonomous actions with Catholicism because of an untroubled faith in the Church as the source of divine guidance and an equally untroubled faith that all the novel programs we were promoting represented our response to the direct inspirations of the Holy Spirit. We were confident that our various pioneering efforts—liturgical reform, greater role for the laity in the Church, laywomen to the missions, modern religious art, modern catechetics—would eventually be approved by Rome.

I can identify a number of milestones on my journey to a feminist consciousness that over the last thirty years have both deepened my insights and increased my alienation from the Catholic Church.

My first milestone was the shattering of my ideas of women's nature by Pellé-Douël's talk and her book *Être Femme*. In Grail courses I taught complementarity: that women and men were equal but essentially different, their different capacities fitting them for different roles in family, society, and church. I even wrote a pamphlet, *The Task of Woman in the Modern World,* in which I made the case for all the stereotypes: maker and lover, rational and intuitive, theory and practice, abstract and concrete, instrumental and expressive, initiator and responder, ruler and follower, self-assertion and self-surrender, originator and nurturer. I saw masculine and feminine qualities as rooted in biology and determining male and female God-given vocations to leadership and motherhood respectively, head and heart in the imagery favored in papal pronouncements.

Pellé-Douël's presentation of human beings as self-defining subjects made clear that humans are always able to take on new roles and to transcend any vocations or definitions that would confine them to supposedly fixed natures.[3] My philosophic training inclined me to take ideas seriously and to seek a coherent view. This big new idea altered my entire mental landscape as I began to work out its implications. No more talk of woman, singular and universal. What exists is women, plural, in all their diversities of race, age, ethnicity, education, class, personal history, individual talents and aspirations. No more talk of woman's nature and her sacred vocation to motherhood, physically for most women, spiritually for all. No more assigning of head to man and heart to woman. After all, every human being has both head and heart. Maybe we should be aiming at wholeness, at competence and compassion as the birthright of each human, whether female or male. My observations of the young Catholic families who were working closely with the Grail strengthened this insight. When they tried to live the head/heart dichotomy, the men tended to become insensitive and domineering while the women became either passive or manipulative. By the summer of 1970, I was ready to call myself a feminist, even though a shiver ran down my spine when I spoke the word.

As I studied the burgeoning feminist literature, I began to develop an analysis of patriarchy as a system of male dominance. I saw that gender roles were largely, if not entirely, socially constructed and began to understand the processes of socialization by which the oppressed internalize the values of the dominant social group. The next milestone for me was the application of this analysis to Christianity, a process that began in a weeklong Grailville program, "Women Exploring Theology," in the summer of 1972. The title itself broke with Father van Ginneken's dictum that systematic theology was for men with their rational powers and that women, with their practical and intuitive gifts, should focus on teaching people how to live the Christian life, how to pray, and how to mortify themselves but were not to pursue formal theological studies.

But there we were, seventy-five women, about a third ordained in various mainline Protestant denominations, a third in seminary preparing for ordination, and a third either professional church workers or active laywomen, launching ourselves into theologizing, beginning from our lived experiences. There were no lectures. Instead, in small interest groups that formed around topics like sexuality, sin, community, or singleness, we told our stories and reflected on their significance, sharing our insights with the total group every evening. It was an exciting week. I could literally see light dawning in the faces of the participants as the new ideas struck home. We spoke of the "Aha" experience and the "Yeah, yeah" experience as we sparked and affirmed new insights with each other.[4] Being in this supportive community made it possible to venture into new territory, to voice the unthinkable questions: Is Christianity irredeemably patriarchal? Can a male savior save women? The week illuminated several issues for me: how having women lead the celebrations at the altar affirmed the women in the pews; how inclusive language changed the images of God; how the complexities of human sexuality contained in our stories revealed the inadequacy of the Church's teaching. We began to read the Bible through women's eyes, rehabilitating Jezebel, seeing her not as the incarnation of female wickedness but rather as the victim of the jealousy of the priests of Yahweh. I began to see how divine revelation had been distorted by the prejudices of male writers and translators, imprisoned in the unconscious assumptions of their own times and cultures.

My problems with the Church increased as I saw the great gap between the gospel values and the behavior of too many churchmen. Why did the institution side so often with the establishment and against the poor, the enslaved, the minorities, and the marginalized? Why were there so many scandals, so many attempts to cover up ugly financial dealings and sexual exploitation of women and children by priests? When I read the history of women's religious communities, I found stories of domination by male clerics that roused my indignation. When I talked to contemporary women working in Church structures, I heard similar stories of gross injustice and contempt for women and their contributions. At present the inability of the hierarchy to listen to the loyal opposition, the stifling of all dissent, the demand for loyalty oaths—all this speaks of totalitarianism rather than a passion for truth, and it certainly has a chilling effect on intellectual life and creativity. I know, of course, that the Church is made up of weak and sinful human beings, that we carry our treasure in earthen vessels; the shortcomings did not destroy my faith, but they were a burden to my spirit.

On the sexuality issues—contraception, divorce and remarriage, ordination of women, mandatory priestly celibacy, homosexuality, abortion—both my studies and my experience led me to part company with the current teachings of the Church. These seem to me instances of what Gary Wills in his recent book, *Papal Sin: Structures of Deceit,* calls "so deficient in intellectual credibility, so disingenuous in their abuse of historical evidence," that those who claim to agree with these teachings betray their own integrity.[5] Take, for example, the question of homosexuality. The Church condemns homosexual acts as serious sins, defines homosexual orientation as "objectively disordered," and assures homosexuals that they have a vocation to celibacy whether they feel drawn to it or not. The position rests on the definition of heterosexuality as the only natural and therefore normal use of sexual powers, ignoring the complexity and ambiguity of human sexuality and the historical evidence that homosexuality has been accepted as a part of many cultures. For myself, as my circle of lesbian friends widened, I saw that the quality of the relationship, not the gender of the partners, was at the heart of the moral question.

Catholic feminists are raising other even more significant questions that reach into the heart of Christianity. Sandra Schneiders's book *Beyond Patching* states a fundamental issue on which the continued participation of women in Christianity depends: Is the God of Judeo-Christian revelation a male being who sent a divine male to save us, thus revealing the normativity of maleness and establishing the superiority of males in relation to females in the order of salvation? Or did God create one human nature in which women and men participate fully and equally?[6]

Despite traditional teaching that God transcends gender, Church language and imagery reinforce the notion that God is father, male, pictured as the all-powerful Roman emperor or the stern, all-seeing judge, determining life or death for his subjects. As Mary Daly observes, "When God is male, the male is God."[7] These images of the divine patriarch ruling heaven legitimize all the patriarchs on earth. The Western tradition—the tradition that traces its roots to the Greeks, the Romans, and the Hebrews—has consistently defined women as relative (Adam's rib), dependent (weak-willed, requiring male guidance), and inferior (less rational, more emotional than men). Church doctrine and practice have supported this view, taught that women were not in the image of God unless joined to a husband, second in creation and first in sin, eternal temptresses, their dangerous proclivities needing to be curbed by either a husband or a cloister wall. Now that secular culture has made these positions untenable, the Catholic Church is teaching that maleness is essential to Christ's role as savior. Only males can represent Christ at the altar. But if women cannot represent Christ, how can Christ save women? What about the traditional teaching that baptism incorporates the individual into Christ's Mystical Body, into a share in his threefold role as priest, prophet, and king? Once again the current teaching puts the seal of the sacred on the male as the norm of the human.[8]

The questions women are posing arise out of basic feminist analysis, beginning from the lived experience of women, insisting on the radical proposition that women are people: that is, fully adult human beings entitled to all the rights and responsibilities thereof. This analysis employs an existential rather than an essentialist framework. It rejects the dualisms of mind/body, spirit/matter, culture/nature, rational/emotional, white/colored, civilized/primitive, transcendent/immanent, immutable/changing, and clergy/laity, as well as the ranking of these dualisms characteristic of patriarchy. It finds the basic paradigm of all these dominance/subjection patterns in the male/female dualism that is the principle of the patriarchal family unit. It traces other oppressions—racism, classism, clericalism, colonialism, ageism, heterosexism, exploitation of nature—to this root. It sees all forms of oppression as interconnected and concludes that sexism cannot be eliminated without a radical transformation of the social order.

Underlying the differences between feminists and the Church are different views of reality. The Church holds to the Aristotelian-Thomistic view of the hierarchy of being, a static universe of fixed natures and predictable outcomes, a universe of law and order sanctioned by an all-knowing, all-powerful, immutable God who has entrusted a revelation to his Church, "a deposit of faith, given once and for all, [that] does not change."[9] For the believer, the Church possesses the fullness of truth about human life, truth binding everywhere and always. Feminists see not a hierarchy but a web of life, an evolving universe, dynamic, egalitarian, in which everything affects everything else. It is a universe of radical openness to the future in which real newness is possible and everything is "continually becoming something else, moving to something deeper. . . . God is not safely ensconced in some heavenly realm unrelated to our world. On the contrary, God is deeply and necessarily involved in the life of the universe."[10] In this universe, revelation is an ongoing process and truth is never complete but part of a historical evolution as our limited minds grow in understanding.

I do not think that Catholic feminists differ from their secular counterparts in their analysis of patriarchy. In fact, it seems to me that Catholic feminist theologians have deepened that analysis as they examine the Catholic Church, perhaps the most patriarchal institution in the Western world. They have pointed out how patriarchy legitimizes itself as both natural and sacred and how this sacralizing has permeated our culture and contributed to the rise of fundamentalisms. They have clarified the interstructuring of the oppressions. Elisabeth Schüssler Fiorenza has recently coined the word *kyriarchy,* from the Greek *kyrios,* lord, to name all the oppressions in which humans—whether emperor, master, lord, employer, father, or husband—lord it over others.[11]

Feminist analysis is not unique to American feminists—it resonates with women worldwide, believers as well as nonbelievers. Catholic feminist theologians are a significant minority in the Church all over the world. They are highly educated, articulate, and influential; their works circulate not only in the academy but also among the growing numbers of Catholic women in the pews who no longer accept second-class status in Church and society. Feminism represents a tremendous challenge to the Catholic Church and indeed to all the world religions. Sandra Schneiders sees the feminist challenge to the Church as similar to the Reformation.[12] Susan Ross suggests that it is analogous to the admission of the gentiles to the early Church.[13]

Is it possible to be both Catholic and feminist? In the Catholic world as I know it, I see four answers to the question.

On the far right there are antifeminist women, Women for Faith and Family, under the leadership of Helen Hull Hitchcock, who would reply with a flat "No." They are against any changes in language, liturgy, catechisms, or Church practices in the name of justice to women. They affirm the Church and its hierarchy as divinely instituted, accept all the current teachings without reservation, and see God as literally "Father."[14]

There are other women on the right who speak of "A New Feminism for a New Millennium," the title of a conference in Rome, May 19–20, 2000, sponsored by Opus Dei. Their feminism is totally reconcilable with Catholicism. They accept the present teaching of the Church on the nature and task of women. Thus, Mary Ann Glendon, Vatican representative at the UN Beijing Conference and presider at the Rome conference, explains that the new feminism "will reflect on feminine nature" and "on feminine spirituality as envisioned by John Paul II in his 'Letter to Women.'" One of the major conference talks was entitled "Woman: Daughter, Wife, Mother."[15] This sounds to me very much like the old Church teaching, woman defined as relative to man, called to put husband and children first, to sacrifice herself to the demands of the patriarchal family.

By far the largest number of feminists I am acquainted with would answer the question with "conflictual but possible." They are like the women described in the book by Miriam Therese Winter, Adair Lummis, and Allison Stokes, *Defecting in Place,* which reports the results of a survey of 3,746 women, Catholic and Protestant, who belong to feminist collectives for support, spirituality, ritual, and action. Some are explicitly feminist; some embrace feminist values implicitly. Some are radical, seeing the need for profound systemic changes; others are reformist, keeping present structures intact but calling for greater inclusion of women. The Catholic women, both religious and lay, feel more alienated from the institutional Church than any other group in the study, although most of them remain members of their local parishes. They tend to be passionately attached to their faith but are full of pain, anger, and frustration with the Church. Many are members of religious communities. Many are lay leaders, active in Church structures as professional scholars and educators or as volunteers, carrying out all the mundane tasks the men don't want to do.[16] It seems to me that the hierarchy does not realize how deeply it has alienated not only the feminist theologians but also the women in parish groups, discussion groups, and diocesan commissions, women who are a core Catholic constituency. While they may not have assimilated the full feminist critique of the patriarchal Church, they are claiming responsibility for their own spiritual lives; they are thinking for themselves, and who knows where that will lead them? Once the questions have been asked, they do not go away; they recur and they deepen.

Many of these women find their spiritual nourishment in their women's spirituality and support groups. They encounter the transcendent, the sacred, in these groups rather than in the sacraments of the Church. Many are members of such dissenting Catholic groups as Call to Action, Catholics for a Free Choice, Women's Ordination Conference, Women-Church, or Women's Alliance for Theology, Ethics, and Ritual. Some stand at the door, daily asking themselves whether to leave. Many of the feminist theologians, among them Rosemary Radford Ruether, Elisabeth Schüssler Fiorenza, Sandra Schneiders, Mary Jo Weaver, Anne Carr, Joan Chittister, Mary Hunt, Elizabeth Johnson, Madonna Kolbenschlag, and Maria Riley, are carrying on a threefold task: (1) recovering the hidden history of women as religious agents; (2) elaborating the analysis of the patriarchy, sexism, and misogyny of the Christian tradition; and (3) developing an alternative vision of Church as an inclusive community, a discipleship of equals. They do not want to abandon their roots in the Bible; they find in the biblical tradition sources for a liberating vision of humanity and our relation to God/dess. These Catholic feminists are putting their energy into creating women's spaces, an alternative reality where they can experience their own way of being and behaving as a basis for a feminist future. They are bringing into being a community that is diverse in age, race, class: inclusive, egalitarian, and committed to relations of mutuality rather than domination/subjection, standing in solidarity with the poor and oppressed in their struggles for justice.

Finally, there are others who have moved from the "conflictual" to a definite "No." I know women who, having completed theological studies and found that the Catholic Church was not willing to employ them, have been ordained priests in the Episcopal Church or have joined other denominations. I know young mothers, themselves raised in model Catholic families, who refuse to have a daughter baptized—"too damaging for her self-esteem." Still others, having suffered disillusion with Catholicism, like Mary Daly, move away from Christianity altogether. For myself, my feminism has led me into deeper and deeper criticisms of Catholicism. After Vatican II, I began to see the Catholic Church as a way, not the way. I found it harder and harder to attend the local parish and finally stopped going altogether. I find my nourishment, my moments of contact with the sacred, in the various feminist circles I belong to. I see the Christian myth as one story among others. It works for some people, giving meaning and direction to their lives. It no longer does that for me. Central doctrines and symbols are so deeply inter-woven with the definition of women as inferior that I'm not able to translate them from their androcentric form to one liberating for women.

Regretfully, I have given up on the institution. I think some insti-tutional form is necessary; otherwise we will slip into extremes of indi-vidualism and subjectivism. I don't think the direction of my life has changed since I was baptized in 1937. I am still committed to a spiritual life and to the struggle for justice in the world. We live in a time of tremendous changes in technology and culture. I see hopeful signs of new life everywhere, significant, widespread changes of consciousness. Perhaps we will achieve a critical mass—the hundredth monkey—that will tip the balance in Church and society toward a profound transfor-mation. Perhaps a new religion will grow out of the present ferment. In the meantime, I have my feminist support and action groups. I remain committed to the task Rosemary Ruether describes in *Women-Church*: "We must begin to live the new humanity now. We must begin to incar-nate the community of faith in the liberation of humanity from patri-archy in words and deed, in new words, new prayers, new symbols, and new praxis."[17]

NOTES

1. Gerda Lerner, *The Creation of Feminist Consciousness* (New York: Oxford University Press, 1993), 217–18.

2. Interoffice memorandum, January 11, 1949, Archives of the Archdio-cese of Cincinnati, brought to my attention by Dr. Patricia Miller.

3. Yvonne Pellé-Douël, *Être Femme* (Paris: Editions du Seuil, 1967), 13, 229.

4. Carol Christ and Judith Plaskow, eds., *Womanspirit Rising: A Feminist Reader in Religion* (San Francisco: Harper and Row, 1979), 200–207.

5. Gary Wills, *Papal Sin: Structures of Deceit* (New York: Doubleday, 2000), 4–5.

6. Sandra M. Schneiders, *Beyond Patching: Faith and Feminism in the Catholic Church* (New York: Paulist Press, 1991), 34–35.

7. Mary Daly, *The Church and the Second Sex* (New York: Harper and Row, 1975).

8. Rosemary Radford Ruether, *To Change the World: Christology and Cultural Criticism* (New York: Crossroad, 1981), 45–49.

9. Mary Jo Weaver, *New Catholic Women: A Contemporary Challenge to Traditional Religious Authority* (Bloomington: Indiana University Press, 1995), xvi.

10. Mary Jo Weaver, *Springs of Water in a Dry Land: Spiritual Survival for Catholic Women Today* (Boston: Beacon Press, 1993), 68–71.

11. Elisabeth Schüssler Fiorenza, *Jesus, Miriam's Child, Sophia's Prophet: Critical Issues in Feminist Christology* (New York: Continuum, 1994), 14.

12. Schneiders, *Beyond Patching,* 110–11.

13. Susan Ross, "Catholic Women Theologians of the Left," in *What's Left? Liberal American Catholics,* ed. Mary Jo Weaver (Bloomington: Indiana University Press, 1999), 39.

14. Mary Jo Weaver and Scott Appleby, eds., *Being Right: Conservative Catholics in America* (Bloomington: Indiana University Press, 1995).

15. Jo Croissant, "Woman: Daughter, Wife, Mother" (paper presented at the International Congress "A New Feminism for a New Millennium," Rome, Italy, May 19–20, 2000).

16. Miriam Therese Winter, Adair Lummis, and Allison Stokes, *Defecting in Place: Women Claiming Responsibility for Their Own Spiritual Lives* (New York: Crossroad, 1994), 30–35, 263.

17. Rosemary Radford Ruether, *Women-Church: Theology and Practice of Feminist Liturgical Communities* (San Francisco: Harper and Row, 1986), 5.

FOUR

Sex-Linked Traits

Jean McGarry

Part I

That winter, 1964, the latest thing was stovepipe boots. I got them for Christmas and wore them to the college lab, where my teacher said, "Those wouldn't fit *my* legs. They wouldn't even fit over my calves." It was the only thing she ever said to me that wasn't angry or harsh. I was fifteen, fat, but the tall patent leather boots fit smoothly to my knees. Her boots covered only her ankles, just shy of the balloonlike calves, pure white, in thin nylons with crooked seams.

"Want to try one?" I asked, without thinking.

"No," she said, looking at them lined up under the radiator, with the stovepipes leaning to one side. She waited to see if I had more to say. I tried to keep my face from smiling, twitching, or otherwise showing that I was having a thought. "Why are you standing there?" she demanded. "Do you think I invited you to work with me just so you could stand around and admire yourself?" I started to grin. "There's nothing funny about it. Did you remember to make fresh medium? You didn't. I can see that you didn't."

She took her own boots off and set them near, but not touching, mine. She handed me her tweed coat to hang and the knit hat: a hand-knitted hat, orange, yellow, and blue, with a snowball on the crown. When she wasn't in

47

the lab, she told me, she knitted and her old mother knitted, or some-times she went to the theater with some neighbors, or played bridge with the VeriDames—the Mothers' Club connected with the college—even though she wasn't married and had no children. "And if I did," she once told me, "I wouldn't send them here!" I asked why. "What do you mean, why? Do you have an opinion? I didn't think so. You're not old enough to think for yourself. You may never be." I was tired from a day of school, and my uniform felt tight, although I was empty, not full, and my face was oily from tiredness and not going home to wash it with a drying soap and cooling alcohol. "You should develop your opinions, you know," she said. "You can't start too young. I have no faith in girls who don't trouble themselves to develop their minds. Isn't that what we're put on earth to do?"

When I was twelve I started a science project at school. Every year after that I worked on one and was picked for the state science fair. The students who worked with Dr. Foley in the labs at St. Vincent's College always won the big prizes, sometimes even money prizes. The Septem-ber I turned fifteen I started going every day to the St. Vincent's labs. On the way over—first I took the bus home from school, then I walked the length of College Drive—I stopped at Janet Conneally's house to see if Janet's mother would let her go to the lab. Janet lived in a big white house on a lawn covered with pine trees. In the middle of the lawn was a statue of St. Francis with birds resting on his shoulders and in his hand. Real birds, Janet told me, wouldn't go near him, although they loved the birdbath in the back yard and hundreds came to eat bread crumbs in the winter and sip the rusty water or peck at the ice. I asked her why and she said that the bluejay who lived in their yard spent his time in the tree next to the statue and bombed it and squawked at it all day long. I thought that was funny, but Janet said her father had to hose the statue down because the jay covered the square pedestal with twigs and leaves and shat on the head and arms. It was a disgusting bird, Janet said, and her brother meant to kill it some night when the next-door neighbors, who could hear and see everything, were asleep. Janet's brother was a freshman at St. V.'s and had made the basketball team, although he hadn't played in a game yet. St. Vincent's was famous for basketball, and it was an honor, Janet had said, just to sit on the bench. Did he know Dr. Foley? I asked. Did he take biology? "Are you kidding!"

Janet had screamed. "You've got to be kidding." Janet was a year older than me and attended the high school downtown, where the tuition was a hundred dollars more and the uniform more up-to-date: plaid skirt and white blouse with a navy cardigan. My uniform was one solid color: blue serge skirt and vest, blue jacket, long-sleeved shirt, and blue bow tie.

Janet noticed the boots right away. It was the first week of January and we were back to school. She looked at them, half covered with melting snow and some sand from the roads, and asked me what color the lining was and to fold down the tops so she could see. I told her I couldn't.

"Why?" she asked. "Why can't you fold them down?"

"They're too tight."

I watched her pull on short boots and then struggle into her fur parka. "I don't think they're supposed to be *that* tight," she said.

I didn't say anything.

"They're too expensive for *me*," she said.

I said they were cheap.

She said she didn't mean that. She meant that having the boots required you to have everything else that went with them.

All the way to the lab, as we walked in silence, side by side, I wondered what else the boots might need. And why a girl like Janet Conneally, rich and the daughter of a big shot working for the city of Providence, didn't already have it. That I had nothing to go with them, not even the thought that anything else was necessary, was no surprise to me. I was a reckless person, impulsive—everyone told me this; I was the one who was always going too far.

I asked Janet why her mother had let her come to the lab without an argument, when usually there was a fight and hard words, and once Mrs. Conneally had bolted the kitchen door and stood in front of it. Why does your mother hate Dr. Foley so much? I had asked, and Janet shrugged. It had something to do with being home alone all those dark afternoons with no one to talk to. Mrs. Conneally was forever asking me why "the girl" couldn't stay put just once in a while—stay at home, do something her mother wanted, for a change!

"What does she want you to do?" I asked.

"Sit in the bedroom," Janet said, "while she puts four coats of polish on her nails, then bites it all off."

We laughed. Mrs. Conneally was known for her nerves.

"Go out shopping, make brownies," Janet went on. "Watch the stories."

"Wouldn't you rather?" I asked her.

"I don't know," she said. "Don't ask."

We walked up the hill to the main campus, a circle of concrete buildings with dirt sidewalks and no trees, and turned left into Feeney Hall. We were late because we had circled past the Smith Street Spa for Cokes and to look at Valentine cards. Sometimes the boys from St. V.'s went there to drink coffee or read magazines. Two were there that day, one smoking a cigarette. He pointed it at Janet, or maybe it was at me, and Janet got nervous. She forgot to pay for her Coke, still on the counter, and the druggist ("Hey, girlie!") yelled from his little window. We froze. Janet's face was red under her angora tam. "Jackie," she whispered to me, "feel this," touching my hand with a hand that was cold and wet.

"I know you girls," the druggist said, when he got to the doorway. Janet handed him a quarter. The boys—I could see them—were laughing.

"No harm done," the druggist said, taking the coin, but he was wrong. I told Janet, when we were halfway up the hill, that he *owned* the drugstore, and could be as rude as he wanted, but she still planned to tell her father, assistant superintendent of schools, and was sure that the guy's goose was cooked. I wanted to tell her to start fighting her own battles, but I didn't like the druggist either.

We knocked on the lab door that afternoon, but there was no answer. The door was locked; only the exit sign was lit. Someone told us Dr. Foley had gone home. When we were late, she often left, and it was—she was always saying—our funeral if the flies starved in the dried-up cake of medium or escaped in the night. Escaped (I liked to elaborate on this when I had my brother Donald as a listener) by collecting in a big army on the underside of the cotton ball that trapped them in their jar. Pushing that cotton with a mighty fly push (I laughed when I told him this story, because he acted it out with a pillow on his head), out they would come. Thousands, millions and jillions of flies, red eyes and white eyes, little flies and big flies, would escape into the lab and onto the campus and into the city until they found the bowl of fruit, especially ("Stop!" my brother would squeal when I got to this part) the rotten bananas and stinky apples and split-open grapes they craved. All those days locked up in their jars with nothing to eat but an inch or an inch-and-a-half of smelly agar-agar. My brother didn't know what that was, and I never told him. The story always ended with him trying to hit me and my mother yelling from the foot of the stairs that we were too loud and too silly at a time when we should be settling down to sleep.

Once, dangling off the bed with his hair touching the floor, my brother said, "I think they'd all go to *her* house."

"Whose?" I said.

"*Her,*" he said. "Roly-Poly."

"Roly-Poly who?" I asked, because I liked this kind of talk, if it didn't get too babyish.

"Roly-Poly Foley," he said, "the Holy Joe with the big fat ass!"

"That's not funny," I said.

"Yes it is!" he said. "Her house is chock-full of fute fries."

"Say it right!" I yelled.

"Flute flies," he said.

I hit him with my pillow, then whispered, "I heard those flies are coming to hide under your bed tonight—to itch you!"

He was quiet, and I climbed onto my bed, still hot from bounding around.

He said, "Don't tell me that, Jackleen, right before I go to sleep."

"Why?"

"I'll have dreams," he said, in a voice a hair away from crying.

I never had one dream about the flies, but Donald always had dreams about everything. He was babyish and dumb for a ten-year-old—that's what everyone told him—but he wasn't a retard, and he wasn't *that* dumb. Now that I was fifteen, and spent my time up at the lab or on the phone with the cord all stretched out, talking about dates I didn't have to my friend Eileen, who didn't have any either, he hated me the way he hated everyone else, except Nana, our grandmother, who lived with us. She didn't get along with anyone either, and stayed up in her room reading mysteries and listening to her transistor. Sometimes Donald went up there and they played cards or bingo. They were two of a kind, my mother said, when she was mad at them: they were spoiled, selfish, and lazy, Nana and her Deedee. "While *you* spend," she would say to me, "every livelong hour of the day up at the college with that harpy, I'm stuck here alone with them, waiting on them hand and foot, and no one to help me.

"I don't blame you, though," she liked to add. "If I had someplace to go, I'd go too, and you'd have to take care of them." I laughed, and then she laughed.

The white-eyed flies, *Drosophila melanogaster,* were just like the red-eyed ones. Their eyes were white because they had received a recessive trait for eye color from both parents. I was working on a genealogy of the white-eye trait, linked with other traits on the sex chromosome. I kept charts of the series of offspring: f_1 and f_2, f_3 and f_4. The percentage of whites varied with each generation, and my job was to mate the flies: pick a male and female from a generation and isolate them in a jar coated with medium and stoppered with a cotton ball, then wait until pupae were stuck to the walls of the jar. When these pupae had hatched, I would dose all the baby flies with ether and sort them under a low-power microscope. I counted the males and females, the red and white eyes, and then I brushed the flies back into an empty jar so they could wake up. They were not supposed to wake up under the warm light of the microscope and toddle off the glass, drop to the floor, and fly away. That would mean I hadn't etherized them enough; the count would be off and the flies would be up on the ceiling, where Dr. Foley could see them. When I watched the flies through the microscope, using the sable brush to roll their little bodies over, I could see everything I needed to see: the tapered male body and rounded female, their different sets of stripes, the eye color, and something that, at first, I didn't understand. I was going to go find Dr. Foley to ask her, but instead I just looked. I looked so long that some of the flies started to twitch and one tottered around like a drunk on legs like threads. I carefully brushed them all into a jar—it was easy to kill them when they were awake, with their wings and legs stretched out—and no flies were lost, none escaped, and no legs or wings were torn or broken.

I made sure the autoclave was off and all the cotton balls were tight on the jars. I looked into the new jar, with the male and female all alone in there, the white-eyed male and the red-eyed female from the f4 generation—now they were f5. The male was hanging upside down from the cotton ball and the female was sitting on the lump of agar—was she stuck? I shook the jar and they both buzzed around.

"You love them flies," my brother once said. "Admit it." He was brushing his teeth and I was sitting on the bathtub rim waiting for him to finish so I could brush mine. "You can brush yours," he had said. "There's room. You think I'm poison!"

"I don't love flies," I said.

"Yes, you do," he said. "Just like you loved your rats last year."

"Why don't you shut up?" I said. I picked up the *Reader's Digest* that was always there on the radiator cover and looked for a joke I didn't already know.

"Talk to me when I'm talking to you!" he shouted.

He spit his toothpaste out. I was trying to keep from laughing. For my last year's project, I had kept three rats in the cellar and was feeding each one a different diet to show the importance of the four food groups. I had to starve two of them because the experiment wasn't working. "Feed your rats!" my mother was always yelling, just to get a rise out of me. My experiment on the value of a balanced diet proved nothing, but my rats almost became pets, letting me stroke their soft backs when I brought them their jelly lids of leftovers from our dinner. One night, though, the biggest rat—the one I was still feeding to make him look better than the rest—locked his jaw on my hand. Then the lid to the cage crashed down on my finger and broke it. "Sickening things," my mother would say, if the subject came up.

I carried the rats and my chart of their diets to the science fair, but I didn't win anything. It wasn't an interesting project, and all the rats looked healthy, even the two I starved. The newspaper took my picture, though, when a reporter spotted my bandaged hand and saw that I had rats. I got twenty-five dollars from the newspaper, for sacrifice in the cause of science. "Take it," my mother said, even if it wasn't for science but for the sake of faking science that I'd been bitten.

I put the jar of new parents down and went looking for Janet, even though Janet was usually gone by then: she hated the lab and left as soon as she could. Still, I always looked for her at seven-thirty or eight, whenever my work of counting and transferring, making up fresh medium, washing and sterilizing jars, and tidying the lab was finished. I went the long route in case Dr. Foley was still working late with her college student. She didn't like me to go home until she went home, and she didn't go home until nine or nine-thirty, sometimes later. If I waited till then, there wouldn't be time to finish my homework, and next day I'd get in trouble with the nuns, which happened a lot. On my last report card, all my marks had gone down. Some of the nuns did it deliberately: they had met Dr. Foley and they didn't like her. They discouraged any of us who were picked to work with her, but once you were picked, as I tried to explain to Mother Francis Marie, the homeroom nun, you didn't have any choice. "Don't be a little silly!" she said, in that automatic way the nuns said everything, but then she said, "Where's your backbone, Jackaleen McManus? And you were the one who was going to show us all."

What do you think I am doing? I felt like saying, but that remark was worth a week's detention, and I'd be late for the bus and late for the lab and late getting home for my heated-up dinner and late for my ten-o'clock five-minute call from Eileen, which lasted at least an hour, or until my father went through the roof and started yelling how he'd rip that phone right out of the wall if I didn't hang the damn thing up, and late for bed—with a slap from my mother for not picking up my clothes or hanging up my uniform—and late getting up the next day and late for school, everyone yelling their heads off. All except Dr. Foley, who didn't care how late we stayed at the lab, the later the better.

Winter nights, when Dr. Foley and I walked out on the hard snow of the campus, nobody would be there, and no sound except the stupid pigeons moaning from the top of the gym, and Dr. Foley, if she talked at all, which she usually didn't, telling me that if I thought *this* was hardship I was living in a dream world. I liked to relax, I was a dawdler, I liked my sleep and my comforts, she told me, and a life in science demanded effort, discipline, sacrifice, patience, good health, mental independence, indifference to what other people think and to the idle way they live. "Are you listening to me?" she once said, when we had got into the frigid car and slammed our doors.

"Yes," I said.

"No you're not!" she said. "You're thinking about yourself. I was young once."

"I know," I said, trying to be tactful.

"No, you don't know!" she said, driving out of the parking lot—as she always did—like a maniac. My mother used to watch for me on school nights from the upstairs windows, until the time she saw Dr. Foley slam on the brakes after squealing around the corner and going up over the curb so that half the car was parked on the sidewalk. She told me my father would come pick me up after that, on late nights, but nothing doing, Dr. Foley told him when he arrived at the door of the lab: "This girl is not finished yet and I'm not letting her go home and throw a wonderful career in science out the window just so your family can lead a tidy life. Go on back home. You're lucky to have a daughter as smart as Jacqueline!"

I couldn't believe she had talked that way to my father, and neither could my mother when he told her. At first, they just yelled and screamed, then they blamed me for the rotten things Dr. Foley had said. I tried to say something, but they kept interrupting to tell me that never in his entire life had my father been walked on that way. I tried to say she was always like that, and if they thought *this* was bad they should hear what she said to me or to the college student she hated so much. This quieted them down, or at least my mother piped down enough to hear about the college student who was Dr. Foley's special doormat. Marguerite Birch, the girl's name was, and she was studying a sickness called PKU, and, according to Janet, she had it. She wasn't smart enough to be a scientist; she was barely going to finish this year at college and then she was going to be put away to die.

"You're making this up," my mother said. "I don't believe you."

My father had already left the room, after giving me a look that said he was too mad to hear this story now but I would hear from *him* later on.

"It's true," I said. "She's already starting to smell bad."

"What's that got to do with it?" my mother said. My brother had come into the kitchen and sat down at the table.

"Don't you be listening," I said to him.

My mother looked at Donald, then rubbed an orange stain from the corner of his mouth with a little bit of spit on her finger.

"It's a free country," he said.

"Is anybody listening to me?" I yelled, and my mother said, "Finish your story and don't be so bossy."

"She's in the science fair," my brother smirked, "so she knows everything."

I couldn't help but laugh at that, and the tone of it: it was as if my grandmother were in his head talking for him.

"You mind your p's and q's," my mother said.

Then my grandmother walked into the kitchen. She had taken a nap and was still holding her prayer book, which she read to put herself to sleep. "Well," she said, "what's going on here, a little party?"

"No one asked you," I said.

"Don't be fresh," said my mother.

"It's a free country!" Nana and Deedee said together, as Nana sat her bulk in a chair, taking my father's place at the table.

Nana took Deedee's hand after she put her prayer book down. "Shh," she said. "Jack-a-leen is talking."

"Now that you're all talking," I said, "I forget what I was going to say."

"Oh, no, you don't," said my mother. "You're talking about how that girl smelled. *Why* did she smell?"

"What girl?" asked Donald.

"Shut up," I said, and then to my mother, "She's also overweight and has a mustache."

"Who?" my grandmother said.

"Don't interrupt!" I said. "The girl at the lab with PKU."

"What?"

"She's dying of PKU," my mother said. "Whatever *that* is."

I told them (it took half an hour to get it out) about Marguerite and how, in her senior year of high school, she'd won the thousand-dollar award from the medical society for her research on mental retardation—it was the biggest prize at the science fair—and how she used the money to spend a year at St. V.'s. And even though it was all boys, they let her in, the only girl, so she could work with Dr. Foley and attend Dr. Foley's classes. "She makes an extra thousand," I said (although I didn't know exactly what she made, if anything), "working for Dr. Foley as a lab assistant."

"What kind of parents," my mother said, "would let their kid spend every waking hour in a lab with that woman?"

"Her parents are old," I said. "That's why she has PKU. Her parents are too old. They had a genetic flaw."

"How do you know how old they are?" my grandmother asked.

I looked at Donald to see how he was taking this.

"Don't be looking at him," my mother said. "*His* parents weren't too old!"

"I wasn't thinking that," I said, but I was still looking at Donald. "You're the only one," I said to him, "who thinks you're a retard. Nobody else thinks that but YOU."

Donald told me to shut up.

"Finish your story," my mother said.

"It *is* finished," I said.

My mother looked at me. "Oh, no, it isn't. You were all set to say something else."

I was simply going to say that Dr. Foley treated her much worse than she treated me, but my father came back into the kitchen. He'd been listening the whole time. Now he wanted to know, too. We were all in the kitchen and everyone was gawking at me.

"What does Foley do to her?" my mother asked.

"Yeah," said Donald. "Tell us."

"I can't tell," I said, and a commotion started around me. "She does to her," I said, when I saw the commotion get out of hand—especially since my father was in the room with his belt on—"what she does to me, but worse." They weren't satisfied with this, but they got involved with each other—my grandmother and my father were never in the same room for more than five minutes without finding fault and treating each other to a stream of insults, which usually got my mother involved on my grandmother's side, and Donald, too. Once I said, "It's three against one!" but that didn't make my father any more a friend of mine, so I didn't say anything when chairs began to scrape the floor and ugly tones and tempers flared up.

But I had wondered myself why Dr. Foley was so ugly to Marguerite, when the girl was completely devoted to science—never washed her hair, never bought a new dress, spent her every waking hour in the lab. And she wasn't really retarded, either, just weird. "Two peas in a pod," Janet remarked one day when we were wisecracking. I had to ask her who the other pea was.

"Foley, you stooge!" she said. "Birch and Foley."

I laughed, even though it was mean. "But are they peas," I said, "or flies?" and then Janet laughed.

The night I was mating the *Drosophila* parents, I found Janet on a lab stool writing on a pad. "What are you doing?" I asked. "I mean, what are you doing here so late?"

"I'm doing my homework," she said, "if it's any of your business."

I went over to look at her sheet of Latin declensions. "We did those already," I said, bragging like I always did about how hard my school was, and how far ahead I was, and a year younger.

"Who asked you?" she said. Then, "If you're so smart, why don't you do a couple for me?"

I looked at them—fifth declension—but I didn't do them. I just said them out loud.

"Again," she said. "Slower, so I can copy."

On the way home in the pitch-dark night, my feet freezing in their boots and slipping on the hard crust of snow ("Here, hold on to me," she said), I told her what I had seen. "To do it," I said, "first they back into each other."

"They *what?*"

"They back into each other." But I couldn't really describe it because she had never seen a fly under a microscope and didn't know what their backs looked like or how their rear ends were shaped differently.

"Tell me again," she said.

"They back into each other and stick there, tail to tail."

"Gross," she said.

"They stick there, squeezed together and all puffed out."

"I don't want to hear about it," she said.

"That's all there is," I said. "It lasts a long time."

"What else happens?" she asked. We were only a few feet from her front door, and the porch light was on. I could see into her house where someone was watching TV, and then her mother came to look out the window. She didn't see us: we were standing in the dark.

"I don't know," I said. "Foley calls it a transfer of genetic materials."
Janet looked at me. "You're so naive," she said.

"Me!"

"Yeah. Plus you're a bullshitter."

I watched her walk up the path and onto the porch. Pretty soon the
door would fling open. "Hey, Janet!" I yelled.

"What?" she said, but didn't turn around.

"Flyshitter," I said.

Now she did turn around, and her mother was behind her. I said it
in a louder voice, adding, "It isn't a transfer of *shit,* stupid!"

"Jacqueline McManus!" her mother said, then dragged Janet in by
the arm and shut the door behind her.

I walked along the sidewalk, carefully shoveled by Mr. Conneally
or by Jimmy Conneally, past St. Francis covered in whatever the jay had
covered him in that day. It looked like nothing from where I was standing, but I knew you couldn't always see what was there—sometimes the
shit was flat and just a gritty streak of green on the white stone. "Stop!"
my brother would say, "you're making me sick on my stomach!"

I finally got a grant for my project on flies, "Sex-Linked Traits," and a
money prize of three hundred and fifty dollars from the Society of Ex-
perimental Geneticists. It happened in June. By the next September,
when I went back to the lab, both Janet and Marguerite were gone,
Janet to college and Marguerite I didn't know where. At first I thought
she was dead, but Dr. Foley mentioned her one day in a fit of rage over
a set of pipettes that were laid every which way in a drawer that also
contained metal objects. "Did you do this?" she said.

"No."

"Then it must have been Birch. I didn't think it was you."

"Why not?" I asked. She looked at me—I was sitting on a stool next
to hers, handing her one prepared slide after another, which she clamped
under the microscope, looked at, made a note about, then discarded, the
little glass smashing in the wastebasket. "Are you telling me I'm wrong?"
she asked, starting with the quiet voice.

"No," I said, "but—"

"Yes, you are," she said, a little louder, taking a slide from my hand.
On it, and embedded in a sandwich of clear gel, was a young moss root

exactly one cell wide and growing by doubling its nuclear material, then splitting. It was a perfect act of asexual reproduction, and her job was to introduce a shock of ultrasound to the splitting cell to alter it in some unpredictable way. First she had to find a root with an engorged nucleus and puffy cell jacket, the sign that it was ready to divide, then rush it into the inner lab—where I was now allowed to enter, as Marguerite had been, and work, and even eat my lunch on a Saturday—and aim a high-speed sound wave at its silvery skin.

"I never expected you to amount to much," she said, when we had taken a slide to the sound room for Step Two. "You come from an unexceptional background and you've had nothing but those mediocrities as teachers."

I stood in the doorway, watching while she placed the slide in the chamber and directed the beam at it. "You're not a natural scientist—some people are, you know. Your friend Conneally—I forget her first name—*she* was. But all she can think about is boys and clothes. Like you. But you impress me," she went on. "You're either the most reckless person I've ever met or your skin is so thick that nothing ever penetrates. Maybe it's both."

She said more, and not just on that day. I worked for the whole school year and entered an ultrasound project, first in the state and then in the national science fair, in Seattle. I won prizes in both, three thousand dollars in prize money. I called her from Seattle and she said, "Why are you so surprised? Do you think I'd work with a loser?" I also met a boy from a Catholic school in Iowa whose project was on fish, and we went out after the last day of the fair. It was my first date, and I didn't have to ask anybody's permission because my sponsor got the measles and flew home. She left me in the hotel with no instructions. "I don't need to tell you how to behave, Jackie," she said. "You could tell *me*."

When I got back from my date—we went to the movies, then had a Coke in the hotel lobby—I had three messages at the desk, two from my family and one from the principal of my high school. On the bed upstairs was a box of flowers: roses and daisies. "You don't often see that combination," the desk clerk said when I came down looking for a vase. There was a card. I found it later, when I went to throw the box out. "Do you think you'd be in Seattle," it said, "or anywhere, if it weren't for me?"

Part II

Part of the fun of being a fiction writer (and what keeps writer and writing from the snare of solipsism) is hearing readers' views of what's what and who's who in one's stories. As a writer who has drawn on "real life" for material, I was never surprised when my stories were sieved for real-life models and situations. "Sex-Linked Traits," published first in the *New Yorker,* then in a collection called *Home at Last,* was no exception to this pattern. But, in this case, reader reaction seemed more off-track than usual.

I wrote the story in 1984, just after finishing the master's program in fiction at Johns Hopkins. I showed it to my writing teacher, who had been, up to then, a real fan of my work. This time, however, he muttered something about "blue-collar realism," adding that it wasn't half as interesting as the things I'd written for him. Stung by his reaction, I reported it to a second teacher, who said: "Of course he doesn't like the story. He thinks you're writing about him." The thought that the eminent, highly cerebral novelist who'd presided over our workshop at Hopkins could confuse himself with the "Dr. Foley" of St. Vincent's College struck me as laughable. But the second teacher seemed to take it seriously.

I asked him where he got this idea. He said, "Reread the last sentence and you'll see." In the story's last line an unidentified (but unmistakable) Dr. Foley, biologist and mentor to student Jackie McManus, telegraphs her at the national science fair with the following message: "Do you think you'd be in Seattle, or anywhere, if it weren't for me?"

I always liked this question—and its position in the story—because Jackie, the story's protagonist, never answers it. But did my writing teacher think that I wouldn't be in the *New Yorker* (or anywhere) if it weren't for him? Or was he concerned about Dr. Foley's feelings?

If this were indeed the case, then he wasn't alone. Other readers, too, expressed their concern on Dr. Foley's behalf. "Sex-Linked Traits" was read by a group of night-school students, mostly women, at the local Hebrew College. These readers saw Dr. Foley as nothing less than heroic: Jackie McManus's savior, the one who rescues her from the hands of the nuns ("those mediocrities") and from the dysfunctional family. They could understand the frustration the teacher felt, which had likely prompted her to send that telegram. Why *wasn't* the girl more grateful to this fierce mentor, who would catapult her beyond the ambit of parochial school girlhood?

And why was I so surprised to hear my character singled out for praise? Writers are normally grateful that their characters seem real enough to elicit a strong response (even if it's the "wrong" one). But I wasn't grateful or even pleased. I hadn't meant to cast Dr. Foley as feminist hero. In constructing the story, I saw her as foil and antidote to the McManus family. As a human being—mean-spirited, pig-headed, vain, colossally tactless—she is, as my father might say, "no bargain." The McManus family, on the other hand, is no great bargain either. Fractious, smug, ingrown, the family is about as torpid and unambitious as anything Tennessee Williams could come up with.

Given these contesting elements, the story "idea" was to place Jackie in a world where ambition (the life of science Dr. Foley emulates and exalts) is as problematic as its opposite. Where Dr. Foley raises Jackie's sights (and her consciousness), she also poses certain problems, exemplifying personal success of a dubious quality. If you need to be this obnoxious to succeed, who would want to?

But it wasn't until the session at the Hebrew College that I saw how I had underestimated the might of my character. Was she also more appealing than I thought? Doubtful. Still, the story needed all of its forces and elements to defeat her. And was she defeated? Her question, at story's end, still reverberates.

In a more schematic way, Foley also embodies (about a decade before its time) the ideals of the women's liberation movement of the 1970s. To excel as a scientist in a man's world (and in a men's college), she defies and routs the feminine paradigm: self-denying, passive, modest, altruistic. *She* wants that same excellence for Jackie and means to bully her through teenage vanities, family loyalties, and even the snare of early success (to shed the best possible light on her angry telegram) to see that she gets there.

That said, I still think of her not as heroic but as comic—if not quite a caricature, then more a foil. The qualities that she lacks (humanity, common sense, good humor), and that might make her whole (or less flat, in E. M. Forster's terms), can be located in none other than the apathetic family, so typically Irish Catholic in their shortage of funds and drive and abundance of conflict and clutter. If, at the lab, Jackie absorbs a sophisticated dose of genetics and the scientific method, she's learning something at home too, something to temper Foley's excesses. What would those excesses be? Her exploitation of the hapless Marguerite Birch, her possessive jealousy of Jackie and her friend Janet, her rigid faith in the scientific imperative. For all her sharpness, Foley is also naive: she prides herself for being that bolt of intellectual ultrasound that will zap (and "permanently alter") an ordinary girl like Jackie Mc-Manus. What she doesn't see is the arrogance of that self-conception and her own vulnerability. The telegram claiming full credit for the science fair success gives her away. She wants something more from Jackie and Janet—and even Marguerite—than their achievements. She wants what she so painfully lacks: affection, admiration, some emotional return on her teacherly investment.

Jackie notices this and other cracks in Foley's armor because she comes from a family with a keen eye for a human foible. It might be worth walking through a few scenes to see just what Jackie perceives and where this talent for insight comes from.

In the opening scene Jackie has just received a pair of trendy new boots and wears them to the lab. Predictably, Dr. Foley is enraged by sight of the fancy boots. Instead of developing her opinions, which, according to Dr. Foley, "is what we're put on earth to do," Jackie's been wasting her time and money on impractical fashions. Instead of criticizing them, though, she observes that the boots wouldn't fit her own legs. Jackie offers her one to try and receives an even stronger blast. Why would Foley care if they fit? Why does the fact that they wouldn't make the stovepipes even more objectionable?

While the biologist is checking out the boots, Jackie is taking another kind of mental inventory. For all her rugged independence, Foley makes her home with her mother and has the habits and hobbies of a homebody: she knits her own hats; she attends meetings of the college (St. Vincent's) Mothers' Club, although she has no children, and even if she did—as she tells Jackie—would never send them to St. V's. So why is she a member of the Mothers' Club? And why run down the school she teaches in? Why is this woman so angry? The question is never explicitly raised (or answered), but it prompts further observation.

The second scene takes Jackie to a girlfriend's house. Janet Conneally is also a budding scientist and—somewhat like Jackie—torn between the domestic and the lab. Janet's mother makes it clear that she resents every minute her daughter spends in Dr. Foley's lab. Jackie asks Janet what Mrs. Conneally would have her do instead. Keep her lonesome mother company is the gist of the answer. Compared to cooking up fly food and facing the daily tantrums of Dr. Foley on the icy campus, Mrs. Conneally's stay-at-home program has its appeal, a fact both girls grudgingly admit. The actual scene suggests that the divide (lab versus home) between the students and their mothers is a painful one and that crossing it is not always definitive:

I asked Janet why her mother had let her come to the lab without an argument, when usually there was a fight and hard words, and once Mrs. Conneally had bolted the kitchen door and stood in front of it. Why does your mother hate Dr. Foley so much? I had asked, and Janet shrugged. It had something to do with being home alone all those dark afternoons with no one to talk to. Mrs. Conneally was forever asking me why "the girl" couldn't stay put just once in a while—stay at home, do something her mother wanted, for a change!

"What does she want you to do?" I asked.

"Sit in the bedroom," Janet said, "while she puts four coats of polish on her nails, then bites it off."

We laughed. Mrs. Conneally was known for her nerves.

"Go out shopping, make brownies," Janet went on. "Watch the stories."

"Wouldn't you rather?" I asked her.

"I don't know," she said. "Don't ask."

Somewhat later in the story, Jackie faces the same resistance from her own more beleaguered mother. "While *you* spend every livelong hour of the day up at the college with that harpy, I'm stuck here alone with them [live-in grandmother and son], waiting on them hand and foot, and no one to help me."

Mrs. McManus has more of a sense of humor than Janet's mother and perhaps can also see where the hours spent in the lab might be more fruitful in the long run than housework and babysitting. She admits as much: "I don't blame you, though," she says to her daughter, right after scolding her. "If I had someplace to go, I'd go too, and you'd have to take care of them."

Implicit in both mothers' claims—and in both daughters' sheepish and/or sullen reactions—is the trace of another ideal that predates the feminist: that of the Catholic woman, as exemplified by the Blessed Virgin Mary and the female saints—not to mention the "mediocrities" who've given their lives to God and to teach the likes of Janet and Jackie.

By that standard—especially a pre–Vatican II version of it—Jackie and Janet, perhaps, *should* stay home. Earlier generations would have— to judge by the number of older women in my Irish Catholic neighborhood who forewent marriage and family, or a career and education, to care for sick or elderly family members or to put older or younger brothers through the seminary—not to mention the ranks of those who, like the mediocrities, "gave their lives" to God.

Nowhere in "Sex-Linked Traits" is Jackie forced to take this route. To the contrary, even the nuns are ambitious for her. "Where's your backbone, Jackaleen McManus?" says Mother Francis Marie, when Jackie slacks off at school. "And you who were the one who was going to show us all." They know, and she knows (and Foley also knows), that Jackie is not going to stay at home or "enter" the convent. As "the one who always goes too far," she's going to have the boots, the boyfriend, and the science fair. But the counterpressure is, nonetheless, felt, often exerted by the family, who feel that Jackie owes them—at the very least—a thumping good report from that exotic world that is so harsh and competitive, a world to which Jackie has been sent as a kind of emissary, a canary in the coal mine.

This brings us to the story's climax, a scene at the kitchen table wherein the young scientist takes on the whole family. Jackie is in a tight spot, having just witnessed a scene where her father is cruelly (even sadistically) dressed down by Dr. Foley. Mr. McManus is sent to the college by Jackie's mother, tired of watching for Jackie "on school nights from the upstairs windows, until the time she saw Dr. Foley slam on the brakes after squealing around the corner and going up over the curb so that half the car was parked on the sidewalk. She told me my father would come pick me up after that, on late nights, but nothing doing, Dr. Foley told him when he arrived at the door of the lab: 'This girl is not finished yet and I'm not letting her go home and throw a wonderful career in science out the window just so your family can lead a tidy life. Go on back home. You're lucky to have a daughter as smart as Jacqueline!'"

The kitchen battle scene follows this outburst. Jackie tries to distract her father from thoughts of how he's been "walked on" by Dr. Foley. She can only think of one way to do it. The bile Foley spews so freely on Mr. McManus is nothing compared to what is dished out to "the college student she hated so much." And so Jackie offers the story of Marguerite Birch.

"This quieted them down," Jackie reports, "or at least my mother piped down enough to hear about the college student who was Dr. Foley's special doormat."

Unfortunately, the strategy backfires. Mr. McManus is too mad to listen to this tale and leaves the room in a huff. The shaggy-dog story, and its reception, are further complicated by an unfortunate comparison of Jackie's younger brother, Donald, with the afflicted (and possibly retarded) Marguerite. Speculations are made about the kinds of parents that would produce such faulty offspring. (Jackie's genetics experiment, "Sex-Linked Traits," prompts this explanation, but so does the contrast between the McManus siblings, with Donald, a natural homebody so unlike his sister that he seems a different species.) One thing leads to another and a fragile family peace is shattered. The father reinvolves himself, and all hell breaks loose.

Jackie may be quick-witted, as the scene demonstrates, and good in science, but she's no wiser than her irascible father in the handling of people, especially the members of this droll and volatile family. But she does understand its workings, and she judges it with fairness and a nice sense of absurdity. "My grandmother and my father were never in the same room for more than five minutes without finding fault and treating each other to a stream of insults, which usually got my mother involved on my grandmother's side, and Donald, too. Once I said, 'It's three against one!' but that didn't make my father any more a friend of mine, so I didn't say anything when chairs began to scrape the floor and ugly tones and tempers flared up."

The story ends, of course, in Seattle, in the world of science, of achievement and ambition, where Jackie probably belongs. It's not going to be an easy life, if Dr. Foley's growing embitterment is any kind of indication. As she picks Jackie for her ever more sophisticated projects, moving closer to her own field of interest (where they're nearly partners), she's even more hostile and derisive in her speech.

In an exchange reminiscent of the scene with the boots, Foley discovers some glassware sloppily stored in a drawer and is quick to blame the hapless Birch, but Jackie insists that she could just as well have done it. Jackie may be defending "poor" Marguerite, but it's just as likely that she's defying Foley for the fun of it. (The recent family set-to may have played its role in motivating Jackie's righteous stand.)

The defiance predictably brings on a flood of insults and corrections. Foley never expected Jackie to amount to much, she says, coming from so ordinary a background and with only a mediocre education; worse, she's not even a natural scientist like her friend Janet. How is it that such an average girl could succeed in such a demanding field? Foley offers three solutions to this mystery. The first two she gives on the spot. In themselves they don't seem particularly apropos: "You impress me," the teacher says, "You're either the most reckless person I've ever met or your skin is so thick that nothing ever penetrates. Maybe it's both."

It's the third that Dr. Foley has most faith in. Jackie McManus has succeeded, in short and in fine, because of the labors and sponsorship of a scientist like Foley. "Do you think," she writes on the card, sent with two kinds of flowers, "you'd be in Seattle, or anywhere, if it weren't for me?"

She's right, and Jackie, I think I can say with some confidence, knows she's right. The credit she would give herself is earned. That she has to ask for it, though, and in such a belligerent way, and at such a moment, shows that this very considerable intellectual accomplishment comes with no refining grace, insight, or humanity.

Jackie knows this, and the McManuses know this.

Jackie may be in Foley's world (Seattle), but she retains the feminine (boots, boyfriend) and the Catholic correction—at least, I hope she does, to judge from the parting comment of her chaperone. Jackie reports from Seattle: "I also met a boy from a Catholic school in Iowa whose project was on fish, and we went out after the last day of the fair. It was my first date, and I didn't have to ask anybody's permission because my sponsor got the measles and flew home. She left me in the hotel with no instructions. 'I don't need to tell you how to behave, Jackie. You could tell *me*.'"

But, as I mentioned, this is not the story's last word. That place is given over to Dr. Foley and her reverberant question. But let's try to answer that question. One answer is no: without Foley, Jackie McManus would not be in Seattle. One answer is yes: Jackie McManus is in Seattle, but Janet Conneally isn't, and neither is Marguerite Birch, both of whom had the benefit of the teacher's intervention.

The correct answer might be: no and yes. If it hadn't been for the "home" schooling, Jackie McManus wouldn't have stayed on in the lab as long as she did—longer than Janet, longer than Marguerite. To be tolerated, Foley's strong dose needs the correction the family provides. Is this how Catholicism tempers feminism? Not exactly. Writers don't usually start out with so defined a program, but looking back, I see that the story settles comfortably into that reading.

Reconciliation might be too kindly and too inert a term for feminism's reaction with Catholicism (at least as far as the story is concerned). The action of one on the other is volatile and doesn't bring about a clean, easy, or permanent resolution. *Dialectic* or *struggle* might be a better term—I seem to have favored the word *correction,* which carries with it the mortifying but bracing lash of a long-lasting Catholic education.

NOTE

The story "Sex-Linked Traits" (Part I) was originally published in the August 27, 1990 issue of the *New Yorker,* and is reprinted courtesy of the author and the *New Yorker*. The essay following it (Part II) is original to this book.

FIVE

Serviam

Madeleine Blais

We were, in a way, saved by the nuns.

My mother had driven me to Ursuline for Mission Day, a chaste little carnival that had in my opinion only two advantages. Classes were canceled, and we could wear normal civilian clothes. Throughout the day a girl in a white dress, wearing a crown, circulated the gym, dispensing robotic hellos. She was our Mission Day Queen, elected solely on the basis of her goodness, which meant she had, during private consultations about her spiritual future, let it be known that a religious vocation was not entirely out of the question. A car was raffled. Elaborate exhibits showed foreign children in uniforms studying at Catholic schools supported by events like our fair. There would be scads of offspring, barefoot and brown, standing in front of smiling parents with downcast eyes. The parents were forever being quoted as saying that as long as you had faith, food didn't matter. You could purchase pictures of saints and pricey rosaries and little pins with the school motto, which was the same as that of the Jesuit school attended by Stephen Daedalus in *Portrait of the Artist as a Young Man:* "*Serviam,*" Latin for "I shall serve."

Mother Francis and our mother discussed literature that day. Not much later, a phone call came.

Ursuline was expanding; lay teachers were needed to complete the staff, especially at the coed elementary school level. My mother's salary of two hundred and seventy dollars a month would be sweetened with free tuition for all four girls. And now all the Blais girls were guaranteed that Ursuline gloss.

On the surface the biggest differences between Ursuline and public school were the absence of boys and the uniforms, ugly gray blazers, box-pleated green gabardine skirts, loafers, and nylons. But more than that, the nuns had a way of micromanaging our social interactions, ensuring that even the sorriest girls had some kind of circle. Someone who in a different school would have been ripe for hazing, given her assorted social handicaps—such as never shaving her legs, never closing her mouth, or possessing a retarded aunt—even she had friends. The nuns made a point of informing us that the more humble and penitential our behavior in this life, the more days we could lop off purgatory in the next through a complicated system of plenary and supplementary indulgences. Their main disciplinary strategy was to treat misdemeanors as if they were felonies. You earned demerits if your nylons sagged or had runs: a messy outer life announced an equally sloppy inner one. In between classes we walked in silence in single file. Lunch consisted of a bleak sandwich composed of a lonely piece of see-through meat. Most of us were so hungry we kept secret bags of chips and candy in our blazer pockets, which we learned to extract piece by piece during class and consume noiselessly without ever being caught.

One time, some girls got suspended for playing Spin the Bible with some elementary school boys on the bus. Their faces were stricken and frightened when they were summoned one by one from their classrooms to explain themselves to the principal.

Encouraging kissing games was bad.

Using the Bible for twisted purposes was worse.

The combination of the two?

Unspeakable.

At each report card, the students who were well behaved got a blue ribbon to wear on the sleeve of their blazers. Girls who were good, and bright to boot, got blue and gold ribbons, and once in a while a brilliant sinner merely got the gold, a cold secular trophy revealing a weak nature and an underdeveloped conscience. Our grades were arrived at with pinpoint precision: "Math 86.7%." When I flunked a major chemistry final during my senior year, the grade was written on my report card in red ink: "67%." I asked Jacqueline, "Do you think Mom will be mad?"

"Try her," said Jacqueline.

She wasn't mad at all. "Don't worry about it. You won't need science. I never did."

At Ursuline, we were, most of us, the children and grandchildren of immigrants. The Cuban girls were the only genuine newcomers. They showed up overnight, mysteriously, shortly after the Bay of Pigs, their only baggage their colorful pasts, musical accents, and pierced ears. The principal, the daughter of a Bronx cop, used to brag, "This is a dictatorship, not a democracy," which must have been especially disappointing to them. When we prayed we listed our intentions, and after Conchita and Mercedes arrived, we added our hope that someday they would get good enough in English to dream in it.

Our last names were Marinello and Giamalvo, Cosgriff and Glynn, and Conway and McCarthy. Although in 1960 a Catholic was elected president, we still imagined we were living on America's margins, fearful of quotas and closed doors.

It was also a tricky business, back then, the education of girls. No one worried about our sabotaging ourselves with bouts of low self-esteem; society had ensured that would be redundant. We knew our education had a hothouse ornamental quality. After disappearing into our grown-up fates, all that Latin and all that business with Bunsen burners would be useless. We were to marry: Jesus, men, or Service to Others in the form of spinsterish devotion to jobs at, say, the soul-eroding Registry of Motor Vehicles or in mournful classrooms filled with interchangeable unruly pupils year after year. If we didn't watch out, our intellects would be like all those Christmas trees on curbsides in January, denuded, discarded, and all that would be left would be the impulse to duty and good deeds. We prayed in Latin, English, and French. Amen with a toga, amen with a baseball cap, amen with a beret.

Very few of our mothers worked outside the house. The fathers had Chevrolet dealerships or practiced medicine or did legal work for the diocese. Tiny, freckled, with a high happy voice, a girl named Connie Breck, about whom everyone said *she has good hair, thank God,* was our only celebrity. Her father was a shampoo and hair conditioner magnate. This was the golden era of the famed Breck ads, with their idealized girls with their gleaming hair and glowing complexions, fixtures in every reputable magazine with a female clientele. "Who is the girl in the Breck portrait?" the ad would ask itself. "She's a teenager in Tucson, a homemaker in Fargo, a career girl in New York. She's like you in many ways. Loves the things you love . . . home, family, children. Most of all she loves to be loved."

It really said that: *Most of all she loves to be loved.*

We asked Connie how it was that each Breck girl possessed the exact same degree of prettiness as the next. At first she wouldn't tell us, holding us at bay until finally, clearly against her better instincts, she relented and whispered, in strictest confidence, of course, what we took to be a well-guarded company secret: "It's all in the lighting."

The nuns gave us lessons in graciousness. Now that a Catholic president was in the White House, our horizons as young women had suddenly expanded. They saw us all as future Jacqueline Kennedys, an amazing leap when you consider that we all had Frito breath. But still they persisted in seeing us in the most hopeful light, the way the Irish describe vicious downpours as nothing more than an overactive mist. Maybe we too would marry a world leader, in which case we had to know where to stand in a reception line, how to curtsey around a monarch, and what to say during conversations with men of substance at a state dinner. "What would you do," we were asked, "if by chance you were seated next to a nuclear physicist? What would you say to him?"

Our blank faces must have been frustrating.

The nuns provided the answer. "Talk to him about himself and his work, of course. Find out where he's from. Ask: What's nuclear? What's physics?"

"Girls, here's something to ponder," said the priest who was leading our weekend retreat. "What age would you be if you could be any age at all?"

We were all fifteen. Our answers did not vary much. Sixteen, seventeen, maybe twenty-one.

"Does anyone want to be younger?"

No one did.

"An infant, perhaps?"

Again, no takers.

His face lit up: bull's-eye. "No one would ever choose to go back to being a baby, yet that is exactly what Jesus Christ our Lord and Savior was willing to do when he came down to earth in order to die for our sins. That's just one more example of the kind of sacrifice he made so willingly, and look at you, not one of you willing to be even one day younger. How many of you have heard the song that goes, 'To know, know, know him is to love, love, love him'?"

We all knew and liked the song by a group called the Chordettes.

We all guessed, correctly, that he was about to ruin it.

"What does it mean? Does it mean that the more you get to know a boy the more you like him?"

We exchanged glances: this guy was a real genius.

He moved in for the kill. "The same is true for our Lord, you know.

"Some of you, I know, are wondering about the ways in which you can honor the Lord. Every day, he gives us the opportunity to honor him in large ways and in small ones. Let's look at one of the small ones: lipstick. Many of your parents have asked that you wait until you are older before you start wearing lipstick. Why? Because you are vessels of the Lord, you are his handmaidens, and the wearing of excess color can be an invitation to lust. A modest amount can be an enhancement in a much older woman, but you girls are still very young, and surely nature at this stage requires no enhancement. It will ergo be considered a violation of your uniform if you paint your face in an excessive manner. We must constantly remind ourselves that we have been conceived in Original Sin, and we are born into a state of darkness, from which the Lord in his infinite mercy has seen fit to rescue us through the Blessed Sacraments of baptism and Holy Communion. For these blessings we must offer constant thanks and daily witness, through prayer and in our actions. Our lives must be conducted in a meritorious fashion so that eventually we can enter the heavenly kingdom ruled by the almighty risen Lord and we can achieve the highest goal of mankind: we can bask in the Beatific Vision, the dazzling light of his goodness.

"The eating of meat on Friday.

"The missing of Church on Sunday or on Holy Days of Obligation.

"The failure to perform one's Easter duty.

"The tragedy of marrying outside the faith.

"These are the large transgressions with which we are all familiar. But sometimes I fear that in our enthusiasm to avoid these sins we relax our vigilance against Satan's less dramatic beckonings, the small moments that are also sinful but perhaps not as public in their depravity. I am talking about some of the thoughts that might occur to you as you bathe. I am referring to the sin of self-pollution. I am referring to the all too popular custom of close dancing, to driving around in cars sitting on the laps of boys, to the lure of liquor in all its cheap perdition. Convertible automobiles, racing toward pleasure: a prime example of the insidious nature of Temptation, arriving as it does in the finest of outward apparel, masking its rotten core. The serpent did not appear in a swamp; he came to Adam and Eve in a garden. Let us now pray to our Blessed Mother for divine guidance to recognize Satan in all his guises, great and small. Mother, most holy, tower of strength."

Every first Friday of the month as well as on Holy Days of Obligation, we celebrated the mass. Because the altar boys were at their own schools celebrating their own masses, we females were allowed as an assembly to give the response to the priest, and to this day when some middle-aged man is discovered to be an altar boy of that vintage, I will challenge him to see who can remember the most liturgical responses, a contest I sometimes win, my one shiny nickel in a mainly male arena, the verbal equivalent of a three-point shot.

Once and only once as I recall, a priest was brought in to hear everyone's confession: I've wondered since then if he didn't have a secret task of ferreting out a rumored pregnancy.

We filed into the makeshift confessional, reciting the boilerplate offenses for girls our age:

Bless us, Father, oh how we have sinned: We listened to the radio after lights out, we snuck a cigarette from our mother's purse, we sipped some beer at Polly's New Year's Eve party, we stopped at Friendly's when we said we were coming straight home. And then pausing, our voices becoming softer and more serious: we had touched ourselves, we had allowed ourselves to be touched. More details: the edge of someone's underpants had been stroked by a boy on the dock outside Doreen's beachhouse in Old Lyme one summer night, a bra had been loosened from its mooring after dark in some boy's car. The vision of all of us in our turn confiding to a dark shapeless creature, dressed in robes, seated inside a box has a lingering air of the absurd and frightening and the kinky: Samuel Beckett meets the Inquisition meets *Penthouse* magazine.

For people who had taken a vow of chastity, the nuns certainly enjoyed talking about sex a lot, only they called it fancy names like "concupiscence" and "the marital debt." Out-of-wedlock babies were a major obsession, and the nuns all had well-thumbed pamphlets, supposedly actually authored by a fetus, before it died in an abortion. They would reach inside the billowing black folds of their habits and read details about each of the fetus's developmental triumphs, such as its first little kick or faint heartbeat, leading up to Month Three and the startling revelation, "Today my mother killed me."

The nuns believed in something called moral hygiene, a loophole that meant that even if you were inclined toward wrongdoing you could cleanse your soul with really good deeds. Every now and then we got to go on class trips, but it wasn't like at the public school where the kids took big yellow buses to Mountain Park or Riverside and got to ride on the Cyclone all day and gorge on cotton candy. We drove around in each other's mothers' station wagons, and our excursions were designed to result in a corporal or spiritual work of mercy. And we didn't sing fun songs like "99 Bottles of Beer on the Wall" either. We sang songs like

> An army of youth
> Flying the banner of truth
> We're fighting for Christ the Lord
> Heads lifted high
> Catholic action our cry
> And the cross our only sword

One time we brought brownies and root beer to an orphanage. A little boy who kept scratching his head tried to sell me a slingshot. Another time we gave homemade sock puppets to some people at a hospital who drooled and made noises you couldn't understand, but which the nuns said meant thank you. Then it was off to a home for veterans. During "Jingle Bells," an old man reached into his pants and started singing along, the same words but totally off-key. Later, he asked one of the prettiest girls if she liked sarsaparilla, which he said would put hair on your chest, and then collapsed into a smoker's hacking laughter at the word *chest*. On the way back it was decided that we made a mistake when we sang secular songs about reindeer and white Christmases and that we should have stuck with the holy ones, with their calming emphasis on sleeping infants. The orphans and the sock puppet recipients and the old soldiers were united by one redeeming characteristic: they were all Catholic.

One nun stood out as possessing a gypsy streak—our mother's benefactor, the French teacher, Mother Francis Regis, or Franny, as we called her behind her back. Franny was by far the most temperamental and as a result the most invigorating of our teachers. Her favorite fillip was "*Pensez-y et profitez-en.*" Think about it and profit from it. She was Miss Universe for *le mot juste*. She had those frequent displays of impatience that often characterize teachers of foreign languages, and her way of showing it was to recruit some sorry specimen to stand in front of the room and be the object lesson for the words that embodied our failings:

Mademoiselle is messy.
Mademoiselle has holes in her clothes.
Mademoiselle has scuffs on her shoes.

Franny reserved the worst circle of hell for mumblers. "How can it be," she would rail at some girl whose natural-born shyness caused her chin to be devoured by her neck, "that despite all my best efforts I have failed so totally to turn you into an exhibitionist!"

Franny was also the drama coach, a title she welcomed because it gave her the chance to travel from Stockbridge to Boston, to cut loose and indulge certain flesh-driven cravings. It was well known that she never refused an offer to stop along the pike at Howard Johnson's for their all-you-can-eat fried clam special.

When she wasn't goading us to do better, she would invite us into her special club involving male-female intrigue. She was the driving force behind our tea dances, awkward daylight events in which the partners were often each other's brothers or cousins, with the exception of the occasional paper boy innocently delivering the *Union* only to be collared by a large nun and ordered onto the dance floor. While inside the school, we would be shuffling our feet to the music, Franny would stand at the door, scanning the horizon for more male recruits. These dances were always held in the winter, and she would pretend to be drawn to a snowfall. "Ah," she would say, quoting, I believe, James Joyce, "the filigree petals, falling so purely, so fragilely surely," clasping her rosary against her bosom, secretly praying, "Dear St. Ann, send a man."

Although not in the world in the least, she was clearly drawn to it. She told a story that was both confused and sorrowful about how as part of her religious training she was cloistered for a year in the early 1940s, cut off from all communication. During the war, while transferring from one convent to another by train, she entered a car filled with soldiers close to her in age.

"Pray for us sister," they said.

"Of course I'll pray for you. Is there any special reason?"

"You know the reason, Sister. We're going to war."

She gazed at them and did not dare ask, "What war? With whom?"

She hid *Life* magazines under her mattress because in the convent they amounted to contraband, filled with shocking information about parties and the Pill and movie stars of dubious virtue. She would sneak them into class, drawing them forth from the folds of her habit, and whisper, "Look here, girls."

"Brigitte Bardot," she would tell us, "is a famous French actress. Let's hear you say it right."

"Bridge Eat Bar Dough," we would reply.

"What's the terrible thing that happened to Clark Gable shortly after he filmed *The Misfits* with Marilyn Monroe?"

"He died of a heart attack."

"En français, s'il vous plait."

"Monsieur Gable est mort d'une attaque du coeur."

"What kind of woman is Marilyn Monroe? En français, s'il vous plait."

"Une femme fatale."

We followed Franny, those of us who also wanted to break loose, to the various contests in which we intoned passages from *The Hunchback of Notre Dame* ("Sanctuary, sanctuary") and invoked the oratory that preceded the death by hanging of Irish Freedom Fighters, as well as recited the more maudlin poetry of William Butler Yeats, including "The Ballad of Moll McGee." This doomed soul, Moll McGee, had the horrible misfortune of lying on top of her infant baby and suffocating him after a long day of work at the salting shed.

> There, little children,
> Don't fling stones at me
> Because I mutter while I go
> But pity Moll McGee.

Franny was the coach when I entered the Voice of Democracy speech contest and helped me write a tribute to Herbert Hoover, that often overlooked statesman who as a child helped support his widowed mother with a paper route, working his way slowly but surely to the top, becoming president of the United States, then through his actions helping to create a Depression, thus affording millions of other youngsters the chance to follow his lead and raise themselves up by their bootstraps.

The dramatic selections for the girls of Ursuline on Plumtree were always safe, laudable, and above all clean. Other students from other schools performed the more daring works of Edward Albee and Tennessee Williams, who would have been considered too modern and transitory and crass for us to study formally. Albee's Everyman on the bench in *The Zoo Story* who felt that sometimes you had to go a long way out of your way to come back a short way correctly, and Williams's flighty character in *A Streetcar Named Desire*, Blanche Dubois, the one who depended on the kindness of strangers: Who needs them? Iffy, iffy.

To the Blais family, the Kennedy White House was proof that we had arrived. If, as it so often seemed in our world, the highest status accrued to families with a priest in their ranks, because then you had your own special pipeline to the divine, having an Irish Catholic in the White House had the same feeling of privilege and intimacy. The whole nation had been shrunk to something smaller and more manageable, to parish. One of ours was at the helm.

We followed the entire presidency, of course, but we were most enamored of Jacqueline Kennedy's televised tour of the White House. She had grace and class; what's more, she wasn't afraid to express her opinions, telling the audience: "When General Grant became President Grant, he put false, elaborate timbers across the ceiling and furnished the room in a style crossing ancient Greece with what someone called 'Mississippi River Boat.'" In that famously breathy voice she praised Gilbert Stuart's portrait of Washington but also complained, "So many pictures of later presidents are by really inferior artists. . . . I just think everything in the White House should be the best." Of course, we concurred.

At home, we played a game based on the Kennedy women. Our mother wanted to know which one she most closely resembled.

We were honest.

"Not Joan," we said. Too young and too fluffy.

She seemed to agree.

"Not Ethel, either." Ethel was too toothy and too "tennis, anyone?"

Again, no argument.

We paused when we came to President Kennedy's wife.

Maureen Shea Blais looked up, hope flashing.

We knew we would hurt our mother's feelings, but we all need to face facts. "Not Jackie, either." No, not Jackie with her perfect hair, perfect pearls, and perfect life.

There was one right answer: "Rose," we said with a flourish, yes, yes, yes, Rose, with her hats and her head held high, her daily mass and her constant campaign teas for her baby Ted.

The static-swaddled crackle of the voice of the principal came over the intercom: Mother Mary Austin, announcing the news that the president had been shot.

"There has been terrible news about President Kennedy. The president has been shot."

Stunned, silent, without being told, we knew we should fall to our knees onto the hard linoleum, a torture we gladly endured because after all Christ had allowed himself to be crucified for our sins and you had to ask yourself, which was worse, and we began to pray for his recovery. The prayers, of course, did no good: Kennedy died soon after we heard he had been shot, but still we remained kneeling, shifting gears, praying now for the repose of his soul, as if there could be any doubt that someone as handsome as he was, from our own home state no less, a devoted father and family man, a believer in the one true holy apostolic faith, would have any trouble whatsoever getting into heaven. "Think about it," said one of my classmates, like all of us a sudden expert on the subject of eternal salvation. "If anyone deserves to bask in the Beatific Vision, surely it is President Kennedy. We are talking state of grace to the nth degree."

At home, we spent the weekend watching scenes of the First Lady climbing on top of the car, ruining her suit with blood, wearing, if truth be told, that unflattering little hat. Later, we witnessed the commotion at the jail when Oswald suddenly slumped over and Jack Ruby was arrested for his murder. We watched the funeral cortege—a new big word—with the riderless horse clomping down some big wide street in Washington. The horror and the spectacle were a leavening force, humbling evidence that everyone could have it tough, even the high and mighty.

Cliches are the most self-respecting of phrases; you don't get to become one unless you embody an extreme and unassailable truth. The more I thought about the randomness at the heart of human existence and the more I contemplated the bullet from the textbook depository, the more anxious I became. I said three Hail Marys to myself at the drop of a hat, and I made the sign of the cross all the time, unremarked, in the palm of my hand. I knew a girl at Ursuline who liked to invent self-inflicted forms of penance. She put rice on the stairs and walked up them on her knees; at school she would offer to sharpen everyone's pencils. I thought if I wanted to enter a similar black hole of pain and frustration, I could always try to match all the socks in our house.

In Franny's class, for weeks on end, the formal study of French was suspended. Instead, she read the accounts of the funeral out loud:

The terrible ordeal of Mrs. Jacqueline Kennedy reached its final phase today.

The widow of the dead president, still bearing up proudly three days after her husband's murder, chose to walk instead of ride behind the caisson bearing her husband's body to the funeral mass.

Before that, the thirty-four-year-old Mrs. Kennedy, who marked her tenth wedding anniversary in September, made her third sorrowful trip to the Capitol in less than twenty hours this morning. This time it was to accompany the body to St. Matthew's Cathedral for a low Pontifical Mass.

Mrs. Kennedy left the White House shortly before 10:30 A.M. EST to go to the Capitol. There she stood on the steps as the flag-draped casket was slowly brought from the Rotunda and placed on the horse-drawn caisson. A dirge sounded in the background.

She visited the casket in the Rotunda three times and kissed it twice.

"Girls," said Franny, smuggling forth yet one more piece of paper from her capacious sleeve, "I have here a quote from the *London Evening Standard* that says it all: 'Jacqueline Kennedy has given the American people from this day on the one thing they have always lacked—majesty.' Repeat after me."

And we did, our voices lingering on the word *majesty* as if it were a crown in and of itself.

My sisters and I did what insecure people so often do in the face of overwhelming external events that have no clear connection to their lives: we found one. As fatherless children, John-John and Caroline were now, on some level, like us, a blood brother and a blood sister. Our feelings were mixed. While it was heady to be considered in their category, it also made us less singular. They would know, as we did, death's great contradiction: the profound presence of those who are forever absent.

NOTE

This essay was originally published in *Uphill Walkers: Memoir of a Family* by Madeleine Blais (New York: Atlantic Monthly Press, 2001) and is reprinted courtesy of the author and Grove/Atlantic.

SIX

Telling Old Tales about Something New: The Vocation of a Catholic and Feminist Historian

Linda A. McMillin

Recently, I met a woman at a conference with whom I felt an instant kinship. We had much in common: both forty-something feminist academics, single parents, natives of southern California, and products of sixteen years of Catholic education. The last launched an evening of playing "Can you top this?" with parallel childhood misadventures straight out of *The Trouble with Angels:* fierce nuns, horrid uniforms, pagan babies, and fractured theological aphorisms. The next morning, we went running together, and the conversation turned confessional. "Are you still Catholic? Do you still practice? Do you still believe?"

Catholic baptism leaves an indelible mark on the soul—a mark neither of us fully embraces but one we cannot easily erase either. Neither of us still believes in the patriarchal god of our childhood. But on good days and in some circumstances, we both still want to embrace faith—in life, in forgiveness, in Jesus, in ultimate meaning. And we both still practice—continuing to find meaning in the rhythm of a weekly liturgy celebrated in a community of faith. However, my new friend is no longer Catholic. She attends an Episcopal parish led by a female pastor. Her decision to leave was a result of her desire not to raise her two daughters in a church that devalued and limited their possible roles and contributions. This is a logical and understandable choice. I remain a practicing Catholic, however, a choice often hard to explain both to friends and to myself. Indeed, I sometimes feel like an oxymoron—trying to be both a feminist and a Catholic. I am a woman who can deconstruct the misogyny at the heart of the Roman Church yet still be nurtured by the familiar word and ritual of Sunday mass. I am a historian who can document the struggles of religious women for space and a voice through two millennia yet still actively participate in a local Catholic parish: teaching Sunday school, singing in the choir, and raising my son in this sacramental community. For me, to be a feminist and a Catholic is to live with contradiction and to continue the struggle for a voice in a church that is at times inhospitable but is also the place where my hope of faith is best nourished and supported.

Growing up Female and Catholic

One of my earliest parochial school memories is of sitting in the mornings with friends on the steps of a large, two-story convent. When our first-grade teacher, Sister Rosa Maria, emerged in a rustle of voluminous dark skirts and heavy veil, we strained our eyes to catch a glimpse inside the mysterious house. Rumors abounded about that sacred space and its occupants, fed by miraculous images from hagiographic collections for children. On the one hand, the sisters themselves were powerful women who ran our school and commanded our respect and fear. I had seen Sister Rosa Maria handle horned toads, snakes, and tarantulas. She had singled-handedly rescued me from the far reaches of our playground during a fierce dust storm. A look from her could freeze and silence forty first graders. She was also brilliant, able to answer all the questions I could pose about God or any other mystery of the universe. Then there was the physical space of the convent—a separate women's place that even Monsignor did not venture into uninvited. Indeed, the majority of the rooms were off-limits even to him. Sister Rosa Maria had allowed me to carry her books into the foyer once and had led me down a hall to see the small chapel full of light and flowers. The swish of a habit and a strong nun's voice are the first strains I hear when I think about growing up female and Catholic.

Of course, counterimages fill my childhood memory as well: the privileged men and boys who could enter the sanctuary, serve at liturgy, preach, and "do the magic" in sacramental action. Despite the power of the sisters, men were in charge—of congregations, of public celebrations, of rule making and rule enforcing. These men heard my confessions, gave me penance, and fed me Jesus. I remember the jealousy I felt of my brother, who could be an altar boy and who always got to pass out the Necco wafers when we played mass. "Why can't I be the priest?" I complained one day as we set up for another imaginary liturgy in our living room. My grandmother's response was clear: little girls are not made for such roles and need to accept their place in the Church. Nuns might be formidable and have their own space, but it is not the main stage. The sanctuary is the domain of the male and the cleric. And the justice of such arrangements is not to be questioned; it is simply to be accepted as part of the natural order of things. So I also learned early that female and Catholic has a countermelody: subordination and silence.

I grew up Catholic in southern California in the 1960s and 1970s. The church of my youth was a bundle of post–Vatican II contradictions. San Bernardino was on the fringe of the San Diego diocese—far enough from the bishop to be a place of disfavor for priests who challenged tradition. And Nuestra Señora de Guadalupe competed with Saint Patrick and Saint Anthony for novenas and fiestas. So the leading disputations were not primarily about gender but about language—Latin, English, Spanish; about race, class, and ethnicity; and about the desirability of reform and the loss of tradition. The religious women of my youth took an active role in these conversations and brought them to the classrooms of which I was a part. From first grade through high school, in my undergraduate theology classes, and in the two years I spent as a faculty member at a girls' prep school, my education was punctuated with the voices of these women. To a person, they spoke on behalf of justice, of siding with the poor and oppressed, and of caring for those in need. These women taught me to act as well as to speak. One asked me to raise money to care for "pagan babies." Another recruited me to visit prisoners in Juvenile Hall. One sent me to work at a Franciscan mission in Mexico between my sophomore and junior years of college. Still another hired me to teach classes on social justice to privileged white girls in the San Fernando Valley. These notes, too, become part of harmonizing female and Catholic: serving others, speaking and acting in the name of justice.

While I respected and admired the many sisters who were a part of my life, I spent much of my youth living in fear that God would call me to be a nun. I knew from early on that I wanted to be married and have children. I was very bright, was expected to go to college, and was often told that all careers were open to me. Still, talk of "vocation" always presented a dichotomous choice: marriage or convent. Each involved sacrifice. On the one hand, the only Catholic women I knew with careers were nuns. As teachers, nurses, administrators, they obviously enjoyed their professional roles and were seriously engaged in the life of the mind. But for this privilege, they had sacrificed physical intimacy and motherhood. By contrast, motherhood clearly meant career sacrifices, subordinating intellectual pursuits to care for husband and children. While all the mothers in my family worked, they did so out of poverty and necessity. Their jobs put food on the table but did not bring much intellectual challenge or personal fulfillment. Motherhood was a laywoman's primary job and would be her sole occupation if only the family could reach a level of middle-class comfort.

Of course I secretly wanted both family and a career, thinking I might be clever enough to balance both. But it really was not my decision. After all, God determines vocations. He calls and you obey. So I dutifully prayed for the religious vocations of others, always adding, "But not me, Lord!" And throughout my childhood, I courted danger, risking to be pious, daring to sing in the church choir and be a youth leader for high school retreats, and having the audacity to major in theology as an undergraduate. To my great relief, God's voice did not direct me to the convent. My vocation lay in the other direction: I got married and had a child. And I carefully pursued a career path that allowed me to obey the rules and keep my familial roles primary. I put off graduate school to support my husband's education and gave up a scholarship to Fordham to give birth to a son. When I finally entered a Ph.D. program it was at a local public university, where I patched together courses and mentors sympathetic to my religious interests. The final notes in the chord of growing up female and Catholic are sacrifice and obedience.

Becoming a Historian

My favorite subject in school was always religion. I was a pious child and faith came easily. I was confident of God's care, and our dialogue inside my head formed a constant backdrop to life. I loved to hear stories of biblical heroes and saints. I had a good memory and could recite great chunks of the Baltimore catechism. I even got the coveted role of Mary in our third-grade Christmas pageant. In high school, my older brother and sister joined a fundamentalist group and urged me to "accept Jesus" and abandon Catholicism. I was happy to comply with the request of my siblings—accepting Jesus was easy; I didn't ever feel like I had lost him. But the simplicity of the local Bible study could not keep me engaged. Rather, I found the scholasticism of my high school religion courses fascinating. I discovered the rich intellectual traditions of Catholicism, where faith and reason did not have to be mutually exclusive. Thus, my intellectual journey toward becoming a historian began in childhood piety, detoured through fundamentalism, and then meandered off through Thomistic apologetics.

I chose to continue my Catholic education after high school at Loyola Marymount University and pursued a major in theology. At first, I continued to focus on scholasticism and reveled in its wonderfully logical "proofs." But such mind games did not hold up to my expanded scrutiny, and I eventually abandoned systematic theology as too far removed from experience. While I had yet to really discover feminism— that would have to wait for graduate school—I can speculate that even then I was uncomfortable with knowledge systems that placed such a divide between mind and body, thought and experience. In my junior year, I fell in love with historical theology in a class taught by the only woman in the department, Sister Marie Anne (nun and Ph.D.!). In history I found a way of understanding the present by understanding the past. God interacts with us in history, in human experience, in a way much more concrete to me than absolute philosophical categories. That I first learned these lessons from my only female professor is also significant. Not only could women teach children, they could be university professors as well. Sister Marie Anne was an exempla, a role model, a signpost pointing toward history as a subject to study and as a profession to pursue.

In graduate school I focused on the Middle Ages as an essential key to understanding the modern Church—the last point where the center seemed to hold before falling apart in the Reformation. Here I encountered a complex world where the human and the divine, the living and the dead, the saintly and the profane were constantly interacting within the same Church; where great variations in doctrine and practice could ruminate within a single faith; but where living with difference sparked consequential and dangerous conflicts. It was in graduate school that I also began to learn about feminism. In a yearlong seminar on women's history, I discovered Scott's work on gender as a category for the study of history and Lerner's on the creation of patriarchy.[1] This seminar was a model of feminist pedagogy as well: in the second half of the course we met over a potluck dinner in my living room (so I would not have to hire a babysitter for my toddler) and read and critiqued drafts of each other's research, with our professor submitting her latest work for our perusal as well. My dissertation grew naturally out of both foci—medieval studies and feminism—and I decided to write about nuns, those powerful Catholic women of my youth. My thesis advisor, an indulgent Jesuit, suggested I focus my research on the Benedictine house of Sant Pere de les Puelles in Barcelona. Even though my gender questions were of minor interest to him, he was sure that the modern convent's rich archives—dating back over 1050 years to its founding—would provide ample material for a good social history. With his blessing, I decided to focus on how the community fared in the twelfth and thirteenth centuries, when the traditional strength of early medieval women's houses was waning. I wanted to understand how Sant Pere survived and thrived. So I began the final leg of becoming a historian—the thesis—with a medieval map and a feminist walking stick.

Throughout college and graduate school, I continued to be an active Catholic. I led music for weekly liturgies, worked in Catholic orphanages in Tijuana, had a big church wedding, and baptized my son. While I had begun to understand feminism, the personal was not yet political for me. In many ways I created separate silos for thinking about the world. I could be a Catholic; I could be a feminist. The two touched in my historical work but not in my personal life. God and I still had that internal dialogue going, and I was confident of the rightness, the righteousness, of my life. Sure, I "dissented in conscience"—a handy rubric—

on the issue of birth control, and I sympathized with female friends who sought ordination. But these were intellectual debates. I did not allow my intellectual journeying to transgress the territorial confines set in my Catholic youth. In my heart, I was still following my grandmother's admonition and accepting my place. I was obeying the rules, putting my husband and child first and pursuing my work second.

In 1989 life changed. The great juggling act that I thought I had mastered—balancing marriage, child, graduate school—came apart. My marriage ended that year and no amount of sacrifice and obedience could save it. I found myself outside the boundaries of acceptable Catholic womanhood. As neither nun nor wife, I had lost my place in the Church—in life. There was no third path in the list of vocational directions from my childhood. So either I had misheard or God had miscalled or. . . . I began to suspect that my dialogue with God was, in fact, my monologue in a silent universe, a crutch for my own hubris, a childish naïveté that could not hold up to the harsh realities of life. Work now had to come first—specifically producing a dissertation—so that I could get a job, so I could feed my son. I spent six months in Barcelona on a subsistence-level stipend, living in a one-room apartment, caring for a four-year-old, and spending long days struggling through mountains of Latin documents. The fragility and risk experienced by women of the past and present who try to survive in a patriarchal society—a central lesson of feminism—became a lived reality for me that year. Neither husband nor Church nor God was going to take care of me. I was on my own in an uncharted wilderness.

My means of survival became my work. And my work became the site where my separate identities as feminist and Catholic hammered away at each other. Each provided a context for my reading of the past and of my own present. The lens of feminism allowed me to see the ways in which a patriarchal tradition had undermined and undervalued religious women in the Middle Ages and had done the same to me. If I took this reading to its most radical conclusions, I would have to consider that the struggles of religious women in the past were in vain and that the ways in which they had found meaning—had found the divine—within their tradition, despite its patriarchal trappings, were misguided and illusionary. This would also make my own struggles to remain faithful and obedient equally absurd. However, my experience of faith, especially the faith of the religious women of my youth, pushed me to look for some middle ground, some place where tradition and feminism could together chart a new course. Ultimately, I needed both my understanding of feminism and of Catholicism to map the story of the twelfth- and thirteenth-century nuns of Sant Pere in all those Latin parchments. And I needed both, along with the nurture of the modern nuns of Sant Pere with whom I worshiped and conversed, to find the path of my own life again as well.

Religious Women of the Past

Historical research is a painstaking process. One must stitch together a story—"what happened"—out of random bits of information recorded and saved by chance. In the archives of Sant Pere, I found several threads that together allowed me to write a central chapter of my dissertation about a thirteenth-century conflict between the nuns of Sant Pere and their local prelate. The first thread I found was a document that records several days of trial testimony in which the abbess of Sant Pere and the bishop of Barcelona both claimed the right to appoint clergy to a parish church in a local village. The abbess locked the bishop out of the parish and appointed a cleric; the bishop excommunicated the cleric; and this pattern repeated itself several times. The bishop claimed to have authority over the convent. The abbess brandished a papal privilege, thereby claiming to be answerable only to the pope. But no judgment was recorded. Then I discovered a second thread: more trial testimony taking place twenty years after the first. The nuns of Sant Pere continued to defend their rights to the parish, despite an armed confrontation. The nuns were said to sing loudly and ring their bells despite being placed under interdict by the bishop. The testimony was lively and included the abbess calling her opponent a liar. Again, much was made of Sant Pere's papal privilege. But no verdict was recorded. After more research, I located the third thread: a short document of minor note that calmly recorded the appointment of a cleric to the parish by the abbess some seventy years after the first confrontation. My conclusion: the convent won.

When I found that final document, I was greatly relieved, for I had feared a different outcome. My own experience told me that such confrontations do not always end in victory for women, even with the pope on your side. I had learned this firsthand back in grade school. In third grade, I discovered that nuns had knees and hair. Vatican II had happened. The Immaculate Heart of Mary Sisters who taught at my school took quite seriously the directive to religious communities that they reform and update their constitutions. The habit was out, blue polyester was in. In our school liturgies, Latin and organs were replaced with English and folk music. Sister Carla, my third-grade teacher, was our local version of the singing nun. Her guitar rested on a high shelf in the corner of the classroom. After hours of good behavior, my classmates and I would sometimes be treated to a sing-along of three-chord Ray Repp tunes: "Here We Are," "Sons of God," and "They'll Know We Are Christians by Our Love."

In 1969, all the Immaculate Heart Sisters—including Sister Carla and Sister Rosa Maria—disappeared from our diocese. After several years of being on the leading edge of reform, their community was decimated in a confrontation with Cardinal MacIntyre of the Los Angeles Archdiocese. Their crime was responding to papal directives at a speed and in directions that their local prelate found unacceptable. Four hundred of the 450 Immaculate Heart Sisters chose to leave their order rather than submit to the cardinal's discipline and reverse their reforms. Of course, that meant losing their jobs at diocesan schools. This loss affected me tangentially; I had already switched to a different school run by a more conservative Dominican order. But I remember my mother explaining that our former sisters had been disobedient and could no longer be in the convent. Unlike the medieval nuns of Sant Pere, these strong women were cast out of their sacred space and tossed into the streets for being too uppity.

These two stories, from the distant past and from my childhood, encompass the best and the worst of being female and Catholic. Women of faith are not silent or invisible in the Catholic tradition. The Middle Ages are rife with clever religious women claiming a voice and a space— using family connections and wealth, playing one male authority off another, relying on visions: "I'm just a poor little woman, but God spoke to me this morning and is She pissed!" They use their spaces to create artwork and music (Hrotsvit of Gandersheim, Hildegard of Bingen), to teach children and care for the poor and sick (Dhuoda,

Bridget of Sweden), to learn philosophy and write theology (Heloise, Teresa of Avila). And they use their voices to call popes back to faithfulness (Catherine of Siena), to rally troops to save kingdoms (Joan of Arc), to demand resources for the needy (Clare of Assisi), to describe the most intimate mystical experiences of the divine (Julian of Norwich). But such "disobedience" is always risky. The boundaries between saint and witch are constantly shifting—just ask Joan of Arc. And the border patrol is always male and clerical. Unlike Joan, at least the Immaculate Heart Sisters only lost their jobs.

The first article I published on Sant Pere was the story of their victory over episcopal authority. Weaving together this tale was my first public act as a historian. In this work I began to plot a course toward a vocation I had not anticipated, had not seen in the two paths presented to me in childhood. Whose voice called me to such work? God's? My own? That of the women of Sant Pere? All I know is that I needed to tell this story, to not let it be forgotten, and to offer it as an alternative ending for the Immaculate Heart Sisters. I wanted my voice to join with both groups of women in song, ringing bells while bishops fumed.

Religious Women of the Present

The convent of Sant Pere gave up its medieval walls in the late nineteenth century and moved to the Barcelona suburb of Sarria. It is to this modern house with its large shady garden that I came to do research. Its chapel is a center for Catalan liturgy and music, and my son and I attended overflowing Sunday masses. People visit daily to seek the nuns' counsel and prayers. Each morning, I passed a line of young women with babies and elderly men waiting for alms to be distributed from the front gate. The scriptorium is still active, and the nuns who work in it always responded with lightning speed to my requests to repair documents I needed for my work. The convent archives are housed in a small room right above the sanctuary of the chapel. I often heard the nuns file into their stalls at the appointed hours, and their music surrounded me as I struggled to decipher the medieval scribal hand in which their story was recorded. Thus, in the midst of my examination of their distant past, the nuns of Sant Pere constantly reminded me of the continuing beauty and meaning of their communal life.

Sister Roser, the archivist, always took a special interest in my work, telling me that, while others had used the archives for various projects, I was the first foreigner to be interested in the convent's own story. Sister Roser herself was an accomplished Latinist and historian, but she had little time to spare for archival work. At fifty-five, she was one of the youngest members of her community. She had many responsibilities in the upkeep of the convent buildings, the managing of community finances, and the care of aging sisters. When I showed her a document from 1248 in which the community decided to cap its number at fifty, she smiled and responded, "We are still fifty, but not for long."

Sant Pere, like many other traditional women's communities, is dying. JoAnne McNamara summarizes the situation like this: "In the last decade of the twentieth century, with the median age of sisters now set at seventy and rising and no new generation of recruits in sight, the death of the feminine apostolate, at least in the United States and Europe, seems to be inevitable."[2] I am sad to think of a future without the women of Sant Pere and others in traditional communities like it. I know that I owe much to these foremothers, "who, for two millennia, have broken new paths for women in a hostile and forbidden world. They served their God and their church and in doing so they fulfilled themselves and laid a foundation for all women. Without the daring sacrifice of these nuns, it is impossible to imagine the feminist movements of modern times finding any purchase in the public world. They created the image and reality of the autonomous woman. They formed the professions through which that autonomy was activated."[3] Sister Roser was philosophical about the future: "God has blessed us for over a thousand years. Now He will do something new. Nothing lasts forever."

"Something new." Sister Roser's words haunt me. She died two years ago and I miss her. Like my first-grade teacher, Sister Rosa Maria, Sister Roser was a beacon in a tempest. During some of the worst months of my life, she was the daily smiling face that welcomed me to the archives, to work, and to heal. She listened to my story of a broken marriage and a broken life. She reassured me that I had made wise decisions under difficult circumstances and that the present was not a punishment for disobedience but an opportunity to make "something new." She believed in and encouraged my work. We debated how to read the past with feminist lenses that were faithful to a tradition and how to value the experiences of women of the past and present who struggled to keep and even expand their space and voice within the Catholic Church. She had no answers for me but offered only the wisdom of holding contradictions in tension. And she invited me to liturgy and to prayer with her community—not promising me the voice of God but providing me with a place to listen. Her voice made the universe less silent.

So what is the "something new" that God will do with religious women now? A remnant of the Immaculate Heart Sisters has morphed into the Immaculate Heart Community—noncanonical, ecumenical, with male and female, married and single members. Their community is not unique. Other groups experimenting with varying degrees of shared life abound. The world is a less hostile place for those of us who live on our own as well. Making a life outside the vows of both marriage and convent has become a viable, even preferable, option for more women today than ever before. So am I a part of that "something new"? Perhaps. The work that I have taken up as a historian, that sustains and heals me, and that has given me an unanticipated vocation, this work also draws me back into the practice of Catholicism. It gives me something to contribute to devising new possibilities. As a historian, I know that imagining a future is dependent on the stories that are told of the past. A future for Catholic women will come from knowing and telling the stories of our foremothers, of retelling the history of the Catholic Church in ways that see religious women as an important part of God's interaction with humanity. I can do that—in my research and writing, and in my teaching.

Religious Women of the Future: Catholic and Feminist?

The Gospel of Mark tells of the Syrophoenician woman who seeks out Jesus to ask a cure for her sick daughter. Because she is a foreigner, a pagan, Jesus refuses her request by saying that it is not fair to take the children's food and throw it to the house dogs. The woman persists. "'Ah yes, sir,' she replies, 'but the house dogs under the table can eat the children's scraps'" (Mk 7:28–29). Her daring speech is rewarded, and Jesus cures her daughter. In this tale, Jesus has a specific, but limited, understanding of his mission and how it connects past to future. However, when the Syrophoenician woman tells Jesus a new story, he is able to imagine a different future, one in which his good news is not just for Israel but for all peoples.

The stories women tell have played a role in the shaping of Catholic identity—in imagining who we are and who we might be—from the Gospels forward. These voices must continue to be a part of our Church's future. I remember the nuns of my childhood—strong women with their own space, serving others and speaking and acting for justice. I want my Church to value such women. But what of the counterstories: subordinate women, silent, obedient, sacrificing and sacrificed? Can I be part of an institution that so deprecates women? I ask for more than scraps but a place at the table—even to see women preside at table.

I continue to practice, to be nurtured by my local community, to listen to the gospel proclaimed, and to participate in the sacraments. I continue to teach—at a Lutheran college where over half of my students are Catholic. In the archives, in my classroom, and in my parish, I continue to discover and tell stories of religious women with strong voices—both past and present. And I try to imagine a future and the "something new" that God will do. But the contradictions remain, and so do the risks. I claim a space in the Catholic tradition and a voice in articulating both where that tradition has been and where it is going. But I am "just a poor little woman" without male clerical power and authority. And the boundaries between orthodoxy and heterodoxy—especially for feminists—remain murky, creating discomfort both for those of us trying to stay within the fold and those who would prefer to drive us out. As one respondent to a survey of Catholic feminists remarked: "I perceive the greatest difficulty to be in retaining one foot in Catholicism and one foot in creating the new. The ambiguity and the need to stay in dynamic tension is too hard for some."[4] So I admit that the temptation to join my friend down the road at the Episcopal church with the female pastor can be quite strong at times.

"Conventional wisdom says that orthodoxy must use its power to eliminate conflicting interpretations, but it is possible that orthodoxy must welcome conflict in order to survive," writes Mary Jo Weaver. Conflict, questioning, dialogue are necessary because "God and human interactions with God are mysterious, elusive, and often terrifyingly unclear." The best theological reflection arises out of the "deep questions at the heart of faith . . . troublesome questions—like those raised by feminists."[5] To her way of thinking, the "patriarchs" and the feminists within the Catholic Church need each other. I agree. They needed each other in the Middle Ages and in the parochial schools of my youth. As competing pieces of my own identity, I have needed them both to construct my own story. Perhaps together we might "invoke a reading of orthodoxy or catholicity that knows when to bow to paradox and believes that it can find, in the ironies of human fallibility, a more capacious language and a more graceful vision of the divine/human interaction than either patriarchy or feminism, alone, dares to imagine."[6] This is the hope that Sister Rosa Maria, Sister Carla, Sister Marie Anne, Sister Roser, and so many others have taught me. It is with this hope that I remain Catholic.

NOTES

1. See Gerda Lerner, *The Creation of Patriarchy* (New York: Oxford University Press, 1986) and Joan W. Scott, "Gender: A Useful Category of Historical Analysis," *American Historical Review* 91 (1986): 1053–75.

2. JoAnne McNamara, *Sisters in Arms* (Boston: Harvard University Press, 1996), 631.

3. Ibid., 6.

4. Rosemary Radford Ruether, "Women-Church: An American Catholic Feminist Movement," in *What's Left? Liberal American Catholics,* ed. Mary Jo Weaver (Bloomington: Indiana University Press, 1999), 62.

5. Mary Jo Weaver, "Feminists and Patriarchs in the Catholic Church: Orthodoxy and Its Discontents," *South Atlantic Quarterly* 93 (1994): 678.

6. Ibid., 688.

SEVEN

The Elephant Is Slow to Mate

Flavia Alaya

Admirable creature, the elephant, who Pliny the Elder says mates in secret—out of modesty—only once every two years, and then "for five days . . . and not more." This gift for delayed gratification has true stoic dignity for the old Roman, who finds something appealing—perhaps a touch of postcoital *tristesse?*—in its deliberately slipping off, after sex, for a cleansing dip in the river. Among elephants, he declares, "adultery is unknown."[1]

Such solemn Roman authority must have seemed unimpeachable to the Middle Ages, and Pliny's dignified and rather asexual elephant enjoyed a long heuristic afterlife in Christian devotional literature. In a brief survey of this tradition, Uta Ranke-Heinemann suggests it starts somewhere in the twelfth century, advancing over the years to reach a pitch soon after the Council of Trent in Francis de Sales's *Introduction to the Devout Life* in 1609.[2] Here Pliny's original emerges more fastidiously asexual than ever, for not only is the lag between amorous encounters now stretched to three years, but this more Catholic elephant rushes in an anxious and "immediate" gallop to the river to "cleanse himself."[3] *Himself,* significantly, for we see that the Christian centuries have turned Pliny's amiably galumphing creature, gender unspecified, into a post-Tridentine metaphor of masculine purity.

Of course, the world did not wait eleven centuries for such apologies for purity, and if feminist scholarship has made anything a commonplace of historical Christianity it is that sexual pudency, if not outright disgust, is a harping theme of the earliest patristic pronouncements—perhaps the only theme on which certain fathers seem to have had anything truly memorable to say. Also that women, to whom they normally attached their disgust, were being lashed into virginity quite early in the evolution of doctrine.

But to mark an ideological growth spurt in the twelfth century, I confess, suits the purposes of my theme, for it is also about this time we find Pope Innocent II announcing to the Synod of Clermont that even the chastest marital sex is so low as to be offensive to their dignity as priests. And although Innocent was already building on the authority of two of his most vocal papal predecessors, Leo IX and Gregory VII, it was he who finally achieved, nine years later, what had long eluded them: the first official canonical *thou-shalt-not* for the long-debated issue of a married priesthood, when the assembled bachelor-doctors of the Second Lateran Council finally pronounced for the Catholic universe what many of their more conservative forebears had sought for centuries.

To bring in the elephant, we might at least take this as a significant ideological time capsule, a moment when an old idea resounded within new sexual as well as ecclesiastical politics. Browning's Fra Lippo Lippi may have been oversimplistic when he later placed the notion of *sex* or *no sex* squarely within the ontological context of the debate over "the value and significance of flesh,"[4] but conceptually it has a very robust appeal. For it seems to me quite momentous—quite momentously anti-incarnational—that we can point to this discrete moment some eight centuries ago when the Church authorities definitively opted for *no sex*.[5] Of course, what they said was more mystified, more politic and political: that no marriage of an ordained priest should be "valid," or, more precisely, that priesthood constituted an implacable "impediment to marriage."[6] Yet even if such language is arguably too legalistic to bear such a heavy theological burden, it nevertheless exposes the decision in all its deepest realpolitik. The day had clearly arrived to declare for the principle of (male) asexual political superiority—that is, *no sex* over *sex*—not simply as the benchmark of holiness (which the Council might have endorsed while still making celibacy optional) but as an ultimate symbol of power.

Grant that the science of this hypothesis is compromised by my oxymoronic status as a priest's widow, for in such matters I may be no more deeply learned than Chaucer's Wyf of Bath, who took "experience" as her authority, just as she had once taken a young cleric to husband and spoiled a priest.[7] Yet I think it might stand the scrutiny of learning to suggest that the churchmen's intent was to exercise the new power they gave themselves, like a very indulgent pay raise, qua power: hierarchical, ultimately centralized, and definitively male. Obviously it resolved all questions about the transmission of "Church" property by making the illegitimacy of a priest's offspring decisive. But even this economic enhancement, however vital, appears less significant on its face than as a secure guarantee that the "mystical body" would permanently be headed—indeed be owned—by clerical bachelors. Scholars have made much of the theory that an unmarried priesthood helped ensure undeviating loyalty to the papacy, turning it back from the "margins"—what we might today call the base communities. They have made less, too much less, I think, of how it enhanced the capacity of men up and down the flowchart, deeply steeped in misogyny, not merely to control uppity women but to dictate chastity to the masses, male and female, from the cathedra of an enshrined sexual abstinence that excluded and "othered" them.

Legally and politically, the celibate clergy had defined for themselves an "authentic" privilege from which to elaborate a hierarchy of masculine purity.[8] For celibacy gave them political—public—authenticity, however *in*authentic the private purity: inauthentic not just because the celibacy was not always celibate but because, notwithstanding the canon law, there wasn't then and has never been a clear or outright "vow of chastity" for final orders. This often surprises people, and it should. Yet even defenders of a celibate priesthood admit that the "vow" is "tacit," a commitment presumed and predicated on the will to accept the sacrifices demanded by the sacrament.[9] Even when the Council of Trent later invalidated any marriage without the official sanction of the Church, it was only to further superlegalize an already legalistic norm and to snare would-be-married priests at the altar.[10] This remained the approximate sum total of the Church's official injunctions till more recent papal *obiter dicta* on the seriousness of the law.[11] Yet even now nothing else has changed: the promise a priest makes retains its vagueness, its discretionary laxity, not unlike the expectation of what constitutes good faith in keeping it.[12]

The equivocation might seem a good deal less cynical if the issue were not enforced celibacy. And it is "enforced"—isn't it? Surely there are—there must be—disabilities explicitly laid down for the offending priest in his own person. But what are they? The law doesn't say that the sacraments he performs are ineffectual (quite the opposite), or even that if discovered in flagrante he will be summarily prevented from performing them.[13] Indeed, it appears that in speaking only to the *validity of priestly marriage* the Church has actually constructed an arena of illegitimacy where the punitive effect, then or now, has almost never fallen upon priests, but almost exclusively on the women who have entered into unsanctioned relationships with them, and on their children. Remarkably, in synod after historical synod, it is the women and children against whom the holy fathers fulminate with increasing violence, who are condemned to social extinction. "Disabilities of all kinds," we are told, "were enacted and as far as possible enforced against the wives and children of ecclesiastics. Their offspring were declared to be of servile condition, debarred from sacred orders, and, in particular, incapable of succeeding to their father's benefices."[14] We are told this by a distinguished *Catholic Encyclopedia* authority on celibacy, whose general lofty tone would impress you, along with his defense of the moral authority of the Middle Ages. Not a single disclaimer of the cruel and unequal meting out of punishment by self-serving ecclesiastical courts to women wicked enough to have loved and been loved by priests; only the rigor of a declaration like that of the Synod of Pavia in the century before the Lateran Council, which defined the wives of priests as "slaves, the property of the Church," for the rest of their lives. Or the Synod of Melfi, after the Council, which declared the "wives and concubines" of any cleric, even a subdeacon, "liable to be seized as slaves by the overlord."[15] These are not cited as atrocities; they are simply used to establish an official paper trail, as proof of the Church's long-standing intent to make the worship of Jesus contingent on extirpating the unspeakable vice of concubinage.[16]

I want to savor this unsavory history not just as a woman, a feminist—a post-Catholic—but as a writer whose voice, though perhaps sufficiently irritating, has not yet been quite silenced on that account. To

savor it as a human being, bittersweetly, deeply conscious of the waver-
ing of the world on the subject of the value and significance of flesh; as
a woman who, once upon a time, enfranchised by a more Christian
Catholicism than any we have known for at least a millennium, might
perhaps have been married to a priest in a marriage of the sacrament
and not just of hearts and minds. I say bittersweetly, because as a feminist I know what any history of struggle teaches us: that things change—
change, and change again; that the voices silenced by enactments like
these are still tribute to a history of contention and courage. That even
as Catholic officialdom trumpeted virginity and engaged in the obscene
and disingenuous discourse of cleansing Mary's vagina from immaculate conception to virgin birth, it took a thousand years for it to enjoin
a celibate priesthood. A thousand years—ten full Christian centuries
without making the authority of married bishops a sacrilege or giving
scandal to the existence of priests' wives!—a thousand years of seeking
that still-elusive scriptural injunction against priestly marriage like some
vanishing grail. A hundred thousand Christians, in the Church or driven
out of it, struggling to bequeath the world a faith that honored women
and sacramentalized the sexual incarnation.[17]

II

I feel obliged to ask, where are they now—the feminist theologians, the
scriptural scholars and historians, outraged by this record or stirred by
this struggle? Apart from Ranke-Heinemann's, whose voice is raised to
declare "concubinage" a feminist issue, who says we must put a feminist analysis to the situation of millions of real women, historical and
contemporary, not would-be priests but real priests' wives?[18]
    I feel obliged to ask. But I confess, in my more serene post-Catholic
moods, I no longer even hope for this. What the Catholic Church has
already done—this and so much worse than this—is already done. I
sometimes feel like Mary Daly, unbound by its history, in some sense
prometheanly unbound from it, loosed from its pernicious injunctions.
The world has turned. I have permission. I wake up in the morning and
thank God I was born a woman.

And at the end of the day, I have less interest in the arguments—the history, the inventory of canonical crimes, generalizing and detached—than in the true article, the stories women tell. They are women like me and unlike me, women who have resisted the implacable *mulier taceat* that poisons us with our own spit. Women who have loved men not in spite of their being priests but because of it. They talk to me. They write to me. One once stopped me in mid-path as I walked with my son—my son and Father Browne's—across St. Stephen's Green. They are glad I've told the truth; I am glad my candor inspires them. They tell me that they too have had the equivalent of long and faithful "marriages." They didn't seduce their priests, nor were they seduced by them; rather, they fell in love in the usual way, the way the Church persists in declaring appalling. And in the usual way they were loved by them in return.

Love. It is certainly a Christian issue. Is it a feminist one? Can it be? I am an accomplished enough woman, they tell me, married, but (or is it *and?*) with an independent life, a life as writer and activist that enjoys the perfect feminist credential (if I may say so) of being irritating to my husband—not a priest—who wishes I would be done with it. Yet it is probably safe to say that I have never been anything quite devoutly except a "relative creature"—daughter, wife, mother, grandmother. Like my own mother, I have found my religion in the blessedness of these relations. That can be—must be—feminist too. Yet even as I say it, I think, *It is also Catholic.* Maybe it's the ultimate bridge between feminism and Catholicism—the bridge I cannot seem to burn. I take comfort from Nancy Mairs when she speaks of the principle of deity as verbal, of a "Godding" as opposed to a "God,"[19] but while I love the audacity of this and of her will to image God as female, none of it can make her actual *conversion* to Catholicism, her *choosing* it, less astonishing to me. I doubt I would be any kind of Catholic if my Sicilian mother had not called herself one. My father, *napolitano,* passionate, possessive, anticlerical to the bone, did his work well, teaching me the meaning of patriarchy on the authority of my body, teaching me how to resist it.

But it was Irish American Annie Murphy and her definition of herself as a "bad Catholic" that lately brought me as near as I have ever come to Olympian laughter on this theme. "Being a bad Catholic," she says, "is the best religion. Turn its beliefs about behavior upside down and, behold, fulfillment."[20] How perfectly perverse, perfectly targeted to all that Catholic thunder about carnality, meant to secure the power of sexless bachelors over the kingdoms of heaven and earth! Frankly, I'd avoided reading her memoir about her relationship with Bishop Eamon Casey till I'd finished writing the story of my own life with Harry Browne, telling myself I needed to preserve the clarity—the naïveté—of my own experience. True in its way, for in this respect a memoir is the hardest thing to write: it keeps on slipping its shape, every new experience altering how you remember your past. Yet I ask myself now, truthfully, How much naïveté could I preserve as a teacher of literature, a voracious reader, almost from the cradle, of novels about obstacle love? Didn't I actually draw the line between me and Annie Murphy out of disdain? Didn't I think her scandal somehow less meaningful than mine—my socially activist, politically significant, long-lived secret romance—more than a romance because it was all these things besides?

Now that I've read her book, I admit without shame that I wept over it too. And wept without shame even as a writer, because where they were not her own words it was enough to know she knew they'd told the truth. And there were the parallels between us: the wounded girl she'd been when she met him, just ending a life passage and starting another, the trip abroad—an escape but also a return, a return somehow to a place she'd never been but where the roots of her being were sunk. That uncanny fact of a *place* having brought them fatally together.

Then there was the difference in ages with its own peculiar psychic electricity, and the complex dance of coming to love him in full consciousness of his hypocrisy. Strange how, for her as for me, the disloyalty, the dishonor of his "breaking his vow" seemed so irrelevant, a sign of a weakness that was not of the essence of him except in its humanity, demanding a secrecy that was annoying, sad, and also hopelessly funny. Like Harry Browne, Eamon Casey knew he had never really taken a "vow" of chastity. He knew he could—and would—be forgiven for "breaking" it if only he avoided scandal. And Annie knew this too, understanding that his real dishonor was a failure of self-knowledge, a childlike need to construct an elaborate mythology of denial, of excuses for loving, and, later, for breaking faith with his love. Harry had done the same at first, putting a gulf between himself and his moral vision, failing deeply his own insight as a historian into the long shame of the Church's treatment of women. He finally understood this, long before he left, but when he left, it was an announcement of this knowledge. "What does the Church's stand on celibacy do but endorse concubinage?" he was to ask the bishops assembled in 1976. Did Bishop Eamon Casey ever understand? Does he now?

Reading Annie, I knew again how we may be overpowered by the beauty of a strong man's weakness, how she could be drawn to Eamon Casey by his energy, his amazing laughter, that radiant healing genius staggering under the weight of a millennium of admonitions and breaking itself loose in an electric shattering that sometimes seemed like pure light to her, the visitation of an angel in a dark place. She loved him as I loved Harry, for the dangers he had passed, for his refusal of darkness, for his subversive sense of carnal beauty and awareness of the world's hurt. She gave the lie to the Church's major premise about such relations: she would not have stood in the way of his ministry any more than I would have Harry Browne's, any more than I did. I declare myself Annie Murphy's sister. I pity the pain she has suffered since the age-old witch burners got hold of the truth of her life.

III

Last year, when my book was in the last stages of preparation for print, I had an absurd anxiety attack over a passage in it about a moment late in our lives together, some years after Harry had left his parish and a little more than two years before he died. In his palmy days as a scholar and professor at Catholic University, before we met, Harry had written a life of the first archbishop of New York, John Hughes—a plum assignment for the pet diocesan Church historian he'd been. The near-finished but unpublished manuscript, though widely known in Church circles and frequently consulted by historians, had never seen print for a variety of foot-dragging reasons. But in 1977 the Paulist Press suddenly published a life of Hughes—Richard Shaw's *Dagger John*[21]— without consulting Harry in their peer review, without a word about his prior work in the acknowledgments or in the notes. Harry had felt certain Shaw had drawn on his manuscript, which lay quite accessible in the archives of the New York major seminary in Yonkers, but his protest fell on deaf ears at the press. They told him Shaw admitted having read the manuscript but not having used it in any way.

Harry felt dead—worse than dead—extinguished. For years after the illness that took his life I couldn't touch the old Hughes manuscript among his papers, weighted with so much vicarious and desperate anguish. So much had seemed to be invested in it, in the idea that he would someday finish it—publish it. Betrayal, or the sense of it, had plowed a hole through his heart. When it came time for me to write about it, someone at the press reading my draft said I risked libel if I even suggested plagiarism. So I restructured and rewrote.

But I couldn't rest. I needed to see Harry's "Hughes" again, see it for myself. I applied to the seminary to read their copy—Harry's work for hire, so to speak—because it was the text Shaw himself had consulted. To my surprise, the keeper of the Dunwoodie archives proved to be a woman—Sister Marguerita—stern but not inhospitable. Not to me, at least, who was still unknown as the scarlet author of a scandalous memoir, though early on, as I negotiated my visit, there were moments of particular severity when I wondered if my name hadn't somehow already ripened in the old diocesan gossip about Father Browne, and reached the motherhouse. But after all I must have seemed a harmless enough drudge when I appeared, my aura of temptress burnt off in the crucible of time, my hair white, short as any nun's, my person inconspicuous, studious of inattention.

And so I read the manuscript over several visits, under her vigilant gaze. It was the passing of a strange and uncanny time with the scholar-Harry before I knew him: that tight-lipped, emotionless author-voice rich with facts, the notes thick with documentation, the insights acute but restrained, impersonal, without particular irony or humor; the voice of a man withholding himself, not so much eagerly reclaiming a life as giving it a dispassionate accounting. Oh, yes, I could see what Shaw must have owed him and should have credited—the laborious newspaper research into the same primary sources he'd quoted, the life neatly structured into its epochs of meaning; but that was all. Book to my left, manuscript to my right, I could find no passage pilfering, nothing the least visible in style or tone that betrayed his debt. Shaw's practiced writer's hand had quite independently known how to make the man live.

But there was something I found that I hadn't come for: Hughes himself. For if it was true that Harry's book refused to underscore its own ironies, it didn't altogether lack them, and even without introduction or conclusion there was an estimate of the man that she who runs might read. Hughes had been coolly intelligent, gifted, driven, relentlessly political, an autocrat once he was secure in power—*Dagger John* indeed. Shaw had caught this too, caught it with a certain zesty approval, perhaps with a certain frank political indifference to what it had meant, for Hughes had set the tone of unbending obedience to hierarchy, lay as well as clerical, for generations of American Catholics.

Obedience his mission, obedience his message—and the medium of his message. No wonder Harry—Hell's Kitchen Catholic Worker to the bone—had never exerted himself to publish this life, a life whose political meaning could never have been a matter of indifference to him, not of any kind. I wondered, then, had obedience—and its dark other, *dis*obedience—always been his theme? Though his loyalty to the corps might have made it unbearable self-knowledge, had he known what I hadn't till now, that his gift for resistance had perhaps not needed me?

Those visits to Dunwoodie became the scene of some of the most important encounters with Harry I have ever had in my life. They were also the most replete with love. I even fell in love with Sister Marguerita, stirred by her inexpressible mix of self-consciousness and self-possession, by the grace of her uncomplaining silence during those long, gray, room-darkened hours, as she sat there, two desks away, patiently waiting for me to be done. Time passed; we became friends almost by vibration. I felt secretly anguished at how soon she would know that I had in some sense deceived her. How depraved she might think me then, to have sat there before her still loving this forbidden man—this man in some sense still forbidden—straining for the sound of his voice in the text, choking back tears at the sight of those unguarded pencil scrawls in the margins, that familiar block-printed handwriting, aggressive, instinct with the life he was alive with again, a visible occasion of sin.

Perhaps she saw and felt none of this. Her last gift to me was a tour of the archive portrait gallery of archbishops from Hughes to O'Connor, her eyes shining as she briefly, reverently detailed each life. We parted friends—sisters—and I passed back into the world, out of the inner *sanctum sanctorum* of the archive reading room, through doorway after protective doorway, back into the chapel, back into the cloistered yard green with summer, back into the grand entrance corridor with its superb devotional statuary and well-carved moldings, its high ceilings and ringing marble floors subduing my footsteps.

More pictures lined these walls, large framed photographs of every seminary graduating class, *seriatim,* since it had begun producing diocesan priests in the early century. I held my breath, counting down, stalking his. And there he was, class of '44, front and center—front and center as anybody could be, sitting at the right hand of the rector. Looking fiercely at the looker. Looking at me. His black-dark eyes burned in his square face under a mound of dark hair in all the animal beauty of his young manhood, the inverse crown of his widow's peak more sharply etched on his smooth forehead than I had ever known it, when it had nevertheless been the mark of him, digging into his forehead like a penetrating thought, a tooth of mind.

Here had been his mission, his corporate loyalty, his devotion. Here had been the well of his capacity for praise, to give it, to receive it, sudden and fresh. Here was that something deeply existential, deeply incarnational, that was the best thing about him, about the priesthood, about Catholicism, that sense that the God-like did most truly, most violently, most purely, inhabit human flesh.

My homage to him in that image was, irresistibly, homage to the institution. It had not after all failed him in all his mortal needs. It had rescued him from poverty of mind as well as body. It had offered him the mystery of evil and the deeper mystery of the need to meet and thwart it in a dedicated lifetime. But my homage was to that rebellious spirit, too, that *non serviam* he spoke when the institution failed him— failing his deeper insight into the real power of the Incarnation.

IV

D. H. Lawrence, from whom I take my title,[22] may have been only a latter-day prophet, but I am reminded by his take on the slow-mating elephant that the celibate priesthood is a metonym of self-transcendence and in that sense a poem—the *poesis* of such self-transcendence in an ancient and dead language. It is a magnificent ruin, speaking to us of the godliness that inhabits—that can inhabit—the merely human, heroic, sacred, sacramental. This is, I suspect, why it is still holy to those for whose faith it can have no meaning otherwise. In the mixed social justice "faith community" of New York's West Side where Father Harry Browne and I once worked, I would have been rebuked by communists, had some of them known our secret, for putting our political work at risk. These people would never have made the celibate sacrifice, were perhaps incapable of it, yet they construed his (supposed) radical chastity as an outward sign of his inner commitment to the selfless service of the people, the loss of one capable of implying the loss of the other. They were a little like the Catholic Church in this. They would have found it easy to say to me: don't get in his way, don't give him a household, a child, a mortgage, to make a coward of him—not knowing that the Harry Brownes of the world are not cowards with ten children and ten mortgaged houses, let alone three children and one house and a dog and a cat. Not knowing that even if I did not minister, we were a ministry of two, and three, and so on . . .

I thank the God who made sure that Annie Murphy had a baby and that I had three. I am forever endeared to a former parishioner of Harry's who wrote me after my book appeared to say that genes for genius like his (and, bless her, even courage like mine) should never be wasted. Someday the human genome project may find some coding for priesthood, some peculiar something—is it a gentleness sometimes beyond gentle, a shamanistic intuitive gift, a motherliness in the man, a fatherliness in the woman? It is not so far-fetched after all. Might we, then, consider the genocidal impact of celibacy on the true *bios* of priesthood? Or thank the concubines for its survival?

NOTES

1. Pliny, the Elder, *Natural History*, bk. 8, chap. 5, p. 13, trans. Harris Rackham, ed. W. H. S. Jones (Cambridge, Mass.: Harvard University Press, 1940).
2. Uta Ranke-Heinemann, *Eunuchs for the Kingdom of Heaven*, trans. Peter Heinegg (New York: Doubleday, 1990), 13–14.
3. *Introduction to the Devout Life,* trans. John K. Ryan (1972; New York: Doubleday, 1989), 229 (third part, 39).

4. Robert Browning, "Fra Lippo Lippi," in *Men and Women, and Other Poems*, ed. J. W. Harper (1885; Totowa, N.J.: Rowman and Littlefield, 1975).

5. On this theme, see Mary Ann Cejka, "Making the World Safe for Incarnation," *CORPUS Reports* (Jan.–Feb. 2000), retrieved from CORPUS Web site: www.corpus.org/archives.cfm.

6. The operant canon law term is usually *diriment* (or nullifying) *impediment*.

7. Geoffrey Chaucer, *Canterbury Tales* (New York: Modern Library, 1994). Chaucer understands the antisex debate as a woman's issue.

8. See Pope Damasus I, as quoted in P. Delhaye, "Celibacy, History of," in *The New Catholic Encyclopedia* (New York: McGraw-Hill, 1967), 372.

9. J. W. Rehage, "Celibacy, Canon Law of," in *The New Catholic Encyclopedia*, 367. See also Herbert Thurston, "Celibacy of the Clergy," in *The Catholic Encyclopedia* (New York: Encyclopedia Press, 1913), also available online in *The Catholic Encyclopedia Online Edition*, 1999, retrieved 2002 from http://newadvent.org/cathen/03481a.htm.

10. Ranke-Heinemann, *Eunuchs*, 100.

11. John Paul II, *Pastores dabo vobis* (1992), retrieved from Vatican Web site: www. vatican.va/holy-father/john_paul_ii/apost_exhortations/documents/hf_jp-ii_exh_25031992_pastores-dabo-vobis_en.html. See also John Paul II, *Ordinatio Sacerdotalis* (1994), retrieved from Vatican Web site: www.vatican. va/holy-father/john_paul_ii/apost_letters /documents/hf_-jp-ii_apl_22051994_ordinatio-sacerdotalis_en.html. See also Paul VI's encyclical, *Sacerdotalis Caelibatus* (1967), retrieved from http//listserv.american.edu/catholic/church/papal/paul.vi/sacerdot.caelibat.

12. Thurston, in "Celibacy of the Clergy," implicitly favors the morality of continence over the morality of justice to women and children (12). Rehage, in "Celibacy, Canon Law of," speaks of "the Church's power to dispense from this impediment, since it is merely of ecclesiastical origin" (367).

13. Rehage, "Celibacy, Canon Law of," 368. See also the decree of Gregory VII at the Council of Rome (1074) (Mansi XX. P. 404), partial text retrieved from Internet Medieval Source Book Web site: www.fordham.edu/halsall/source/g7-reform1.html.

14. Thurston, "Celibacy of the Clergy," 10.

15. Ibid., 13, 14.

16. Thurston is unrelentingly precise about the English Church, which he says in the fifteenth century refused "to recognize any such entity as the priest's 'wife.' It knew nothing but concubinae and denied to these any legal right whatever or any claim upon the property of the partner of their guilt" (ibid., 13).

17. Ranke-Heinemann's *Eunuchs* is especially good on this theme of resistance throughout.

18. An issue completely omitted, for example, from Rosemary Radford Ruether, "Feminism in World Christianity," in *Women in World Religions,* ed. Arvind Sharma and Katherine K. Young (Albany: SUNY University Press, 1989), 228ff.

19. Nancy Mairs, *Ordinary Time* (Boston: Beacon Press, 1993), 11.

20. Annie Murphy, *Forbidden Fruit: The True Story of My Love-Affair with Ireland's Most Powerful Bishop* (New York: Warner Books, 1993), 61.

21. Richard Shaw, *Dagger John: The Unquiet Life and Times of Archbishop John Hughes of New York* (New York: Paulist Press, 1977).

22. D. H. Lawrence, "The Elephant Is Slow to Mate," in *The Complete Poems of D. H. Lawrence,* ed. V. De Sola Pinto and F. W. Roberts (New York: Penguin Books, 1964). The poem begins with the title line and continues in part: ". . . slowly the great hot elephant hearts/grow full of desire,/and the beasts mate in secret at last,/hiding their fire."

EIGHT

After Sufficient Reflection: Catholic, Feminist, and Divorced

Victoria Kill

I met Val, a Jesuit friend, for lunch, and when I hugged him I thought back to the first time my breasts had touched a priest. Clothed breasts, to be sure, but still perhaps a sin? My fiancé and I had just finished our final marriage preparation class, and our parish priest offered congratulations by pulling me into a rather robust embrace. I was married a week later without confessing this mash of chests, the corresponding thrill, or my libidinous loops of fantasy about taking down a priest—an act that realized would be a mortal sin worth hell, plus some. Such sins are simple math to call, and such fantasies, I know, not foreign to Catholic female imagination.

I had rescheduled this lunch with Val three times because I both wanted and did not want to talk with him about sin (mine), an untested topic of conversation between us. Val is my friend, a fellow writer and teacher, fond like me of long walks, beer, and no-rules tennis. He is not my confessor. This lunch, however, was for advice about my soul. I was dying to determine if I was going to hell. And I was chagrined beyond measure that the most reassuring strategy my feminist mind arrived at was to ask a man.

Nonetheless, across salt and pepper shakers and a saffron daffodil, I told Val about reading Louise Erdrich's latest book and about a camping trip with my daughters. And then without a pause I said that, by the way, I was ending the Catholic marriage I hadn't talked about much, the one begun twenty years ago, about the same time as that first breast memory of a priest's hug.

"Twenty years," Val echoed, and I met his gaze that did not feel like damnation. He had been a priest about that length of time.

"How do I know," I asked, "if breaking the sacramental vows of holy matrimony condemns me to hell? Is there a way," I asked, "to escape this being a mortal sin? What," I asked, "is a good enough reason? How," I finally asked, "can I confess a sin that I will never repent?"

Then I stopped talking and looked almost directly into his eyes and waited, planning to believe whatever he told me. I was desperate to make the move from questions to consequences. My hands were fists in front of me, and Val's hands reached across the table to cover them.

"I have an Italian friend," he said, "who lives outside of Florence. There is a cemetery on his monastery grounds where members of his order are buried. I walked through that cemetery last summer, and I was struck by the dates on tombstones. 'Emilio Petro Benveniste, born 14 January 1737, ordained 26 July 1761, died 11 December 1780.' 'Gabriel Horatio, dedicated to Holy Orders 13 June 1121, died 4 April 1141.' 'Carlos, Eugenio, Nicolas: ordained at twenty, dead at forty.' Those men were priests all of their adult lives, which equaled about twenty years.

"I have come to think," said Val, "that those sacraments which bind up our years may well have been based on life spans much shorter than ours." His hands on mine possessed electric weight, and I experienced Val's touch as holding my soul in solution. In absolution? He said: "Perhaps you might decide you've done your twenty years."

Growing up Catholic in the fifties and pre–Vatican II sixties got me well educated in a belief system whose basic tenets are firmly grounded on the ballast of mortal sin. My child's-heart Roman Catholic faith involves always being afraid for sulliedness of soul, knowing that I live in a world where venial and mortal sins are easy to come by. Sin lessons constitute my cerebral cortex. Strung end to end and side to side inside my skull, their integration throughout my childhood was sometimes masked as entertainment.

Theater, for instance. I remember first grade and the play that fourth graders put on for the rest of the elementary school every year. I was in the first grade but not too young to understand the exquisite symbolism of a set of palace pearls that must be polished each night. The princess and prince neglected this chore a few times, and the consequence was dark spots that no amount of polishing could remove. They were in despair until their fairy godmother came to tell them they had another chance with a second set of pearls. I think they kissed her feet at this news, or at least I know I wanted to. The children polished the new pearls faithfully every night, and then one day a circus came to the palace and kept them up late.

I could see what was coming, and watched in terror as the children crawled into their beds without a glance at the pearls. More indelibly than the permanence of goldfish deaths, this finality of no more chances took up residence in my consciousness, displacing me existentially and ruining my life at six years. My grief-driven wail became so loud that I was removed from the auditorium to wait in the principal's office for my mom to come and get me.

Mortal sin is like that. It leaves stains that neither toothpaste nor industrial strength cleaner can remove. Baltimore Catechism Question 55: "Why is this sin called mortal?" Answer: "This sin is called mortal because it deprives us of spiritual life, which is sanctifying grace, and brings everlasting death and damnation on the soul." I did not have the appropriate analysis until years later, but it is clear to me now that, by mortal sin standards, the children in the play were unfairly damned; their sin did not meet the prerequisites. Baltimore Catechism Question 56: "How many things are necessary to make a sin mortal?" Answer: "To make a sin mortal three things are necessary: a grievous matter, sufficient reflection, and full consent of the will." Divorce, for example, fills all three damning conditions.

I have been constructed in the language of the Baltimore Catechism and as well in the pictorial images of *Lives of the Saints,* a one thousand and one installment series for teens about saints, mostly martyred ones. Grace lessons were no less terrifying than those about sin. *Hermione crawled steadily forward, dragging her crushed leg, moving with determination toward the crucifix which lay buried under the spittle of her tormentors. Holding her nearly severed left breast in its approximate place, she pressed hard, determined to stanch the flow of blood long enough to reach her goal. Then, horrors!! A laughing assassin aimed his dagger at Hermione's spine. He threw his weapon, and it pierced her heart, from back to front, just as she stretched to touch the cross, and to humbly murmur: "All for thee, Sweet Jesus."*

Hermione was safely on her way to sainthood as I sat reading about her in my small hometown, drenched with envy at her opportunity for martyrdom. I lived in such an uneventful place that I could not step in front of a car for Jesus without the car braking before it hit me. The secret of life, according to my young Catholic reality, was to figure out how to die while saying "All for thee, Sweet Jesus." I probably missed about three years of conversational development because I spent all my time muttering this line, knowing that I could not count on being forewarned of the moment that would be my last.

The saints, I figured, had it so good. They simply got trapped with a loose lion, or set up on the rack, or any one of the multitude of meaningful preludes to death graphically depicted in my Martyr Mutilation Monthly magazine, and then it was no sweat to figure that their last moment was near. A few minutes of "All for thee, sweet Jesus" and they had it made. If they were female, they would know as soon as their bodice got ripped to start the prayer; predictable as clockwork, they would be home free, dead in minutes, with grace to spare if they were violated on the way.

My life, by comparison, was unpredictable and boring. Long after I had given up all hope of being boiled alive or flayed dead, I still yearned to be machine-gunned down on my way home from confession or attacked by a nest of rattlesnakes as I walked to a Lenten morning mass. But the good old days were gone, and I had to settle for risking myself in secular ways.

Catholicism was slip-knotted to my guts by stories like Hermione's, and it lived there, less than thoroughly unexamined, until I decided to leave my marriage. My four divorcing years were an agony of thresholds: I lost solid days trying to estimate when any particular move on my part would put me across the mortal-sin line. I knew that unquestionable mortal sins were those like killing someone or stealing from the collection plate when you didn't need the money. Something like hurting, leaving someone, however, was one of those tricky calls; you could do it—hurt someone—and it might or might not blacken your soul. It depends on things I often do not fully understand. I am neither proficient nor comfortable about drawing lines between duties to myself and others. The following, specifically, is a problem: I was raised by my parents to take care of men. Like the hardwired tutelage of the Baltimore Catechism, nothing I have learned about the pitfalls of such projects has entirely erased such training.

Scene: a divorce workshop for women, seven of us taking advantage, at bargain Women's Center rates, of three sessions with a lawyer and a financial planner. My husband has told me that if ever the time for divorce comes I will not need a lawyer, that he would not be able to live with himself should he be less than fair. I believe he means this, but his business world has educated him in different ways than my world has, and I need to learn some of the things he already knows. He takes great pleasure in his work, on behalf of clients, in making bankers and lawyers and IRS agents and estranged spouses agree to things they had not planned.

So I find myself in a small room, with six other women holding pain more or less closely. Some need to talk, need listeners to hear about husbands who are cheating, beating, leaving. This is an informational presentation, and the rules seem to be that emotional discharges must be wrapped into questions, stuffed into too-hearty laughter, borne out in sympathetic eye contact and other sisterly physical languages. This is no space for confessions of Catholicism. One woman needs only translations: English is not her first language, and she knows that all is at stake in words. She is right. I am suffocated by the words of the Church.

But I am here for facts and not comfort, which works out well because I find myself unable to speak throughout the first three-hour session. I am mute with compassion for other women in the room, including the wife of thirty-one years, kicked out of the house in which she raised five children, psychologically abused, financially ignorant and insecure. This muteness is to my credit, certainly, but the deepest reason I am silent is in fear of my life: I quickly become concerned that this roomful of hurt women might hurt me when my questions make apparent that I am the spouse who is ending the marriage—when they identify me, like their husbands, as the villain.

I decide, during the second session, that I must ask the questions I have paid to ask, and I begin with a safe one about children's involvement in the "parenting plan." This is a fairly obscene document that requires the geopolitical parsing of children's years: With which parent will this child spend Memorial Day? His or her birthday? His or her mother's birthday? My state requires that this plan be filed as a condition for granting divorce.

I later gather my courage to ask another question. This friend of mine, I finally say, wonders what a judge will do if (1) he does not want the divorce, and (2) he will support his wife if she stays with him, and (3) he has asked his wife not to throw away a perfectly good person. Given these things, will a judge penalize this wife for being unreasonable? Will a judge be less inclined to sympathize with a wife walking away, by her own choice, from this situation? Wouldn't a judge just say: I do not reward stupid people? Wouldn't a judge just tell this wife to grow up and quit being so stupid and selfish? Wouldn't a judge tell her to get her head out of the clouds and stop dreaming that common priorities have much to do with staying married anyway?

I do not entirely trust my memory, but this is the gist of what I asked, I think. After I stopped asking, I braced myself for accusations of betrayal from the divorce collective in the room, but this did not happen. What followed reminds me of the way the Dutch film *A Question of Silence* ends.[1] In this film, three women are on trial for the unpremeditated murder of a shop owner, a stranger to them, their actions largely premised on the fact that he's a man. The film asks viewers to understand the women's act as sane, not necessarily justified, but a choice motivated by the daily little murders they experience as women. The film narrative follows the education of a female psychiatrist, expert witness for the state, who is expected by the legal system to verify the women's insanity. She does not, and the film's penultimate scene takes place in a courtroom where all of the women present become participants, one by one, in powerfully disruptive laughter that marks the absurdity of explaining the reasons for this crime in legal terms.

What happened at my divorce workshop was an affirmation in the smiles and nods of approval that followed my question. I realized that these women liked me, despite my role in making a divorce. They liked me because I was hurting a man. This made sense and it was so sadly wrong. The painful tension of these realities kept me from returning for the third session.

Some time after the divorce, I tried annulment. I thought I could shape it into a healing event. My chosen and officially designated advocate was feminist and wise. Our satisfying conversations breathed grace through interstices of papers and rules and cups of tea, but the process was nonetheless painful at every turn. I still have the letter from the tribunal responding to my advocate's notice that I did not wish to continue the process. It asks her to please assure the petitioner that her case can be reactivated at any time. It says the case is indefinitely suspended in accord with Canon 1520. The letter was kind and the people involved were all kind. But the process, in the end, was brutal and undoable.

Part IV, Question 3: "Please describe the day of the wedding and the honeymoon." Part V, Question 10: "What do you think was missing from the beginning, had it been there, the marriage would not have ended?" I had answers to these and other questions that my archdiocesan tribunal asked, and with my advocate I might have shaped them within the shelter of her spiritual guidance toward greater self-knowledge. I also knew that I could write convincing and sincere responses for the tribunal. I would tell a truth that set aside paradox. I thought of Maxine Hong Kingston's Woman Warrior, who said she practiced "to make [her] mind large, as the universe is large, so that there is room for paradoxes."[2] With large mind, I embraced my long marriage as both a sacrament and not a sacrament, as both valid and a nullity. But I was also prepared to honor the annulment process by making my mind small in order to focus on one thread whose lessons I was hungry for—the defective part of my marriage reality.

Many of the Church's intentions for the annulment process, I am convinced, are good: they involve exploration and movement toward wisdom and self-knowledge for the annulment seeker, and they include possibilities of growth that might foster future sacramental relationships. But the process is also riven with adversity and adversarial machinations, and its focus is invasively public and legalistic.

I deeply appreciate the written testimonies of people like Sheila Rauch Kennedy, and I identify with others who write and lobby about the abuses inherent in annulment and who are activists for change.[3] Tribunals don't operate in standardized ways, but they all require the involvement of several parties, and they force the dredging up of memories for analysis by people who at best have little to gain for their efforts and at worst are subjected to psychological brutalities. Witnesses to the history of the marriage are contacted and deposed. The formerly married parties become petitioner and respondent, and the respondent is encouraged to produce an independent version of the marriage for tribunal judges who then judge its quotient of sacramentality.

An annulment may have done my private soul some good, but not my soul in community. The process for my former husband would have been a painful indignity, whether he chose to engage in it or not. And the only witnesses qualified by ongoing knowledge of the twenty-plus years' relationship were my family members. My brother pled youth and ignorance about a courtship that occurred while he was a teenager, and my sister begged not to have to participate in anything that might further hurt the brother-in-law she cared for. I was forced to turn to my parents, who were still grieving the divorce I had put off so long telling them about.

Dear Mother and Daddy,

It was wonderful to get your letter saying that you are once again settled for the winter in your Mexican village, and that all is well with you and your RV. What luck to run into the Hansons at the border, and to have them for travel companions all the way to Hermosillo. Your volunteer work at the mission sounds interesting, and I'm happy for you that so much English is spoken.

Oh Mom. Oh Dad. This is not really another in my series of "don't be tourists" lectures. We have such different experiences with Mexico and Mexicans, and raising this is an effort to avoid writing about something else anyway. What I really want to say is how great it is that you have the health and one another's company so you can make these extended trips. I marvel at the long marriage that makes it possible for you to realize your planned travels together. Your relationship has not been without its rocky times, I know, but here you are, and if I cannot always imagine staying married to either of you—as much as I love you both—well, here I am. I have something impossibly hard to tell you. Where I am, it turns out, in spite of tremendous effort to avoid it all, is not being able to stay married. Life works out as planned, sometimes. Sometimes not. I am ending my marriage.

I am so sorry for the pain of this news, but I need for you to know that I am incredibly, increasingly, wretched, and making this change feels like saving my life. I am going on the fourth year of despair about financial risks and our separate lives. I can no longer bear for my daughters to think that this is how a marriage looks.

I will not lie and say I would rather be talking to you in person, although I feel that might be the principled thing to do. But that would be too hard to bear. Please understand that my married feelings have been disappearing for years. I have tried very hard but I cannot get them back. This does not mean there is anyone else, although there are times I wish this were true, times I feel overwhelmingly lonely.

It does mean that when you return home in time for our Catholic family Easter, you will find that I sleep in a different room, and I decided that even if I meet you at your car when you arrive, this is all too much to get explained between the street and front door.

I will be the one to leave, this summer. He wants the marriage to continue, for reasons I think are habit, given the broad separations of our lives these past several years. We have tried very hard to both continue living here, unmarried together, so that each of us might participate in the dailiness of the girls' lives, but I cannot do this much longer. We care about one another, and I think we will some day go on to be friends, but living together on terms of such different desires makes friendship now difficult. I had thought I could stay long enough for him to let go, but I think that staying is making this impossible.

The girls are fine, and I have to say—because I hear so clearly your question about how can I do this to them—they are surely better educated by my leaving this painful relationship than remaining in it. It would devastate me to think that they would stay in such a loveless arrangement, giving over their lives, out of duty, to something that no longer makes sense.

Both girls want to move with me, but I am scared that one of them may decide her dad needs her more, at least to begin with, and I do not know how I will bear this. Please pray for me, and especially for your son-in-law, who, most days, thinks I am ruining his life. But please, please, if you love me, do not pray for our marriage, as success with this prayer will surely kill me.

I am so glad the fishing is terrific, Daddy, and if, when we next see one another, you can possibly look at me with eyes not grief-gouged by certainty that your fallen daughter is condemned to hell, I will be so deeply grateful.

I love you both and shall write again soon.

I signed and mailed the letter and thought: spare me, dear God, my father's eyes. They are blue, and they have seen so much, and I already cannot suffer the work of looking into them. At first, my mother will not tell me that she understands, although she always understands more than I think she will.

It was good to have the letter sent, and these last hardest people to tell, told. This was not their problem, and I invented irritation at them in an effort to make the telling easier. Mostly it killed me to have them know I could not do this right, that my self-care resulted in messed-up lives for others. I knew they would call the day after they got the news, giving themselves one day to talk and grieve and to begin novenas and missions praying for my marriage.

Mother has followed my feminist education with reservations and interest, no longer convinced that being told she thinks like a man is exactly a compliment, is exactly the point. But she is also convinced that women, necessarily and appropriately, must in relationships do sacrificial giving. I am the first person in my family to attend college, but she will probably figure out, long before I do, exactly how my doctoral education in feminist cultural theories has only confused, and not overturned, my born-in-the-service-of-men ethic. People say I have my mother's eyes.

In the end, my parents agreed to be witnesses for the annulment because it was the proper Catholic thing to do. I knew this meant that my mom would also write my father's statement so that he would not have to do it. Their hearts ached for this deposed son they loved, as well as for me. Their abiding love and care for my former husband was and is a godsend. Before the divorce itself, in all my married years, I had entirely hidden from them my insecurities over financial risks and swings of fortune, all the things they might judge faults in their son-in-law's care for me. When I could no longer remain in the marriage and they had been told, I wanted them to accomplish an emotional fast-forward, to jump to the same page that I was on about the realities of my long-troubled and empty marriage. This was a lot to ask. For purposes of the annulment it would have been agonizing for them to revise, one by one, their past assumptions about my married happiness. It would have been devastating for them to revisit occasions of so much hope with hope now dashed. For many good reasons, not without some regrets, but because I found it the most caring of all alternatives, I turned away from plans for annulment.

Why, I often ask myself, has it been so difficult for my feminism to reach into some corners of my Catholic construction? My answers come slowly, but they are enabled for me by acknowledging and exploring these things: my construction in Baltimore Catechism rhetoric, in Catholic parental example and admonitions about gender roles, and in fantasies of martyrdom. I came to work at a Jesuit Catholic university following my divorce, in part to continue examination of my feminist Catholic self.

Sufficient reflection, one of the qualifications of a mortal sin according to the Baltimore Catechism, is also an affirming practice and survival strategy, I would argue, and possibilities for reflection are enhanced by my workplace among feminists across many disciplines, people who are part of a group Michele Dillon refers to as prochange Catholics.[4] There is a large community of us who contest the boundaries of Catholic identity as defined by the Vatican, not in spite of but precisely because of our passionate embrace of participation in Catholic community. As Dillon's work supports, it is important and life-giving to understand that maintaining Catholic identity in the face of differences with Rome is both feminist and Catholic work.

NOTES

1. Marleen Gorris, *A Question of Silence (Der Stilte rond Christine M.)*, Dutch with English subtitles (New York: New Line Home Video, 1982), video.

2. Maxine Hong Kingston, *The Woman Warrior* (1975, New York: Vintage-Random House, 1977), 35.

3. Sheila Rauch Kennedy, *Shattered Faith: A Woman's Struggle to Stop the Catholic Church from Annulling Her Marriage* (New York: Henry Holt, 1998). An Episcopalian, Kennedy forcefully objects to the insult of an unwanted annulment obtained (to facilitate a second marriage) by her former husband following their amicable divorce. Leaders on issues of divorce, annulment, and remarriage for Catholics include Charlie Davis of Call to Action/Northern Virginia, Maureen Fiedler, S.L., of Catholics Speak Out, and Janice Leary of Save Our Sacraments. One recommendation of these activists is that most cases of annulment and remarriage should be handled at the pastoral level through the internal forum option provided for by existing canon law.

4. Michele Dillon, *Catholic Identity: Balancing Reason, Faith, and Power* (Cambridge: Cambridge University Press, 1999). See chap. 1, "Pro-Change Catholics: Forging Community out of Diversity," which introduces the three prochange groups that this study analyzes: Catholics for Free Choice, Dignity, and the Women's Ordination Conference. Dillon's first book is a study of divorce in Ireland: *Debating Divorce: Moral Conflict in Ireland* (Lexington: Kentucky University Press, 1993).

NINE

Dis/Re/Com/Union

Nancy Mairs

When I had been married for half my life, the whole rambling, precarious, cockeyed structure George and I had
banged together almost toppled down around our ears.
The collapse—nothing so definite as a disaster, just a slow
sort of dry rot in the posts and beams—really wasn't our
fault, I think today. We'd had about as much chance of
constructing a shapely and sturdy dwelling place as a
couple of blindfolded children turned loose with a heap of
toothpicks and marshmallows. Nor was it the fault of
anyone else. Calamities are seldom the result of isolable
personal shortcomings. They have a genius of their own.

Which is not to say that there weren't good reasons
for our marriage to founder. They were endless and excel-
lent. When I think of how poorly couples are prepared for
this undertaking, I'm astonished that only one marriage
out of two fails. People who wouldn't dream of permitting
a child to set off into the wilderness without providing
maps and charts, a compass, a Swiss army knife, raingear,
sturdy boots, a snake-bite kit, a flashlight, sunscreen, in-
sect repellent, and as many firsthand accounts of previous
treks into the territory as they can collect send the same
child into marriage with the equivalent of a new pair of
tennis shoes and maybe a handful of band-aids. By general standards, George and I weren't all that poorly prepared. The details of the marriages we had known may
have been carefully shrouded, but at least the marriages

appeared stable and even satisfactory. We knew such an arrangement could be made to work, even if we had no idea how.

Even with more accurate information, however, I suspect our idealism would have blurred our vision, both at the outset and as we went along. "For better or worse," I'd vowed, dutifully parroting the minister's solemn intonation, but I hadn't really meant it. *For better,* I'd meant. *And better. And better.* My prevarication, all unintended, stemmed from the sense of magical immunity that youth and ignorance confer: I knew that some people's marriages got into trouble, but I didn't believe that ours could ever make us unhappy—at least nowhere near as unhappy as it eventually proved capable of making us. We believed ourselves exceptional, just as every other bride and groom do when they publicly pledge themselves "for better," "for richer," "in health," secretly leaving the "worse" and "poorer" and "sickness" for some other, unexceptional couple.

Ready or not, George and I were married just as a social upheaval was beginning to call traditional institutions of all kinds, not merely matrimony, into question. Quickly, "doing your own thing" assumed a kind of moral force, making it possible for me to write a decade after our wedding: "George and I now know that we may not be married forever—that we are committed to personal growth, which necessarily involves the risk of growing apart." It doesn't necessarily involve any such thing, but an alternative model—a model in which the commitment might be to generating and sustaining an indissoluble relationship, from which personal growth would result, if not necessarily, then at least probably, simply because so difficult a task tends to force development—was hard to conceive during the heady self-celebration of the sixties and seventies.

Acting on the premise of personal growth (inasmuch as I can be said to have acted on anything so rational as a premise), I permitted myself from quite early on to have extramarital affairs: infrequent, short-lived, noncommittal, generally discreet. And passionate. That's what I loved about them, their capacity for waking me from the torpor into which my spirits habitually sank to such terrifying depths that I couldn't tell whether I was dead or alive. I was neither, I know now; I was floating in the half-drowned state of clinical depression, and if I had been medicated consistently, I might never have needed these rough rousings. Can

biochemistry legitimately be held responsible for sin? Can psychophar-
macology be employed to prevent it?

Not that I thought of these affairs as sins. *Sin* is not a very seventies
word. I'd have been mortally embarrassed to admit it into my thoughts,
much less my conversation. I don't think I actually condoned my adulteries. Sometimes I even dreaded them. But I believed myself powerless
to resist them: "Goddamn men for their largesse with trivial attentions,"
I wrote at the first signs of one that blessedly failed to materialize.
"They're like stupid zookeepers who casually saunter into the cages of
sleeping tigers; and when the creatures stir and growl, they say, 'Go to
sleep again, good pussies.' Don't they understand that an aroused beast
does not go to sleep—it rages?" Patristic texts at their most virulent do
not surpass the misogyny underlying this image: I, the trapped feral
animal, all sleekness and grace and fury, carelessly kept by the man who
should guard and tame me.

No wonder I was morally vacuous. Tigers do not by any stretch of
the imagination fret over their possible or actual trespasses. They just
do what comes naturally. Even years later, well after my conversion to
Catholicism, as I was contemplating whether to begin what would turn
out to be my last affair, I didn't employ moral terms: "Having an affair
requires a lot of effort, a lot of attention to another person. Sometimes
I feel like bothering, but often as not I don't." The ghost of the tiger
lingers, tolling in the shade, amber eyes slitted sleepily as she watches
the heedless man and sniffs his tantalizing scent. He's not awfully plump,
but she's a little hungry. Is he worth the effort of eating?

Fidelity, I had begun to think after the first hectic conjugal flush had
faded, condemned me to a life of self-deprivation. That it offered me a
means for self-discipline never crossed my mind. *Discipline* had only
cheerless connotations; parental spankings, after-school detention, parking tickets, all measures to make of me a more compliant person than
I was sure I cared to be. To the extent that it entailed choice, it obliged
me to take the most distasteful option available: cramming for a biology
exam when I felt like writing a poem, going without a new dress in
order to pay the telephone bill. I never associated it with satisfaction,
certainly not with joy, and its relation to personal growth entirely escaped me for nearly twenty years.

I'd like to claim that a flash of moral illumination put an end to my infidelities, but I can't even do that. I simply lost interest in men in that way. Perhaps the highs and lows wore me out. Or perhaps I'm only suffering from sour grapes, since within a few years I'd grown too old and crippled to interest men in that way. Certainly it's more than coincidence that my depression was brought under medical control at about the same time. But no, gradually I've come to discern a genuine moral dimension to my changed attitude. I lost interest in men because I began to assume responsibility for rousing myself: not a somnolent tiger, not a beast at all, but a woman, a writing woman, a woman inscribing a life. Such a process necessitates moral choice. I'd been choosing all along, of course, but obliviously; now I had to attend to what I was doing.

Now I was capable of sin. If only I could figure out what sin was. This task ought to be simpler than I've found it. I don't mean I had trouble discovering what deeds are deemed sinful; no student of literature with a special interest in Old and Middle English can help but have the Seven Deadlies inscribed on her brain. Nor was the sinner's fate in doubt: "*In this life sinners suffer* from remorse of conscience, fear, and unhappiness. Their *sin often brings* upon them *disease* or *death,* the *hatred* and *scorn* of their fellow-men, and other temporal punishments," says one particularly lurid religious manual, and after death "the unrepentant sinner is punished in *hell.*"[1] But the truth is that I've known all kinds of furious, greedy, lustful, jealous, slothful, gluttonous, vainglorious people (though seldom all at once) who were clearly having a whale of a time. My own adulteries didn't make me wholly miserable; to be honest, I had some lovely interludes. If I believed in hell, perhaps I could take some satisfaction in believing that they'd get theirs, and I mine; but on the matter of hell I remain on the skeptical side of agnostic.

Yet I now believe that adultery is a sin and that sin is retroactive— that is, that whatever I've done is no less wicked simply because I didn't perceive it in that light at the time. In part through reading and reflecting upon Christian teachings from the Gospels onward, but also through the very experiences I now renounce, I have come to apprehend sin as the state into which I'm thrown whenever I choose, consciously or not, to act in a manner that frays or severs the bonds of love between me and my fellow creatures, between me and the God present to me through those creatures. Viewed in this way, in terms of conditions and consequences, no deed can be judged sinful outside its context, and the definition of a deed's sinfulness can be disconcertingly ambiguous. If you take pride in your child's performance as a Thanksgiving turkey in the school play, for example, your delight and praise will strengthen her for the next challenge, and even open boasting, though it may bore your friends, is no sin. But if you treat her badly—make her mop up a glass of milk you later discover she didn't spill, say, or refer to the first boy she ever loves as a mooncalf—and are too prideful to apologize to her, your offense is great. Transgression consists not in breaking an inflexible rule against pride but in disrupting mutual affection.

I married for love—most everybody does these days—and when I pledged, in the course of the Christian marriage ceremony, to forsake all others so long as George and I both lived, I affirmed marital affection to be not merely mutual but exclusive and perdurable, qualities annulled by adultery. Although legally I could unspeak my vows at any time, thereby altering the context of my actions, a web of other forces—largely social and financial to begin with but over time spiritual as well—permitted me to transgress but not to dissolve the conjugal bond. I couldn't shake the sense that marriage was something more than an economic contract between two men, the father who bestows and the husband who receives the bartered bride, and that, although the practical benefit of fidelity is to ensure the legitimacy of the husband's offspring, it holds a symbolic value as well: the gift of self, freely and lovingly dispensed as a sign of abiding commitment. Violating my vows did not absolve me of them, I felt sure, as long as I persisted in believing that what God joins, no one—not even I at my wickedest—may put asunder.

Nevertheless, I was free to violate them if I wished. Sin is always an option. As is its opposite. One of the splendid features of the liturgical year is that the same stories come round again and again, at least once every three years; if you go to church over a long enough span, you get second and seventh and twentieth chances to tease out their meanings, which multiply as your experience deepens. Jesus did not condemn the woman caught in adultery, and far from punishing her, he protected her from punishment. "Go," he said to her then, "and do not sin again." Clearly, I recognized after who knows how many readings, he believed her capable of choosing this course of action without being threatened and of carrying out her choice. Being a faithful wife meant more than denying myself the giddy rush brought on by a new lover in order to preserve myself from hellfire I didn't even believe in. It meant choosing George over and over and over: a lifetime of weddings.

With the irony only real life permits, just as I gave up trying to escape marriage and started to settle into it as into a rambling old house, the kind one knows will demand a lifetime in restoration and upkeep but promises to be so graceful and commodious, with its waxed pine floorboards and tall windows and deep veranda draped with wisteria, that no amount of work will seem wasted, George decided to leave. "I've always believed that we'd grow old together," I mourned when he told me, "that he'd make the trip toward death with me and that we'd make that particular hard journey easier for each other. Now he's getting off at a way station. Now he's getting off." We'd been married nineteen years. "But George has never been good at initiating action—tends to wait for a push from me," I observed as he teetered for months on the threshold. "Is it my job now to push him out of my life, whether I want him to go or not, for his own good? I don't want to be without him, but neither can I stand to hold him here with me for my own comfort and protection, knowing that I make him miserable and that he's here only because he's too weak and too kind—a tricky combination—to make a drastic change."

The months turned into years: 1982, 1983, 1984. . . . And because he did not ever physically depart—return to New England to find a teaching job and another woman as he contemplated—George believed that he'd stayed after all. But he went, I assure you, he set off alone into some remote and inaccessible landscape, leaving behind a golem whose hollow presence fooled the eyes of strangers, and maybe even most friends, but tormented me in ways that outright separation might not have done. The golem was not in love with me. When I returned from an out-of-town reading, it told me it didn't care one way or the other, didn't miss me while I was gone, wasn't glad when I came back. Taking a second job, it stayed away from the house long hours; when there, it pottered silently, laying tiles in the bathroom, repairing light fixtures, watering plants. At night, instead of making love to me, it scooted to the edge of the bed and clung there like a limpet. "I'm comfortable with myself," it told me when I suggested counseling, "and don't feel any need to change."

I felt the need, all right, but not the capacity: "I can't 'win him back.' I am, after all, the same person who lost him in the first place. I can't get rid of the things that make me me—my crippledness, my writing, this slow deep steady feeling for George that he would not call love. It's *this* woman that he doesn't love. *This* woman is *me.*" If my faithlessness, now at an end, had worn him out, he never told me so. He was not in the habit of explaining himself. Left to my own devices, I experienced the central issue as a kind of vocational conflict: "*This* woman" could be either an attentive wife or a committed writer but not both, because whenever I became absorbed in my work, he found me cold and remote. "What a bind," I noted cheerlessly. "I don't see how I could survive, let alone work, without him—but when I feel safe with him and thus free to work, I start, through my preoccupation, to lose him." In the gamble of my life, I chose work.

At the heart of this dilemma—a false one, to be sure, but perfectly real—was feminism: "It's that wicked feminism which has stolen away his helpless, guilt-ridden wife who couldn't always perhaps see things in his accurate way but who always tried, at least, and now she's not even trying, she's just balky and stubborn, truly perverse, truly a witch. . . . He's got to have something to blame. The possibility that he's simply been an awful shit—quite unconsciously—all his life is inadmissible. The problem is all in my poor little mind, contaminated now by feminism." This passage, written at my bitterest, caricatures George's response, but in truth he did hold feminism, rather than the extramarital affair in which he was by this time deeply involved, responsible for our marital difficulties. If I'd found out about his infidelity, he'd likely have laid that at my feminist feet, too. He has not been an awful shit all his life, or even very much of it, but here and there he's outdone himself.

His choice of scapegoat seems especially ironic now. But not wholly inaccurate. "Ever since you found feminism," he accused, "you act as though you're on some higher level." Feminism never provided me quite the aura of religious enlightenment suggested by "found"; and "higher" reflects his own anxieties about dominance; but my sense of locus did shift, though outward rather than upward, as I scrutinized my life for the assumptions on which it was based and questioned how I'd come to collaborate in those assumptions. It was this shift that George hated, I think, because it inevitably undermined his own stance. You really can discount the person at the other end of the seesaw as a cold and crazy bitch or any other damned thing you please only so long as she stays in place, but if she dismounts and wanders away, you're left sitting on the ground with your jaw hanging. George scrabbled to his feet and fled.

For me, feminism had several practical consequences—among them directing a project in women's studies, finishing my Ph.D., winning a major poetry award, publishing a book of poems and a book of essays, securing several good job offers and later a sizable advance on a new book—but fleeing was not one of them. On the contrary, even when I decided to teach at UCLA while George remained in Tucson until Matthew graduated from high school, I stated clearly that I considered the arrangement financially necessary but temporary, a "commuter marriage" that would end as quickly as feasible in our reunion. "I guess I've given up on us," George had told me not long before. "I just assume we're going our different ways." "Do you ever say, 'I'm going my different way,'" I asked, or is it always 'We're going our different ways'?" but he was so used to defining the world for both of us that he didn't get the distinction. I couldn't help that. He could go his different way if he had to, but I wasn't going anywhere. Not in the way he meant.

In spite of all these emotional comings and goings, we never actually parted, and I've often wondered why not. My favorite private theory is that we're permanently bonded because we smell right to each other, joined in olfactory wedlock, so to speak, but people generally look shocked when I mention it, there's something so primordial about sniffing each other out, so I guess I should come up with a public theory a little less baldly corporeal. Certainly for years our poverty pressed us to remain together; we could scarcely keep one household afloat, let alone provide adequately for two. Much of the time, an even more powerful factor has been social, and especially familial, expectation. Divorce has not been common in either of our families or among our closest friends. We're Yankees at heart, good Puritan stock, people of our word, hardy and severe: "You've made your bed," we say, "now lie in it." Divorce signifies failure: of love, of course, but also of will. We're too proud for it.

Had we been Catholics from the outset, we might have considered ourselves stuck with each other—body odor, scanty resources, and propriety notwithstanding—since one of the essential properties of marriage defined by canon law is indissolubility. As with virtually every other pronouncement of the Church, I'm of several minds about the intent and implications of this. I have never doubted, before or after becoming a Catholic, that my marriage to George had permanent force. I'd vowed as much in perfectly plain language—"till death us do part"—and a woman must be taken at her word. To the extent that the Church intends to support and strengthen me in fulfilling that vow, I'm grateful for the help. I can use all the help I can get.

But in effect, the Church's stand seems more coercive and punitive than supportive. The prohibition of sexual relationships between single people precipitates risky marriages. The denial of remarriage to divorced Catholics excludes them from a supportive community they may most need. Annulment, which is increasingly easy to obtain, puts people in the emotionally and morally dubious position of avowing that their marriage was never valid in the first place. In bitterness, many may believe this; but for spiritual health, they need to be encouraged to value, not despise, their human connections, to let them go when necessary without repudiating them, and to form new ones with fresh wisdom and care. The Church's inflexibility doesn't prevent divorce and remarriage; it simply drives those who choose them away.

The ones who remain have traditionally been offered a model of matrimony worse than useless. "Every couple should imitate the peace and love that reigned in the home of the Blessed Virgin and St. Joseph, the models of Christian spouses," one manual admonishes.[2] Oh, come on. Who knows what went on behind the mud walls of that carpenter's house in Nazareth? What help does an empty model provide two people for whom the preservation of civility and even sanity is a livelier goal than sainthood any day? In recent years, a less treacly and more pragmatic view of marriage may have emerged, at least among progressive Catholics. Premarital instruction is mandated, and retreats like Engaged Encounter offer couples the opportunity to reflect on their commitment and explore their expectations. Celibate clergy still advise couples on matters they're required never to experience, but at least they are often trained in counseling.

The fact remains, however, that the Church takes its very identity from a marital model based on domination and subordination: Christ is the Bridegroom; the Church, the Bride; and there's no mistaking who's in charge of whom. "Husbands, love your wives, as Christ loved the church," the Letter to the Ephesians exhorts; "Wives, be subject to your husbands, as to the Lord. For the husband is the head of the wife" (Eph 5.25, 22). Now this isn't as bad as it sounds, says the pope, because "in marriage there is mutual 'subjection of the spouses out of reverence for Christ,' and not just that of the wife to the husband"; moreover, *"all human beings—both women and men—are called* through the Church, *to be the 'Bride' of Christ. . . . In this way 'being the bride, and thus the feminine' element, becomes a symbol of all that is 'human.'"*[3]

Listen, guys, you can take it from me, being a woman in our society, even a purely symbolic one, is not all that hot, and any spousal relationship, whether human or divine, that is structured in terms of "heads" and "subjects" violates the radical mutuality of realized love, both ours for one another and Christ's for us. Better we should drop the wedding imagery altogether, corrupted as it is by centuries of inequity, and think of ourselves in terms of identity: not the Bride but the Body of Christ. We enact Christ. Through us Christ enters the world. Christ needs us in order to become present even as we need Christ to give our enactment of that presence significance. This is real love we're talking about, passionate, reciprocal, incarnate. In a church modeled on such love, matrimony becomes truly holy.

Whether this Church will become that Church remains to be seen. If it can transform itself from an exclusive to an inclusive institution, one that views all its participants equally as very members incorporate in the mystical body of Christ, to use the beautiful language of the Book of Common Prayer, new paradigms of partnership, both homosexual and heterosexual, will evolve intermediate between indissoluble marriage and perpetual celibacy. I especially like one proposed by the controversial Episcopal bishop John Shelby Sprong, which provides for the formal betrothal of two people who are certain of the seriousness of their relationship but not of its permanence, freeing them of both sexual guilt and the stigma (though not perhaps the pain) of divorce. Marriage would be reserved for those willing to make a lifelong commitment, especially those wishing to bear and raise children.

The bonds of such a marriage are best thought of as indissoluble so that we'll give them time to work. Otherwise, in a society that throws away diapers after the first soiling instead of dealing with an infant's shit, at the first twinge of conflict or boredom marriage would get sent to the nearest spiritual landfill. But life is very long, and getting longer; and a marriage contracted in one's twenties may no longer be a marriage a couple of decades later. In that case, dissolution has already taken place, Church sanctions be damned, and new arrangements must be worked out without the blame that so often strikes people as an inevitable, even a necessary response when, really, rarely are the actions of individuals reprehensible. We all want to be good to one another, and if we can't manage it under some conditions, perhaps new ones will be more enabling. But surely ascribing blame and taking sides are always disabling.

"Do you believe that you are marrying Eric forever?" I asked my daughter, about six months before her wedding, when she came in during these meditations and plumped down on the shabby sofa across from me.

"Yes!" she said in her of-course-Mother-how-can-you-be-so-dimwitted-as-to-ask? voice. But I do have to ask. She's a whole generation away from me, and of a more pragmatic nature. I'm sure she doesn't think of marriage in terms of a "vocation" or "spiritual discipline," concepts she probably considers pretty goofy. I can see clearly that she has a moral life, but I'm not certain how marriage fits into it. She might have said "as long as it's good for us" or "we'll take it one day at a time"—not bad aspirations but not, I would argue, *enough*. Only forever is enough.

"Oh, good," I said. "I've been writing down my thoughts about marriage," I went on, sheepishly, "and they're . . . conservative." This made her laugh; she and Eric are our resident conservatives. "But I don't see how you can get anywhere, spiritually speaking, if you keep turning in one marriage on another like used cars." She nodded, perhaps remembering how, just a year before, sitting in this little room, I'd told her about her father's infidelity and my determination not to turn the marriage in, perhaps basking in the diffuse joy generated by that decision. She even permitted me "spiritually." I could hardly wait for the wedding.

"Marriage requires the continual breaking of ground, going where one has never gone before," I reflected in 1982 when George first mentioned leaving me. "First marriages, anyway, and second ones that last longer than the first. I hear George saying that he wants to move back, not forward, to go home where it's safe, to do again what he's sure he can do. I wonder if his desire comes out of a fear of death. If he goes on, he has to move closer to dying. If he circles round and starts over, then he's twenty again, not forty. Whatever the cause, I'm helpless in the face of his longing. With me there's no starting over, only going on. I'm aging, fading, before his eyes. With me he can only travel toward death." To go on, and on, and on, God knows where, to have the whole adventure: holy matrimony.

"I, Nancy, take you, George . . ." I had intended to speak firmly this time, but my voice is whispery and tremulous again. Outside the wide window of the little chapel at the Desert House of Prayer, the landscape trembles, pale and dry already in the mid-May heat, so different from wet, wind-tossed maples against a slaty sky that we could never have dreamed it a quarter of a century ago. In place of white taffeta, I'm dressed in heavy cotton knit, cream and tan; George wears not a morning coat but a rose-colored shirt with stripes of cream and blue, a graying beard, glasses. Within a small semicircle of close relatives and friends, we stand with Father Ricardo and make anew all those promises it's a good thing we didn't understand the significance of the first time around. "Poorer" didn't turn out to be so bad, but "worse" has sometimes been dreadful indeed, "sickness" meant cancer and multiple sclerosis, and "death" really will part us, perhaps before very long. The ignorance that protected those children, waifish in their dress-up clothes, smiling, stunned—the ones we always laugh at in the wedding album, exclaiming, "Who'd let two babies like that get married?"—has worn away. We know now. We promise anyway.

Twenty-five years is probably just about the right length of time for a courtship, and I really do feel I'm marrying George in a new way. For one thing, I'm not sick with dread this time. Weddings in our society seem designed to reduce the bride and groom to precisely the condition of those who, because they "lack sufficient use of reason," are "incapable of contracting marriage," according to canon law. What with the gown to be chosen and fitted (smaller and smaller as the strain takes its toll), the color scheme settled on, the attendants' attire selected, the hall hired, the caterer and photographer booked, the flowers ordered, the china and silver and crystal patterns registered, the invitations printed and mailed, the gifts opened and acknowledged (the sixth pair of salt and pepper shakers just as rapturously as the first), the ceremony rehearsed, and the guests assembled, all eyes trained on the happy couple, who are obligated to turn in a perfect performance on this most momentous occasion of their entire lives, it's no wonder if their voices tremble less with joy than with exhaustion and stage fright. I knew I was supposed to look radiant and greet each guest graciously, even the ones I'd never laid eyes on before. No one ever mentioned having a good time. The most telling photographs in our wedding album are the ones in which George and I wear not revelers' grins but the stares of deer caught in the headlights of an onrushing automobile.

After a full day of celebrating their fiftieth anniversary, George's parents exclaimed how much more fun they'd had than at their wedding, and now we know what they meant. Except for a couple of brief conversations with a caterer whose work we already knew and a morning's maddening search for suitable cocktail plates and napkins that weren't all gooped up with silver bows and bells, we've hardly fussed at all. I bought my dress on impulse, with no particular occasion in mind, from a sale rack in a shop going bankrupt. Friends sent us a stunning bouquet of two dozen salmon-colored roses or we'd have no flowers. I woke feeling excited, not nervous (the physical sensations of these two states are almost indistinguishable, but you'll like them better if you call them "excitement"). The tremor in my voice as I pledge to cherish George forever betrays neither fatigue nor fear but the intense thrill of renewal.

This time we exchange our vows as Catholics. Not that the first ones didn't count, even in the eyes of the Church, because of course they did. But they were largely social rather than sacramental in nature, entitling George and me to use the same last name, live openly together, have sexual intercourse whenever we wanted, bear children legitimately, carry them and each other on our health insurance policies, and inherit jointly owned property without putting it through probate when one of us died, all the while enjoying the community's approbation so long as we didn't go too deeply into debt, let our house and yard deteriorate into an eyesore, or scream at each other in public. Viewing ourselves as responsible primarily for each other's spiritual well-being, and then for the spiritual well-being of the world, would have struck me as a ludicrous piety.

Insofar as I involved God in making and carrying out those first vows, he was the Daddy God, pleasing whom entailed a list of onerous prescriptions and prohibitions. The fact that these took their most basic form as commandments suggested that human nature had to be forced into goodness; left to its own devices, it would prefer idols, profanity, leisurely Sunday mornings with bagels and the *New York Times,* disrespect for authority, murder, adultery, theft, lies, and everything belonging to the guy next door. I'm questioning here not these strictures themselves, most of which I accept at face value, but the view of the human creature underlying their form. In it, I was forever on the perilous verge of doing a don't, to atone for which I had to beg forgiveness from the very being who had set me up for trespass, by forbidding behaviors he clearly expected me to commit, in the first place: the God of the Gotcha, you might say. It's awfully hard to achieve spiritual health in relation to a being who appears eager to condemn you so that he can then magnanimously redeem you from your own nasty nature. His power corrupts the bond between you. It's far easier to thrive in the care of one who, thrilled with the goodness of her whole creation, asks for the single act that will make transgression impossible: love.

Oh, how I quail at using that word! It's been so sentimentalized in contemporary culture that almost all its resonances have been smothered in a drift of red hearts and teddy bears: I [heart] NY. I [heart] MY VOLVO. JESUS [heart] YOU. It's a transitive verb whose object is always pleasing; the instant the object ceases to delight, we switch the verb to "like" or "can live without" or "downright detest." But the great commandment permits no lexical shift. The only verb is *love,* and the objects it takes are designated without regard to your pleasure: (1) God; (2) everybody else, yourself included. If you love God with all your heart and all your soul and all your mind and also love your neighbor as yourself, you will naturally carry out all the other commandments as well. Of course, this is a harder task than any they set. I've had far less trouble refraining from adultery, in the years since I discovered I had the power to choose fidelity, than I've had loving Ronald Reagan, for instance; in fact, I've never quite accomplished the latter. Conceiving love only as a warm fuzzy, you can readily forget just how much work it entails. But it's authentic work, strenuous and productive: doing a do, not avoiding a don't. It puts you in a right relation with God and others, reciprocal rather than hierarchical. At one time or another, legal penalties have been imposed for violations of all the ten commandments and still are for some (a "stubborn child" may still be turned over to the state in Massachusetts, for example). But the great commandment is extralegal. Love cannot be forced. It must be chosen. You love not out of dread but out of your own fullness. It's what you were made for. When you fail at it, you aren't sent to prison, or to the electric chair, or to hell. You are commanded again: Love.

By the time I make my marital vows to George for the second time, I believe myself capable of this kind of love: mutual and without condition. As usual, overestimating my spiritual stamina, I'm a little bit right and a little bit wrong—but righter, in this case, than wrong, as I will prove a couple of years after this celebration when I learn of his infidelity. I can indeed love George, more often than not, in a way that reflects the love of God. The terms of our first marriage—social propriety, sexual and intellectual compatibility, personal growth, responsibility for our children—were sound and honorable enough, but they failed to yield metaphors that would transcend the mechanical and legalistic elements of our union. For this we need to set our vows within the Mass, which incarnates love.

"The Body of Christ," George says, placing the wafer on my tongue. The words both describe this scrap of bread and affirm my identity: a double mystery. I eat the Body of Christ. I am—we are all—the Body of Christ. Nourished by God, we must bear God into the world and give God away with ourselves.

As Philip Slater long since pointed out, we are a society of hoarders, not just materially but also spiritually, organizing our attitudes and activities on the premise that there's never enough of anything to go around.[4] Among the myriad and complex consequences of structuring our lives in terms of scarcity rather than abundance is the sense of the self as a depletable resource in danger of trickling away like the dried beans that leaked from my son's childhood pig Wilbur, leaving only a limp rag of purple plush. The self-husbandry that such a concept necessitates—the drive for "personal growth" in the sense of "individual growth"—starves any relationship, but especially as energy intensive a relationship as marriage. Marriage requires a sense of the self not as the tumescent male who fears that, after ejaculation, his penis will wilt and droop never to rise and spurt again, but as the nursing mother who knows that the more voraciously her infant sucks, the more milk her breasts will produce.

"The Blood of Christ," I say to George, and he takes the pottery chalice and drinks. The Eucharist is inexhaustible, we feed on it week after week, and in configuring our relationship to reflect it, George and I nourish and sustain each other. Instead of eating each other up, we find we have enough, more than we'd ever dreamed, a surplus, a super-abundance, plenty to squander in every direction and more where that came from, so much that we even lavish it on our poor foolish corgi, who sighs and rolls his eyes as George scrubs the remains from the yogurt carton off his nose, and the hummingbirds who, hovering around the empty feeder, peer through the back window and screech "juice! juice!" and one day—why not?—even worms, even daisies.

NOTES

This essay was originally published in *Ordinary Time* by Nancy Mairs. © 1993 by Nancy Mairs. It is reprinted by permission of Beacon Press, Boston.

1. Louise Laravoire Morrow, *My Catholic Faith* (Kenosha, Wisc.: My Mission House, 1963), 57.

2. Ibid., 354.

3. John Paul II, *On the Dignity and Vocation of Women,* Apostolic Letter, August 15, 1988, 92, 94.

4. Philip Slater, *The Pursuit of Loneliness,* 3d ed. (Boston: Beacon Press, 1990).

TEN

Respecting Life and Respecting Women's Lives: Abortion, Feminism, and My Return to the Catholic Church

Kathleen M. Joyce

I was eighteen when I told my mother that I did not want to go to her doctor, the ob/gyn specialist who had delivered me and my seven older siblings. My explanation that I would feel more comfortable with a female doctor did nothing to soften for her my rejection of the man who had played such a central role in my mother's life during her twelve years of childbearing. "Don't you realize," she cried, "that you wouldn't be here today if it weren't for him?" My response was a silent, bewildered, uncomprehending look that seemed to upset her even more than my original statement. "Any other doctor," she continued, now actually *crying,* "would have aborted you once we found out that I was exposed to rubella. But not him. He was Catholic, and he wouldn't hear of it. You are here today because he let me continue the pregnancy." I owed this man my loyalty, my mother made clear, because I owed him my life.

I would like to say that I was moved by my mother's tears to a better appreciation of what it had been like for her to carry me inside her, hoping for the best, but prepared for the worst—believing, on the basis of prevailing medical opinion, that she was likely to give birth to a child with multiple disabilities. But I wasn't moved by her tears, and I didn't gain any appreciation for what she had experienced. I thought she was being melodramatic, and I was annoyed with her for giving her doctor so much power and authority. He "let" her continue the pregnancy? Ridiculous, I thought. The man had been on a power trip, encouraging his patients to be much more dependent on him than they needed to be. It was fitting, I thought, that he was Catholic. The priests who told my mother and other women of her generation that it was their duty to have six, eight, ten children (the normal range among my mother's friends) could count on Catholic doctors like my mother's to back them up when Catholic women came to their offices.

I don't know precisely why I was so quick to see my mother's reaction as an exaggeration. After all, the story of her exposure to rubella was well known to me, and I had always accepted her exposure as the source of my own health problems. For I had been born with a disability—a blind eye—and my early years were marked by severe asthma, allergies, and regular bouts with pneumonia that required frequent hospitalizations. But I never saw myself as disabled, and I couldn't—or wouldn't—believe that my time in the womb had amounted to any real crisis for my mother.

Fifteen years later, I was a mother myself as well as a historian studying the history of therapeutic abortion in the United States. I was also, at that point, an ex-Catholic. I had left the Catholic Church during college in search of a tradition that would fit better what I understood to be my spiritual needs and social convictions. I enrolled in a Presbyterian seminary and trained for the Presbyterian ministry. Ultimately, I decided not to pursue a career in the ordained ministry, and I entered a graduate program in religion instead. Still, throughout these, my "Protestant years," I retained an almost mystical attachment to the Catholic tradition. My closest friends in seminary were Catholic, and I became a fierce defender of the Church as I encountered students and professors who seemed to be unfairly hostile to it. I explained this to myself in terms of family heritage. The Catholic tradition linked the generations of my family together, I reasoned, and my attachment to the Church was an extension of my attachment to my family.

Now that I have returned to the Catholic Church, I have come to think that there was more to it than that. My departure from the Church was not based solely, or even primarily, on my opposition to its positions on women's ordination and abortion. I left the Church because I was hungry for a kind of spiritual experience that I felt it could never satisfy. But it is also true that I believed that Catholics were too conservative about women's roles and women's rights and that I would never find a real home within the Catholic Church. Even so, I wouldn't have called myself a feminist at the point of my departure. Like many women of my generation, I left college assuming that I was entering an adult world of equal opportunity for men and women. I thought the battles had all been won, and I often was annoyed with women who complained about gender bias. It was in the past, I would argue, exasperated, why couldn't they just let it go? In my eyes, the gender bias that remained was limited to one institution—the Catholic Church—and to one demographic group, "older people."

My seminary education, and the pastoral fieldwork that went with it, provided a harsh introduction to the place of women in the real world. When I joined the Presbyterian church, I assumed that its support of women's ordination and abortion rights meant that I would be valued as a woman. Instead, what I found was a more subtle rejection of women's gifts that came less from the institution than from the people in the pews. By the time I finished seminary, I had decided that the ordained ministry would lead only to frustration and battle fatigue from the constant challenges to my legitimacy. I withdrew from the ordination process, and I entered graduate school. Angry and disillusioned with organized religion, I drifted away from the Presbyterian church and focused on my own private spiritual life.

At the same time that I was pursuing this private spiritual course, I was also focusing my graduate studies more directly on American Catholicism. I justified my interest as evidence of my contrarian tendencies. The central narrative of religious life in the United States was a story of Protestant institutions, figures, and beliefs. Annoyed by this, I pledged to make Catholics part of the story. Although I believe this impulse was the right one, I also believe that in turning to the Catholic story I was beginning my journey back to the Church. I began my study of American Catholics by writing a dissertation on the history of Catholic hospitals in the United States. The study of hospitals soon led me to the issue of therapeutic abortion, as I tried to determine what impact

Catholic teachings on medical ethics had on the actual practice of medicine in Catholic hospitals. To my surprise, I found that the further I delved into the history of therapeutic abortion, the more I came to appreciate the rich theological complexity of the Catholic tradition. Working my way through literature on therapeutic abortion turned out to be the final step in my journey back to the Catholic Church.

I understand the irony of my admission that abortion helped to bring me back to the Catholic Church. I am a prochoice feminist, and I lived successfully for over ten years on the other side of the Reformation divide. Why would I return to a church that is so firmly, and so actively, opposed to the exercise of a choice I believe every woman should be allowed to make? My answer, like the Catholic tradition itself, is complex. Even as I continue to defend the legal right to abortion, I find myself moved by the Church's compelling defense and embrace of life. By asserting that all lives are of equal value, the Catholic Church dignifies the lives of all people, from the socially privileged to those marginalized by, among other things, poverty, race, or disability. The power of the Catholic faith for me lies in this celebration of life as an incontestable good.

Appreciating this fundamental Catholic reverence for life and the equality of all people does not, however, prevent me from recognizing that the Church often fails to be true to its teachings. By excluding women from the ordained ministry, the Church sanctions the inequality of the sexes. Its insistence, moreover, that complications in pregnancy cannot be resolved through therapeutic abortion historically has led to the privileging of fetal life over the life of the mother. As I think about the ways in which the Catholic Church fails to affirm, in practice, the dignity of women's lives, I find it hard to articulate a justification for my return to it. Indeed, I have come to realize that the only way I can explain my return to the Catholic Church is to describe how I felt, and what I learned about myself, as I conducted my research on the history of therapeutic abortion in the United States.

As I described above, I came upon the topic of therapeutic abortion innocently enough. I was researching the history of Catholic hospitals, and it seemed to make sense to try to learn what I could about the practical impact of Catholic teachings on abortion. I didn't recall at first—at least not consciously—that therapeutic abortion was an issue my mother had confronted during her pregnancy with me, but I quickly became emotionally involved in the stories I read. Initially, my own tears, of sadness and of rage, flowed as I read medical accounts of, and Catholic statements against, therapeutic abortion. The medical accounts were stark and unsparing in their clinical descriptions of women's bodies, and I found myself shifting uncomfortably in my chair, my hand falling protectively over my own womb, as I read them. The physical pain women endured before, during, and after their surgical abortions was made palpable through these accounts, and my own body pulled away, in fear and discomfort, from their harsh realism. The protocols of scientific research did not allow for any direct discussion of the emotional pain associated with terminating a pregnancy, but somehow, despite the clinical detachment of the medical reports, I found myself relating to the pain of the women whose ordeals were described. That I had experienced my own pregnancy by that point surely influenced my response, but there was more to it than that. As I thought about what these women had lost, I found my views on abortion challenged and complicated as they hadn't been by my own pregnancy.

At the same time, as I read Church pronouncements on therapeutic abortion, I became enraged at the tortured logic of the theologians who seemed to put the life of the fetus before the life of the mother. Reading these documents, it was difficult for me to see anything but cruelty and misogyny at work. The theology that said you can't sacrifice one life for another lost its nobility and integrity when it was translated into the practical directives found in pastoral medicine manuals. The writers of these manuals discussed the deaths of women with an air of indifference that I found frightening. For example, Austin O'Malley, the physician who wrote the definitive early-twentieth-century guide to Catholic medical ethics, *The Ethics of Medical Homicide and Mutilation,* was not content simply to pronounce that "therapeutic abortion is never permissible, under any circumstances, if the child is not viable."[1] O'Malley went out of his way to make clear that "if the mother cannot be saved without emptying the uterus, the mother must die; there is no way out of the difficulty."[2] The ease with which O'Malley and other Catholic writers dispensed with women's lives was appalling to me, and my sadness over the loss of the child was overtaken by an angry defense of the priority of women's lives. As I read these Catholic pronouncements, the complexity of feelings that my reading of the medical literature had induced was overridden by an overwhelming desire to protect women. I moved from feeling the need to protect my uterus and what might be inside it to feeling that I had to protect my life.

Immersed in sources from the late nineteenth and early twentieth centuries, I found it easy to be outraged at the Catholic Church's position on therapeutic abortion. Most medical literature emphasized the need to preserve the life of the mother, while acknowledging the delicacy of making this choice when the patient was Catholic. But as I moved my research into the middle decades of the twentieth century, I was surprised to find in the medical literature what I can only describe as a diminished concern for women's lives. Indeed, the practical implications of mid-twentieth-century medical protocols seemed to differ little from those that flowed from Catholic teachings.

This represented a major shift in American physicians' views on abortion. Physicians had been major players in the nineteenth-century campaign to criminalize abortion, but one of the goals of that effort had been to distinguish medically indicated abortions from those obtained for convenience or concealment. The medical elite who controlled local medical societies, wrote medical textbooks, and published articles in medical journals had always assumed that abortion was legitimate and medically necessary in certain circumstances. This assertion of the legitimacy of therapeutic abortion was usually accompanied by statements warning of self-absorbed, manipulative women who might fake their symptoms in order to obtain a medical abortion, but the focus of the medical literature remained on the women whose lives were endangered by pregnancy complications.[3]

By the middle of the twentieth century, most doctors seemed to believe that medical progress had eliminated the need for therapeutic abortion. Women who sought medical abortions were immediately suspect. Doctors accused them of being selfish and unwilling to accept their responsibilities as women. Indeed, the willingness to submit to an abortion became evidence, in many doctors' eyes, of mental pathology. Women who allowed their pregnancies to be terminated were said to suffer from a neurosis rooted in a fear of their own femininity. The humanity I had seen in the nineteenth-century medical literature, which had been in such pointed contrast to Catholic writings on therapeutic abortion, was gone. By the early 1950s, most hospitals in the United States required physicians to obtain permission to perform a therapeutic abortion from formally designated abortion committees.⁴ Although greater consideration was given during this period to the emotional health of the mother, and many women were able to obtain medical abortions for psychiatric reasons, the result was increasing cynicism toward the practice of therapeutic abortion and heightened hostility toward women patients. It was not unusual, in fact, for abortion committees to approve an abortion on the condition that the woman also submit to simultaneous sterilization.⁵

As I read the medical literature of the 1940s and 1950s, I was astonished by the anger and casual cruelty of the doctors authorized to make these decisions about women's lives. I was also disturbed by the obvious inequalities in access to medical abortion. It was clear that white, middle- and upper-class women had a far better chance of obtaining a medical abortion through the committee system than women of other races and lower social position. Although I wasn't willing to champion the Catholic position on therapeutic abortion, I couldn't help but think that by allowing no exceptions, even for the socially privileged, and opposing sterilization, the Catholic approach to therapeutic abortion was more fair to women than the secular system. Even so, the situation for women in this period seemed so bleak that I wasn't prepared to give credit to anyone.

The women whose fates were being determined by the hospital abortion committees of the 1950s were my mother's contemporaries. Curiously, however, I didn't immediately place her, or me, in this disturbing narrative. The images in my mind were of the 1950s women depicted on television and in movies and advertisements. They were not of my mother. This changed, however, and dramatically so, when I came upon medical literature from the early 1960s that discussed maternal exposure to or, more typically, contraction of rubella in the first trimester as legitimate grounds for therapeutic abortion. The issue became even more personal when I began to find references to a rubella epidemic in 1964, the year of my birth. Suddenly, the memory of that summer afternoon fifteen years earlier came flooding back to me. My mother crying in the dining room as I stood, holding myself back from her, in the kitchen. My refusal to believe that she had ever faced any choice, or had any concern, about continuing her pregnancy with me. Now there was no denying it. My mother and I had become part of the history I was writing. Once again, I felt protective of my life, but in a new way. Now I was the fetus in the womb.

As I continued my research, I came across the story of Ruth Smith, a child conceived, as I was, during that rubella epidemic of 1964.[6] Ruth Smith wasn't as fortunate as I was. She was born with severe mental and physical handicaps. At the age of three, when her story was told in a courtroom in New York, she was unable to hear or speak. Her vision was impaired, due to cataracts and a damaged retina, and she wore long leg braces and a pelvic band to coordinate her movement. Her handicaps were so severe, in fact, that no school or residential facility would accept her as a student or patient. The overwhelming burden of caring for Ruth had led her parents to court, where they were the plaintiffs in a medical malpractice suit. The substance of their complaint? That Long Island College Hospital had acted negligently by failing to perform an abortion cn Beatrice Smith, Ruth's mother, even though she was known to have contracted rubella during the first weeks of her pregnancy with Ruth.

Although the judge and jury were not sympathetic to abortion in general, the Smiths nevertheless seemed to have a strong case. Beatrice Smith's doctor had confirmed that she had contracted rubella, and he had recommended a therapeutic abortion. Acting on his recommendation, Beatrice Smith had obtained the necessary authorizations, and she had been admitted to Long Island College Hospital for the specific purpose of having a surgical abortion. On the morning of her scheduled abortion, Mrs. Smith was prepared for surgery and wheeled into the operating room, only to be told that her surgery had been canceled. The obstetrician appointed to perform the procedure had determined, Mrs. Smith was told, that the abortion was unnecessary and that her baby would be "all right." (It is not clear why Mrs. Smith was refused her abortion. Both race and religion probably were factors. Mrs. Smith was black, and the hospital staff was white. The chief of obstetrics was a Roman Catholic who opposed abortion.) The documentary evidence supporting the medical indications for abortion in Beatrice Smith's case were so strong, and the hospital's defense so weak in the face of that evidence, that the jury's verdict was unanimous: $10,000 in damages to

Beatrice Smith, $1 to Richard Smith, and $100,000 to Ruth Smith. The verdict affirmed that Beatrice Smith had not received adequate medical care and recognized the damage done to Ruth as a consequence. One hundred thousand dollars was not enough to pay for the lifetime of care that Ruth needed, but the verdict sent a powerful message.

Two months after the trial ended, however, the judge in the case set aside the verdict awarding damages to Ruth Smith. He did not deny that Ruth's disabilities were the result of her mother's contraction of rubella early in pregnancy. Even so, the judge wrote, "the proof showed that the only way the infant could have been spared being born without birth defects was not to have been born at all. . . . This court cannot weigh the value of life with impairments against the nonexistence of life itself." In the judge's view, the Smiths' had suggested, and the jury judgment had affirmed, that by forcing Beatrice Smith to continue her pregnancy, Long Island College Hospital had violated Ruth Smith's right not to be born. The judge believed that she had no such right.

The story of Beatrice and Ruth Smith, mother and daughter, is disturbing to me for a lot of reasons. The hospital's treatment of Beatrice Smith was awful, and the tragedy of Ruth Smith's severe, irreversible handicaps is more awful still. For a time, as I read their story, I forgot my own connection to the rubella epidemic responsible for Ruth's disabilities. I was too wrapped up, and appropriately so, in the drama of the Smiths' lives to put myself into their story. But as I continued to read an article about the Smith case, I was stopped short by one of the author's statements. Noting that the (then) recent development of an effective antirubella vaccine meant that babies could now be spared Ruth's fate, the author went on to express concern that the public funding needed to carry out an effective vaccination campaign might not be available. "But unfortunately," she wrote, "the public funds so far allocated are far from sufficient to wipe out a disease which produced 200,000 defective babies after the 1964 epidemic."[7]

"Defective babies." I was born in New York State in 1964, just as Ruth Smith was. My blind eye and other health problems were attributed to maternal rubella exposure. Was I one of those defective babies? The words bothered me enormously. What did it mean for a baby to be defective? Cars could be defective. So could stereos and computers. But humans? I was glad that I didn't share Ruth Smith's fate. I certainly couldn't compare my minor health problems with the severe disabilities she lived with every day. But it still made me angry, both on her behalf and on my own, that we rubella babies were stamped with that label. "Defective."

Reading Ruth Smith's story, and finding myself in it, didn't sway me from my prochoice convictions. As a student of women's history, I know how often and easily women's lives are devalued, and I believe it is critical for women to have the right to make decisions about their own lives. My concern for women's rights and well-being make it impossible for me to support any effort to deprive women of the right to a safe, legal abortion. But I remain troubled. My research on therapeutic abortion has forced me to reflect deeply about what makes for a valuable life. It is a question we confront as a society every time we debate the "right to die," the rights of people with disabilities, or the ethics of aborting a "defective" fetus. I can't escape the fact that in championing some of these rights—the right to abortion, the right to die—I am agreeing that there are circumstances under which it might be better not to live. Nor can I escape the fact that in championing these rights, I am accepting that some people will choose not to live with, or choose not to give life to babies with, disabilities that other people not only do live with but also live with in ways that are rich, worthy, and of inestimable value.

My research has forced me to confront these complex, troubling questions, and my study of Catholic teachings has made it impossible for me to deny the weakness of some of the answers I devise. I can't accept fully the Church's teachings, but I recognize in them a moral consistency I cannot claim. I honor and appreciate the respect for the humanity and dignity of "defective" babies and disabled children and adults that the Catholic Church stands for, and I find myself humbled by my own inability to dignify these lives with my own seamless defense of life. In my humility, I find myself more forgiving of others'—even the Church's—sins, and I am filled with awe and reverence for a God who can inspire a community of fallible, fallen people to heights of such selfless love and commitment.

My appreciation for the Catholic tradition's powerful affirmation of the dignity of human life does not prevent me, however, from recognizing the continued failure of the Church to affirm fully the dignity of women's lives. The moral and logical consistency that links together both the Catholic Church's opposition to abortion, capital punishment, and euthanasia and its demands for economic justice and social equality is strikingly absent from its declarations on the role of women in Church and society. Indeed, the theological arguments against the ordination of women appear all the more weak and unnecessarily tortured in comparison to the powerful moral clarity of the Church's stand on issues of social justice and human rights.

But the very starkness of this contrast is to me a source of hope. For with every Vatican declaration on the sacredness of all life, the theology of difference that provides the rationale for the nonordination of women becomes all the more logically indefensible. Ultimately, I believe, the Church will find its prophetic witness undercut by its own failure to respect life—the lives of women—and it will be forced to confront and resolve the inconsistency of its teachings on women's rights and roles.

I remain in the Church because I believe this change will occur. I believe this to be true not only because it is in the Church's pragmatic self-interest to strengthen its position as an advocate for justice but also because I believe in the Church as a fallible human institution guided by a God who constantly challenges us all to be better, truer messengers of the gospel. The history of the Catholic Church, both in my lifetime and in my life, suggests that positive change is possible, and I trust in the power of the God who has inspired such change. I know now that this is the God I was searching for as a young adult, and I believe that the same gift of grace that brought me back to the Catholic Church eventually will lead the Church to become a more just representative of the gospel it proclaims.

NOTES

1. O'Malley's use of the term *viable* is confusing. His categorization of therapeutic abortion included the premature induction of labor in the second and third trimesters of pregnancy. Today, this procedure has been labeled "partial-birth" abortion by its opponents. O'Malley's point was that inducing labor prematurely was permissible only when the fetus was developed enough to survive outside the womb. If the fetus was not viable, doctors were to allow the pregnancy to run its course, even if this led to the death of the mother and/or baby.

2. Austin O'Malley, *The Ethics of Medical Homicide and Mutilation* (New York: Devon-Adair, 1922), 181.

3. For examples of the warnings issued about women who fake their symptoms, see "Symposium on Criminal Abortion: The Duty of the Medical Profession in Relation to Criminal Abortion," *Journal of the American Medical Association* 14, no. 2 (1904): 1890; Frederick J. Taussig, *The Prevention and Treatment of Abortion* (St. Louis: C. V. Mosby, 1910), 163–64; Joseph B. DeLee, *The Principles and Practice of Obstetrics* (Philadelphia: W. B. Saunders, 1913), 1017–18.

4. For a fuller account of changing attitudes toward therapeutic abortion, see Rickie Solinger, "'A Complete Disaster': Abortion and the Politics of Hospital Abortion Committees, 1950–1970," *Feminist Studies* 19 (Summer 1993): 240–61.

5. On therapeutic abortion and sterilization, see ibid. See also Close Hesseltine, F. L. Adair, and M. W. Bonton, "Limitation of Human Reproduction," *American Journal of Obstetrics and Gynecology* 39 (April 1940): 551; Clifford B. Lull, ed., *Management in Obstetric Complications* (Philadelphia: J. B. Lippincott, 1945), 90; J. Robert Willson, Clayton Beecham, and Elsie Reid Carrington, *Obstetrics and Gynecology* (St. Louis: C. V. Mosby, 1963), 188.

6. For the full discussion of Ruth Smith's story on which this account is based, see Marion K. Sanders, "The Right Not to Be Born," in *Abortion: A Reader,* ed. Lloyd Steffen (Cleveland, Oh.: Pilgrim Press, 1996), 9–24.

7. Ibid., 17.

ELEVEN

Irish Women Reconciling Catholicism and Feminism: The Abortion Question

Mary Kenny

I

Abortion politics are different in each culture: I have observed the prolife movement in Ireland, Britain, France, the Netherlands, Norway, and Australia, and in each society there are cultural variants. In France, for example, abortion politics—and birth control in general—are related to the perpetual French anxiety concerning underpopulation. In Norway, the only Scandinavian country with an active prolife movement, they grow out of the very specific form of Norwegian Lutheranism, which is also rather sternly opposed to alcohol. In the Netherlands, the prolife movement is a practical example of Catholic-Protestant cooperation and focuses quite strongly on the social work aspect of crisis pregnancy. In Britain, the prolife movement does things the British way, favoring parliamentary democracy and shying away from direct action: but practical measures to support women in difficult pregnancies are also valued.

In Ireland, abortion politics are about a wide range of subjects. As David Quinn, editor of the *Irish Catholic*, wrote in a recent issue of *Human Life Review,* "The flashpoint in the culture wars . . . is about abortion. It is about the nature and knowability of the moral law. It is about the relationship between Church and State. It is about the rights of minorities and dissenters. . . . It is about the state of modern medicine. It is about the limits and extent of personal autonomy."[1]

It is, of course, also about women, although Irish women, in the main Catholic, or inheritors of a Catholic (and agricultural) tradition, can, I think, generally be said to have mixed views on the subject of abortion. Perhaps that is true of most women, in most places.

Feminism, also, is subject to cultural variations, as I observed when reporting the UN World Conference on Women in Beijing in 1995. Feminists in different countries have different priorities and different values.

II

As a young journalist, I was, in 1970, a founder-member of what was to become an influential feminist group, the Irish Women's Liberation Movement. Like others, I had been influenced by events in the United States in 1967 and 1968, when what was then called "women's lib" became such a well-known and even sensational cause. I was also influenced—as were other women in Ireland—both by Irish traditions of early feminism, which had been focused both on education and on nationalism, and by wider left-wing movements in Europe. As a reporter for the *London Evening Standard*, I had witnessed the French students' rebellion in Paris in 1968, and while the students' objectives were fuzzy ("Power to the Imagination" and "Underneath the Pavement, the Beach," were two of the most popular slogans), their methods were exciting and contagious. When I arrived in Paris in May of 1968, one of the first sights to meet my eyes was that of a group of students dancing around the Stock Exchange ("La Bourse"), which was on fire, crying, "The Temple of Capitalism is Falling!"[2]

This heady student radicalism was also affecting Ireland with the rise of the civil rights movement in Northern Ireland, and when I returned to live and work in Dublin in 1969 I found a society ripe for social change. Women's liberation would be part of this social change, and a group of us younger women came together to form the women's liberation movement. This group included, quite early on, Mary Robinson, who was to go on to become the first woman president of Ireland in 1990, and perhaps a template for other women at the top in Irish political life. Some of the first meetings of the Irish Women's Liberation Movement were held in my apartment in Dublin.[3]

Our agenda in founding this movement was reform and change for women in Irish society, though I believe that some of us (including myself) were also influenced by the spirit of rebellion of the age. Ireland was a highly conservative society until the 1960s, although there were paradoxes even within that conservatism: social observers writing about Ireland frequently described it as free and easy, tolerant of eccentricity, and with some matriarchal characteristics.[4] Nevertheless, there were many laws and regulations pertaining to women's public life that were, by 1970, quite archaic.

As we noted in our pamphlet *Chains or Change,*[5] these were well overdue for alteration or dissolution. In 1970, Irish women were not called for jury duty—they could request to sit on a jury, but requesting to sit on a jury could be, in itself, a disqualification! In opening a bank account or credit accounts, the countersignature of a man was required. Married women could not have a government job, or a job with any semistate body, which at that time composed a large sector of the economy (Ireland was said to be "more socialist than Yugoslavia" in its economic system then). Women who wished to or needed to continue working after marriage could do so only in uncertain "temporary" contractual conditions, and while this was not rigidly applied in the private sector, it was nonetheless frequently the practice. Both widows and deserted wives had poor welfare benefits; unmarried mothers had none. There was no recourse to divorce, although Irish women (as was subsequently demonstrated by two referenda, in 1986 and 1995) were ambivalent about divorce in a society where men still had superior property rights.[6]

Equal pay for work of equal value did not, of course, apply. There was man's work and woman's work; in a culture where employment had always been in short supply, this was not a straightforward issue, particularly for the left, which traditionally favored priority for the man's wage as "the family wage."

And perhaps most controversially, birth control "devices" (this meant condoms and any other barrier method of birth control) were illegal in Ireland by an act of 1935. The contraceptive pill, which was not a "device" but a pharmaceutical, never came under the prohibition. We wanted all such archaic legislation swept away: it was unacceptable in the late twentieth century for customs officers at Irish frontier posts to forage in the personal belongings of visitors, or Irish people returning home, in search of banned contraceptive artifacts.

There were, as I recall, about twelve of us, mostly young Irish women, in this feminist movement at the start, which rapidly expanded and became astonishingly successful in its impact. We had many heated discussions and "consciousness-raising" sessions. But at that stage abortion simply did not enter the picture. We never even raised it: I do not believe it occurred to any of us to do so.

There were a number of different reasons for this. First, there were too many other issues on which there was consensus and that were much more attainable. The social justice issues, such as the plight of widows and deserted wives, had widespread grassroots support. I was the woman's editor of a national newspaper, the *Irish Press,* in 1970, and I recall that we received many letters of support from women in rural Ireland on these basic points of justice.

Second, we thought the contraception issue was the more important area of birth control and human rights. Abortion seemed more marginal, more associated with the hidden and the criminal. Earlier pioneering birth controllers, too, such as Margaret Sanger and Marie Stopes had themselves eschewed abortion, sincerely believing that contraception would prevent abortion.[7]

I now believe, in retrospect, that our Catholic sensibilities also played a part in our attitude to abortion. Although most of us would, at that time, have felt rebellious against the Catholic Church, which we characterized as "patriarchal," and would have disagreed with the encyclical *Humanae Vitae,* issued by Pope Paul VI in 1968, which retained the prohibition on artificial contraception, I think it is probable that most of us young Irish feminists at this time would have regarded abortion as basically sinful. Most (though not all) of the women in the women's liberation movement in Ireland were products of convent education, but it is my experience, in any case, that Irish Protestants and Irish Jews would share many similar cultural attitudes with Irish Catholics. Some Irish Protestants, particularly in Northern Ireland, are as vehemently prolife as Irish Catholics, and indeed when there was a referendum about abortion in Ireland in 1983, among the most outspoken supporters of the prolife cause was the Rev. Ian Paisley of the Free Presbyterian Church, who is also probably Ireland's fiercest critic of the pope and "popery."[8]

In our convent education in the 1950s and 1960s, we were not given what is now called "prolife education": a subject such as abortion would not have been discussed at all, not only in Ireland, but elsewhere too. Piquantly, the word was quite openly used in an agricultural and veterinarian context, where farmers would speak of a cow having an abortion—meaning that the cow had failed to calve. This, too, is significant, however. For rural people, failure in reproduction is failure, and a cow who miscarries is a cow who has disappointed the cowman. Thus, in an agricultural society, the very word *abortion* carries negative baggage, even leaving aside the moral dimension.

III

It seems to me that even before the era of abortion awareness, or prolife education, Catholics absorbed an unconscious prolife culture, particularly in Marian prayers. Ireland has a strong tradition of devotion to the Blessed Virgin,[9] and the most repeated Marian prayer, the Hail Mary, resonates with a strongly prolife message: "Blessed is the fruit of thy womb, Jesus." That the "fruit of the womb" contains the Incarnation itself is an extraordinarily powerful idea, and when the prayer becomes a kind of mantra, it is reinforced with each recital and enters the subconscious and the unconscious. Even without any prolife education, or, as critics would call it, antiabortion propaganda, Catholic women would be imbued with an unconscious hostility toward abortion, which some would describe as a guilt mechanism.[10]

But I also think that we did believe, at this time, that fertility control, including the Pill and forms of barrier contraception, really would provide women with a sense of empowerment over their bodies. This belief was shared by many social reformers in the 1960s, when "family planning" was upheld as the great good that would genuinely "solve" the problems of unwanted pregnancies. Abortion had indeed been legalized in Britain in 1967—one of the first European countries, after

Sweden to usher in such legislation—but the legislation was promoted, at this time, not as a "choice" but as a remedy against special hardship.[11] The 1967 Abortion Act was originally designed to protect physicians from prosecution when they had terminated a pregnancy in good faith, and it was virtually carried by the scandal of thalidomide. Women who were carrying a fetus damaged by the drug thalidomide were flying to Sweden to terminate their pregnancies, and this gave the Abortion Act its vital impetus. (Ironically, many people exposed to thalidomide grew up to live quite normal lives and are themselves now parents.)

But all this seemed, at the time, within the sphere of "hard cases." It is true that British feminists were, by the late 1960s, moving toward more affirmative demands regarding abortion: they wished to normalize it as a woman's choice rather than preserve it as an exceptional measure. By the early 1970s, abortion politics was altering in most of the developed countries, and of course many societies were influenced by the *Roe v. Wade* decision in the United States in 1973.

Not in Ireland. Or not yet in Ireland. In the 1970s, there were too many other social issues: birth control freedom was increasing gradually, but until the 1980s, there remained certain prohibitions on the sale of condoms.[12] For a brief period, birth control was legal only for married couples. However, it is virtually impossible to maintain a social change by political dictate once a wave of social change is underway. Gradually, the market itself orders the pace of change, and today there are no practical prohibitions on access to contraceptives in the Irish Republic.

Abortion still remains illegal and an extremely difficult area in Irish life. Public figures approach the subject with care and tact. And while there are certain individual women, generally known as radicals, who do speak openly in favor of abortion choice, a perceptible curtain of reticence still surrounds the subject among women in general. In November 2000, an Irish Sunday newspaper carried out a survey on attitudes to abortion among female members of Parliament: only four of the thirty-one women in the Dail and the Senate agreed to participate in the survey, and even among these four, response was circumspect. A government minister, Mrs. Mary O'Rourke, said simply that she did have her own opinions on the subject but that it would be "inappropriate" to voice them. On the Opposition benches, Liz McManus and

Jan O'Sullivan, both Labor members, said that they supported abortion "in limited circumstances." An Independent member, Mildred Fox from Wicklow, said "there should be no abortion under any circumstances."[13] Ms. Fox is twenty-nine.

The newspaper suggested that the women politicians in Ireland were too nervous about party or constituency reaction to make their views plain. If this is so, then that in itself indicates that public opinion is sensitive, and still broadly conservative. Opinion polls have certainly shown that antiabortion attitudes are remarkably tenacious in Ireland, and even where attitudes toward other values have altered or "modernized" (such as attitudes about gay rights, or divorce), the prolife base remains strong.[14] Sociologists analyze this in a number of different ways, but I believe myself that the "Hail Mary factor" goes deep into the culture: blessed is the fruit of the womb.

IV

How much does the "Hail Mary factor" establish a tension for Catholic women, especially women living in a Catholic culture like Ireland? (Despite a decline in overall churchgoing and increased secularization prompted by the new-found prosperity of the Irish economy, known as the "Celtic Tiger economy," a report in the Irish religious magazine *Doctrine and Life* in December 2000 indicated that the Irish were still the most religiously observant people in Europe.[15]) This is a very complicated question, but I will return first to the issue of feminism.

Despite some conservative aspects of Irish culture, feminism was reasonably well favored in Ireland in the early part of the twentieth century, and many distinguished Irish women described themselves as active feminists, most notably Countess Markiewicz, who was to become the first woman to be elected to the House of Commons (as a Sinn Fein deputy, she did not take her seat), and Maud Gonne MacBride, who founded "The Daughters of Erin," which advanced the cause of women.[16] Irish feminists, however, tended to throw their lot in with the national movement, and individuals like Constance Markiewicz chose, rather, the path of political rebellion over women's suffrage alone.

With the establishment of the Irish state in 1922, there was a political desire for a period of stability, especially after the disturbing period of Troubles, and this, in turn, led to a more conservative mood. After the Wall Street crash of 1929 and the rise of the European dictators in the 1930s, many cultures came to emphasize what the Third Reich so regretfully defined as the woman's role—"Kirche, Küche, und Kinder"—church, kitchen, and children.

Nevertheless, the tradition of admiring a woman of spirit remained in Irish culture. In his classic study of culture and society in the West of Ireland, the poet Padraic Colum[17] noted that women with strong personalities were always esteemed in Irish rural life, especially since the man of the house might have to be away on long fishing trips or might be a migrant worker in Scotland. Colum notes that articulate women were also esteemed in this society—a common phrase of praise being "a well-discoursed woman." This matriarchal strain in Irish society was also noted by the American anthropologists Arensberg and Kimbell in their 1940 study *Family and Community in Ireland*,[18] and it is endorsed by many other social studies of Irish life. This esteem for "the strong woman" lay as a template for Irish women's empowerment even when the laws pertaining to the public and employed role of women were unreformed and archaic.

This "strong woman" Irish ideal was, I would say, in many respects underlined by the traditional Catholic convent education, where female saints with a distinct line in "autonomy" were upheld as role models (in my own convent, the Institute of the Blessed Virgin, Stephen's Green, Dublin, certainly, in the 1950s and early 1960s): St. Brigid of Ireland, who apparently repelled suitors so she could become a hermit; St. Catherine of Siena, who became a doctor of the Church; St. Teresa of Avila, mystic and intellectual; and St. Joan of Arc, who led an army to rid France of the English (a particular favorite with more nationalistic Irish nuns!). I have no memory of any religious sister speaking to us about our future roles as wives: the Old Testament concept of the woman as the Good Wife was not underlined. Not being themselves wives, perhaps these teaching nuns had little sense of identification with the woman as wife.

In my twenties, when I read the work of American feminists such as Betty Friedan, Kate Millett, Gloria Steinem, and Shulamith Firestone, the one aspect that was foreign to me was the notion that marriage was the only career open to women. This may have been true, or seemed true, in America, which has always favored marriage. It certainly seemed true in the movies we watched from the United States: *Oklahoma!*, *The Tender Trap*, *How to Marry a Millionaire*, and a string of comedies with Doris Day. Marriage was, for women, the be-all and the end-all in this 1950s ideology of Hollywood. But it was much less esteemed as an end in itself by our Irish teaching nuns, who had a stronger vision of women as saints, missionaries, visionaries, musicians, intellectuals.

But there was a contradiction in our values (as there are many in life): women were actively encouraged in education and in fulfilling their talents. Yet through our devotional life, too, we would always have the example of Our Lady's story: how Mary, as an astonished young teenager, accepted the Annunciation, a story that was enacted in our daily recital of the Angelus: "The Angel of the Lord appeared unto Mary, and she conceived of the Holy Ghost." Stories are one of the strongest means of communicating morals and values, and through this story of the Annunciation (said to be the most frequently painted subject in European art), we learned that Mary accepted. She may have been confused and bewildered, but she accepted what was ordained for her. Feminists would later describe acceptance as a social construct of female passivity, but I am sure we internalized, and venerated, the first episode in the Joyful Mysteries of the Rosary.

There is a tension in Catholic Christianity between the choices made by female saints, often headstrong choices, such as that of St. Jane of Chantal, who walked away from her home and her teenage son to found a religious order (he was subsequently reconciled to his mother and went on to become the father of the brilliant French woman of letters, Madame de Sevigne[19]), and Mary's acceptance of a stunning biological fact with the words "Behold the handmaid of the Lord—be it done unto me according to thy word" (Lk 1:38).

However, if there is a conflict between the notion of choice and the notion of acceptance, perhaps we just have to accept that fact. Life is full of such conflicts, and not all of them can be resolved. Carol Gilligan's work has suggested, most plausibly, that women can tolerate conflicting ideas more serenely than men,[20] and Lynda Bird Francke's sensitive study of abortion among secularized American women, *The Ambivalence of Abortion*,[21] more than suggests that inner conflict is inevitable, necessary, and sensitive for a reflective woman with natural maternal feelings.

There are studies that suggest that religious women feel more troubled about an abortion decision than women with no religious sensibilities. This seems no more than common sense, but again, I would suggest there are probably cultural variables: Italy has a scandalously high rate of abortion (almost a third of all pregnancies are terminated),[22] yet Catholic culture has remained quite tenacious in other respects in Italy. Arthur Marwick, in his definitive study *The Sixties,* claims that Italy's long opposition to the death penalty actually derives from its Catholic cultural base in regarding human life as sacred and the death penalty as therefore morally inadmissable. Yet this same Italian revulsion at taking human life seems to have little impact on abortion practice in Italy, where it is virtually customized as retrospective contraception.

Moreover, some women with no religious background are quite opposed to abortion. I carried out a study in June 2000 for the London newspaper the *Daily Express,* which entailed twenty-two interviews with young women in East Kent, England, all of whom had been pregnant as teenagers. Although only two of these young women had any contact with churches, almost all of them expressed a marked repugnance for abortion. This hostility to abortion was even present where the individual had actually had an abortion. A recent study on Finnish women showed that suicide was higher among women in Finland who had recently had abortions, although Finland is not regarded as a religious society and is certainly not a Catholic society.[23] So attitudes toward abortion may not necessarily depend upon religious practice or sensibilities. It seems to me that a great deal more personalized research needs to be done into this subject: exploring women's values and feelings in a descriptive way.

V

Irish Catholic culture is, I suggest, both biased toward certain forms of feminism—admiring of the woman as a strong personality, and deferring to matriarchal figures—and at the same time pronatalist (as most agricultural, and low-population societies are) and in consequence antiabortion. Padraic Colum noted that there were at least ten different words for "baby" and "child" in the Irish language used by the women of the West of Ireland, a linguistic indication of the value placed on the child and on fertility. At the same time, we may suppose that some clandestine abortions did take place in traditional Ireland, or (since the surgical operation of abortion could be very dangerous for the woman until the 1940s), alternatively, infanticide.

In 1998, I had occasion to examine the coroners' records in Dublin,[24] comparing the deaths in suspicious circumstances archived in 1998 with those in 1968 and 1958. Drug deaths (mainly by heroin, or by heroin with a polydrug use) dominated the 1998 statistics but were virtually absent from the figures in 1958 and 1968. But incidents of dead babies left in church porches that had occurred in 1958 were absent by 1998: birth control, or abortion via a trip to Britain, had erased this statistic.

Abortion in Ireland today is still not lawful: a referendum was held in 1983 to enshrine the right of the unborn child into the Irish constitution, and although the turnout of 54 percent was not considered high, the country voted two to one to protect the life of the unborn. It had been a bitterly fought cultural war,[25] though it was more characteristically between liberals and conservatives than between feminists and Catholics, since men were as visible (on both sides) as women. Yet the catchphrase "the right to choose" had broadly spread across the globe during the later 1970s, and younger women and radical women in Ireland, as elsewhere, were tending now to emphasize choice rather than moral coercion, as they would see it.[26] At the same time, there are several high-profile women in Ireland today who would declare themselves to be both feminists and prolife Catholics, of whom the most distinguished is the current President of Ireland, Mary McAleese.[27] Mrs. McAleese, who comes from Belfast and was voted president in 1997, is a confident feminist who has been actively involved with Church issues (she argues persuasively for the ordination of women) and an equally self-assured Catholic who has declared herself opposed to abortion on orthodox Catholic grounds. It might be said that Mrs. McAleese, a mother of three, has most successfully balanced feminism and Catholicism.

It was predicted—wrongly, as it turned out—that the prohibition on abortion in the Irish Constitution would have a deleterious effect on the health of women and mothers in Ireland and that women might even die as a consequence. This did not occur. Indeed, Ireland has consistently come toward the top of the World Health Organization's League of Safe Motherhood: maternity services are exemplary. Maternal deaths are extremely rare, and seldom above 1.5 per 100,000.[28] Recourse to abortion does not necessarily correlate with good maternal care for women nowadays, as the lamentable statistics from Russia and other former Soviet Union countries will show: abortion is common and health care for women in pregnancy and childbirth is often appalling. Objectively speaking, there are too many variables (culture, distance, number of midwives, traditions of health care, financial resources, and so on) to draw any rigid parallel in the modern world between maternal health and access to abortion.

This is also because abortion has indeed reached, in many societies, the aim of being a personal "choice" rather than being a matter of health. Very seldom, nowadays, is an abortion performed to save the life of the mother. As Dr. David Paintin, consultant gynecologist at the Samaritan Hospital in London and a veteran of the prochoice Abortion Law Reform Association, told me in an interview: "Abortion is a social operation, in most cases, not a medical one. If the woman wants the pregnancy, we can now nearly always manage it."

So abortion law—or the lack of it—in Ireland was not to be challenged on grounds of health. But it was to be highlighted by a particularly distressing event, known as "the X Case," in February 1992. The "X" case (so called because the Irish courts said the young girl should never be named but should be referred to only as "X") involved the pregnancy of a fourteen-year-old girl. She was made pregnant by an older man who was a neighbor, and because she was under age (the age of consent in Ireland is seventeen) this counted as a statutory rape. Her parents decided to seek an abortion in Britain and informed the Irish police of their intention. In consequence, she was forbidden to leave Ireland, and when the issue became public, there was a national uproar. The *Irish Times* compared Ireland to the Ayatollah Khomeni's Iran, and there was international media attention on the unhappy "X." Eventually, the case itself went to the Irish Supreme Court, which ruled that, because the young woman was reported to be suicidal, she would be entitled to travel abroad for a termination of pregnancy. (She did so, but it was reported that she suffered a miscarriage before the abortion took place.) However, this has stood in case law as a precedent, and where a young woman is reported to be "suicidal," it is considered legal for her to go abroad to seek a termination of pregnancy. Further referenda were called in Ireland to establish "the right to travel" and "the right to information" about abortion.

And privately, something in the region of six thousand to eight thousand Irish women do travel to Britain each year to have abortions. (Figures are necessarily inexact because they are unofficial.) How the women themselves feel about it is a mystery. An all-parliamentary report that was carried out in Ireland in the winter of 2000 looked at every aspect of abortion and resolved to research further the causes of abortion, but women were extremely reluctant to give evidence of their own experience. Nobody really wants to talk about it, on a personal level, the odd media star aside. Even with the odd media star, there are endless sequelae to a public reference to an abortion experience. A friend of mine wrote an article in an Irish newspaper about how she had chosen to have an abortion when a second pregnancy occurred at a difficult time in her life. Ever since then, whenever she has mentioned her two children, she has had mail—not always unkind, but always insistent—from readers, saying: "And what about the little one up in Heaven that you are forgetting?"

Yet another referendum on abortion was held in March 2002, in which a proposal that abortion could be carried out if a woman was suicidal was passed—but by a margin of only 0.8 percent. The situation at the present time is that in theory a woman could have a legal abortion in Ireland if she were suicidal, but in practice, no psychiatrist or psychologist has yet certified a woman in this condition. Most doctors do not wish to carry out the operation. It is more practical to travel to Britain: Liverpool is only 20 minutes from Dublin by plane. However, the morning-after pill is legal, and an abortion pill will eventually probably change things again. Yet the cultural resistance is stubborn.

VI

Our Enlightenment heritage tells us that problems have solutions, and quite often they do. Medicine cures; science advances; research brings answers. Yet this model cannot always be imported into questions of culture and society. To some problems, there are no solutions, exactly. There are no clear and tidy answers. Or there are many, complicated, personal, and even paradoxical answers, which people will find unsatisfactory but which they just have to accept. I believe there is no real reconciliation between Irish Catholic values and abortion as a feminist cause. There are continuing culture wars in Ireland over abortion, and there will be for a long time to come. By the time this war is brought to a closure, there could be a completely new scientific answer—perhaps fetal transplants (whereby the unwanted fetus can be donated to a recipient), or cryogenic freezing (where the unwanted fetus can be put on ice for some future possible choice of reanimation). Who knows?

There is a prochoice movement in Ireland whose most articulate spokeswoman is one Ivana Bacik, and I do not intend to sound a xenophobic note when I record that Ms. Bacik's ethnic roots are in central Europe. Ms. Bacik is a frequent correspondent to the letters page of the *Irish Times,* calling for the woman's right to choose in the matter of the termination of pregnancy. Some people admire her for her outspokenness, and some agree with her. Some disagree: some think her a crank. But since she is not herself a Catholic, her political or social role has little to do with reconciling feminism with Catholicism in Ireland. Catholicism still represents the deposit of Ireland's historical value system. In June 2001, a Dutch self-styled "abortion ship," calling itself "Women on Waves," sailed toward Dublin harbor (remaining just twelve miles outside the territorial waters of the Irish Republic) offering Irish women abortion and contraceptive advice. As it turned out, the ship was not provided with a license to carry out abortions, so "Women on Waves" was really merely an advertisement for abortion on request. Ms. Bacik, supported by several others, wrote to the *Irish Times* welcoming "Women on Waves," saying that there was a pressing need for their services:

> We are delighted that the reaction of the press and public to the ship's visit has been so positive, and that the visit has helped to reopen public debate on the need to legalize abortion. Most importantly, the visit has highlighted the real experiences of women facing crisis pregnancy in Ireland. Over 300 women have contacted Women

on Waves Ireland over the past week. Many already knew they had to terminate their pregnancies, but were worried about the arrangements and the costs. Some were utterly desperate; many were alone, with little or no emotional or financial support. We have been able to offer some support to them, but the sheer number of calls demonstrates the urgent need for abortion services to be provided in Ireland.[29]

Yet although the media recorded the arrival of "Women on Waves," others objected to its visitation. I heard private mutterings about the "neocolonialist" aspect of a foreign ship visiting Irish waters to contradict Irish law: natives do not always welcome foreigners sailing into their home waters and bestowing upon them foreign liberties. The most radical feminist in Irish political life, the Labor Party member of parliament Liz McManus, would only say of "Women on Waves": "This is a highly controversial issue where politicians tread at their peril."[30] She would not be drawn further. In the *Irish Times,* the columnist Breda O'Brien said that it was "a non-event" and that most people were embarrassed by the episode.[31] This was also the reaction of Frank McCourt, the Irish writer, among others, on an Irish radio panel: it was "distasteful" and "embarrassing."[32] And what about the alleged three hundred Irish women who called "Women on Waves"? We will never know.

About 10 percent of Irish pregnancies are terminated abroad, though the figures will remain fuzzy because some Irish women going to London give British addresses, and some British women, seeking an urgent British National Health abortion, give Irish addresses to facilitate priority. It is likely that many of the Catholic Irish women who choose abortion in Britain do so because they feel that they simply are unable to face continuing a pregnancy, for practical reasons. (Breda O'Brien claims, in the same *Irish Times* column, that a parliamentary committee reported that the phrase women used most commonly about abortion was, significantly, "I had no other choice.") It is likely that they squared it with their own consciences, in the tradition that "necessity knows no law."

It seems, from opinion polls, that Irish people differentiate between citizens making the private choice to go abroad to terminate a pregnancy and endorsement of the practice of abortion within Irish hospitals. For some, this is hypocrisy; for others, it is just the best compromise on offer. Abortions in Irish hospitals would mean the official sanctioning of the abortion culture, which still remains distasteful to Irish Catholic tradition.

There are too many hidden agendas within the Irish collective unconscious to regard abortion as a simple issue of personal choice or to imagine that there can be an easy reconciliation between this issue of feminism and Catholicism. There is the long agrarian history of depopulation; there is the stain of the Great Famine of the 1840s, which is such a living memory still with Irish America. There is the agricultural imperative of fertility and the Catholic imprint of the Hail Mary idea. Fertility is even intertwined in traditional Irish drinking toasts: "Health and long life to you; land without rent to you; a child every year to you; and death in Ireland."

One Irish female member of the European Parliament (MEP), representing the Green Party, Ms. Nuala Ahern, has said: "Abortion is a difficult question. We all have different, and sometimes conflicting, views. We just have to start from the base of accepting the differences and respecting one another."[33] There is no immediate legal solution, but as a recent movie aimed at teenage anguish advocates—"Live with it!" We will be living with this problem for some time to come. But that doesn't mean that in other areas—particularly in education, social change, literary output, economic progress, law and media, justice and equality—Catholicism and feminism haven't been reconciled in ways that are often highly enriching of both.

NOTES

1. David Quinn, "Ireland's Pro-Life Civil War," *Human Life Review* (Winter/Spring 2002).

2. My reports are in the archives of the *London Evening Standard* (May 1968). A useful account of the events of 1968 appears in Arthur Marwick's *The Sixties* (New York: Oxford University Press, 1998).

3. An account of the development of the Irish Women's Liberation Movement appears in June Levine's book *Sisters: The Personal Story of an Irish Feminist* (Dublin: Ward River Press, 1982). I also refer to the background in my own book: Mary Kenny, *Goodbye to Catholic Ireland* (London: Sinclair-Stevenson, 1997).

4. Alan Bestic's *The Importance of Being Irish* (London: Cassell, 1969) and V. S. Pritchett's *Dublin, a Portrait* (London: Bodley Head, 1967) are examples of this genre.

5. Irish Women's Liberation Movement, *Chains or Change* (1970) is available in the National Library of Ireland as a historic pamphlet.

6. Chrystel Hug's *The Politics of Sexual Morality in Ireland* (London: Macmillan Press, 1999) describes the referenda on divorce and abortion that took place in Ireland throughout the 1980s and the social changes affecting homosexuality and birth control.

7. See June Rose, *Marie Stopes and the Sexual Revolution* (London: Faber and Faber, 1992).

8. See Kenny, *Goodbye to Catholic Ireland,* for reference to Ian Paisley's support for prolife policies in the Irish Republic.

9. See Peter O'Dwyer, *Mary: A History of Devotion in Ireland* (Dublin: Four Courts Press, 1992).

10. Letter from Mrs. Barbara Dobson, of Sligo; letter from June Levine, author of *Sisters,* the book that chronicled the Irish Women's Liberation Movement. June Levine, who is now sixty-eight, was brought up in a Catholic-Jewish Irish family.

11. See Madeleine Simms and Keith Hindell, *Abortion Law Reformed* (London: Peter Owen, 1971).

12. See Ailbhe Smyth, ed., *Irish Women's Studies Reader* (Dublin: Attic Press, 1993).

13. *Ireland on Sunday,* November 19, 2000.

14. Mary Kenny, *Goodbye to Catholic Ireland,* 2d ed. (Springfield, Ill.: Templegate, 2000; Dublin: New Island Books, 2000), refers to surveys done on Irish youth attitudes.

15. Andrew Greeley and Connor Ward, "How 'Secularized' Is the Ireland We Live in?" *Doctrine and Life* (December 2000): 581–617, available from Dominican Publications, 42 Parnell Square, Dublin 1. E-mail: dompubs@iol.ie.

16. See Kit and Cyril Ó Céirín, *Women of Ireland: A Biographic Dictionary* (Kinvara: Galway, 1996).

17. Padraic Colum, *My Irish Year* (London: Mills and Boon, 1912).

18. Conrad M. Arensberg and Solon T. Kimbell, *Family and Community in Ireland* (Cambridge, Mass.: Harvard University Press, 1940).

19. Donald Attwater and Catherine Rachel John, eds., *The Penguin Dictionary of Saints* (London: Penguin Books, 1995).

20. Carol Gilligan, *In a Different Voice* (Cambridge, Mass.: Harvard University Press, 1982).

21. Lynda Bird Francke, *The Ambivalence of Abortion* (London: Penguin Books, 1978).

22. Marwick, *The Sixties*.

23. M. Gissler et al., "Pregnancy Related Deaths in Finland 1987–94," *Acta Obstetricia et Gyynecologica Scandinavica* 76 (1997): 651; Mika Gissler, Elina Hemminki, and Jonko Lonnqvist, "Suicides after Pregnancy in Finland 1987–1994," *British Medical Journal* 313 (1996): 1.

24. Research carried out for my book *Death by Heroin—Recovery by Hope* (Dublin: New Island Books, 1999).

25. See Tom Hesketh's *The Second Partitioning of Ireland* (Dingle, Kerry: Brandon Books, 1990), for a detailed account of the 1983 referendum.

26. Letter from Mrs. Maire Collins, of Dundalk, County Louth, writing as a Catholic Irish woman.

27. See the recent biography by Justine McCarthy, *Mary McAleese: The Outsider* (Dublin: Blackwater Press, 2000).

28. Statistics on deaths from maternal mortality all come from WHO annual reports.

29. Ivana Bacik, letter to the editor, *Irish Times*, June 26, 2001.

30. "The P.M. Programme," BBC Radio 4, June 15, 2001.

31. Breda O'Brien, "The Breda O'Brien Column," *Irish Times*, June 23, 2001.

32. Today FM, "Sunday Supplement," Dublin, June 17, 2001.

33. Nuala Ahern was speaking at the Parnell Summer School, Wicklow, 1995.

TWELVE

Reconciling Latin American Catholicism and Feminism

Nilsa Lasso-von Lang

I was born in the Republic of Panama, in a small town east of Panama City. Like most people in Panama, I was brought up in a society where Catholicism is not only a religion but also an essential component of its culture. In fact, I daresay that in my house, we were not allowed to even think about becoming something else. In other words, being Hispanic was synonymous with being a Catholic. I was born in the bosom of the Catholic Church. My family, like most Latin American families, accepted Catholicism as its religion almost automatically, as a family tradition that must be upheld. However, I don't remember having too much spiritual guidance, practicing the principles of Catholicism, or going to church other than for Christmas, New Year's Eve, funerals, or special religious celebrations. Even then, only my mother, my two sisters, and I went to church. My father, like most Latin American men, believed that the Church is "a women's thing."

My experience as a Catholic woman has been full of traditions that view women as objects. In Panama, as in the rest of the Latin American countries, women are victims of cultural attitudes, such as machismo, that are directly or indirectly supported by Catholicism. The Church gives men a more dominant and possessive role and views women as silent members of society. Other cultural attitudes or symbolic myths overshadowing women are virginity and maternity. Virginity is very important in my culture. Church and society are very strict when it comes to women's behavior. I have two sisters. It was very clear to us that we were responsible for the honor of our family—the three of us had to stay virgins for our husbands. We were expected to marry at church and wear a white dress and a bride's veil. My sisters and I were closely observed because according to our society our virginity was a seal guaranteeing our value as people. Without our virginity, we were in danger of losing everything and receiving labels such as "bad woman," "prostitute," "whore," or, as many men would say, "bad merchandise." Paradoxically, staying single and virginal or wanting to become a nun didn't make a Hispanic woman more prized. Some of my female cousins and aunts decided to stay single, and now they are subjected to mockery. People make cruel remarks such as "Yeah! right, like we really are going to believe she wants to become a nun," "Look at her, the train left her, she is not as virgin as she wants you to think," or "Nobody wants to do her the favor."

As a Hispanic, I know very well that in Latin American society a woman's mission and reason for being is still "reproduction." My mother, for example, was responsible for taking care of us and the domestic chores. It wasn't until my youngest sister was in high school and my older sister and I were in college that my father reluctantly agreed to let my mother work outside the home. I guess my sisters and I were lucky to have parents who, in spite of their traditional ways, were wise enough to foresee some social changes in our society. They always encouraged us to become educated and independent. The three of us have college degrees. Indeed, Panama is among the Latin American countries where women outnumber men in college; large numbers of Hispanic women work outside the home. Yet all these women have to endure a *doble jornada*—that is, they work at home and outside the home. Ironically, women's efforts and sacrifices don't entitle them to anything. Traditions and social norms of a patriarchal society determine who is a good or a bad mother.

These beliefs are directly tied to the Church, for the traditional conception of woman as the ideal domestic figure, mother, self-sacrificing, and submissive, is fully supported by Latin American Roman Catholics. Mexican and Mexican American Catholics view the Virgin of Guadalupe as a role model, for she is pure, pious, and divinely appointed as the perfect mother. Other Latin American Catholics have the same role model in the Virgin Mary, Mother of Jesus. She was the exemplary mother, symbolizing perfection, devotion, and suffering.

I have had the opportunity to study the development of feminism in Latin America. Unlike American feminists, Latin American feminists have not had the advantages of living in a pluralistic society. There isn't much room for a multiplicity of positions, disagreement, confrontation, or dialogues among people. A double sign of militarism and Catholicism has marked Latin American history, resulting in two groups of pressure, the army and the Church. They are responsible for the lack of progress in Latin America. Spaniards came to my country holding the cross in one hand and the sword in the other. They brought the Church, which preached conformity and suffering and supported social norms that viewed women as subservient to men; they also brought violence, anarchy, civil war, totalitarian governments, revolts, and revolutions. The first time I got married, I did so under Panamanian laws. As the judge was reading to us our responsibilities to one another, my groom, who was a foreigner, couldn't believe how rigid our civil laws were regarding the woman's role. It sounded more like he was gaining a slave, not a wife. These laws are fully supported by the Catholic Church.

Catholicism teaches that matrimony is a permanent sacrament that only death can break. The Vatican's highest authorities are still firm in maintaining the Roman Catholic Church's traditional laws that condemn remarriage after divorce. When I was getting married, my fiancé and I went to talk to a Catholic priest for the usual premarital orientation. It turned out that my fiancé, who was divorced and a Methodist, had to request an annulment in order to marry me in the Catholic Church. According to the priest, annulments take about a year and are not guaranteed.

Like me, my Mexican friend Lupe was raised a Catholic, but she considers herself a non-Catholic feminist Christian. She says, "I firmly believe that religion in general is being misinterpreted by men in their favor, and also by women whom I called 'patriarchal women,' guardians or supporters of the patriarchal order." She supports her arguments by offering the following examples: "We can only see what recently has happened in Guanajuato, a Mexican state. The law, supported by the Church, has denied the right of raped women to terminate their pregnancies under the threat of incarceration if they 'commit abortion.' There was no consideration of more severe punishment of the rapists." Lupe and I still see women treated as second-class citizens at home and in society. We are not very optimistic about a possible reconciliation between Catholicism and feminism because the doctrines of Catholicism are deeply embedded in our society.

Take a look at Latin American history. In the late 1800s, women found a small place in the public sphere. Lower-class women started to work for manufacturers, and an increasing middle class had the opportunity to receive an education. In the twentieth century, Latin American women started celebrating feminist congresses. Between 1929 and 1961, Latin American women earned their right to vote. In Panama, for example, women won the right to vote in 1946. In the 1970s women celebrated the "International Year of Women." I was in high school when this happened, and my female role models were too traditional to welcome it with open arms. Maybe this explains why I didn't understand it and only vaguely recall what should have been a memorable occasion for all of us girls.

From the beginning, Latin American feminism has identified itself with radical theories. In a nonpluralistic society like Latin America things are black or white, yet there is no clear separation between church and state. Those who disagree with the existing norms have to accept extreme views. Perhaps this explains why most Latin American feminists tend to be more secular. During the 1960s, the Cuban revolution and the doctrines of Marxism attracted many liberal and progressive individuals, among them groups of women. These groups became what were called *feministas comprometidas* (women committed to a political ideology). Other groups of women, not committed to a specific ideology, became pressure groups who organized to denounce acts of violence against people in general. They concentrated their attention on the disappearance of people and torture during totalitarian regimes.

For example, Argentina, like many other Latin American countries, suffered under *caudillos'* authoritarian rule. In the 1970s, a dictatorial government violated human rights, institutionalizing the system of *desaparecidos*. The military government was responsible for the disappearance of thousands of Argentineans. Thousands of Argentinean women, who were later known as "Mothers of La Plaza de Mayo," organized themselves and met daily at La Plaza de Mayo in order to demand information about victims of the military government. Most of these victims were their sons, daughters, and husbands. In the late 1980s, Panamanian women were very active during the protests against the despotism of Manuel Antonio Noriega's government. With the fall of communism in Europe, women have grown less attracted to Marxist doctrines. Feminist groups, regardless of ideology, are joining forces to denounce economic injustice. They deal with other profound and traditional patterns of oppression, such as racial and social discrimination, creating a sense of solidarity among feminists all over the world and other oppressed people, men or women.

Today, I live in the United States. I am happily married to my second husband and consider myself a non-Catholic Christian feminist. I definitely support divorce and remarrying after divorce. Who among us makes no mistakes in life? Every person has the right to a second opportunity to achieve happiness. I am very disappointed in organized religion because of its conventionality. I can relate to those feminists who are Christians and believe that the Bible proves that God doesn't favor the discrimination and subordination of women, since women were created in His image

Even my Mexican friend Diana, who views herself as a nonfeminist Catholic woman, admits that Catholicism has created serious problems in Latin America. "Catholicism," she says, "can be blamed for the lack of progress in Latin America. The doctrines brought to Latin America by the Spanish conquistadors, along with retrograde, antidemocratic conceptions of society, are responsible for the systems of thought that prevail in Latin America, such as machismo, class divisions, and a cult of spiritual values." Like Diana, other Catholic Hispanics are growing increasingly aware of the need for change in our society and questioning the retrograde conceptions that characterize it. Juan, a Catholic and a good friend, believes that "Catholicism is embedded in our culture. When you walk by a church you see people almost kneeling and crossing themselves, as they say, 'In the name of the Father, the Son and the

Holy Spirit.'" Smiling, he adds, "Even those who are not Catholic show their respect to the saints when walking by the church."

Some of my other Hispanic Catholic friends and relatives will say, "Catholicism means well" or "I am Catholic because it is the first and true Church." To me, these rationalizations indicate that Latin American Catholics are aware of the serious problems with their religion. They see it as an inherent part of their culture. In other words, they are Catholics because it is their nature. Today, more born Catholics, like myself, seem to be moving from rationalizing and justifying to openly admitting that Catholicism is failing them and calling for social changes, especially those related to the role of women. My cousin Nubia, a nonpracticing Catholic, observed that feminism has been very positive for all women, for it has given us the opportunity to become active members of society. Still, she believes that Catholicism and feminism are incompatible because of the patriarchal views of the Church. This attitude, she says, needs to be changed. Older women like my mother and her sisters, who have been housewives most of their lives, don't seem to have a clear idea of what feminism is. Nevertheless, they know that it has something to do with them as women. Not surprisingly, they are prolife and believe divorce is needed only in extreme situations. They hold a more traditional view on issues such as women's ordination. They don't hesitate to say "No" when asked if women should be allowed to become priests. "Why?" I ask. "Because we are used to having men priests," they reply.

For some women in my culture, Marxism served as a means to feminism. It provided a political vehicle for them to voice their feelings and attempt to elicit social change. In other words, this radical theory that revolutionized our world gave Latin American Marxist feminists the opportunity to see themselves as active members of their society. I, like feminist Marxists, defended a feminist theory that posits equal political, economic, and social rights for men and women. However, I don't think Christianity functioned for me as Marxism did for them. First of all, Christianity didn't serve as a means to my becoming a feminist. In fact, I used to believe that a woman couldn't be a Christian and a feminist at the same time without compromising her faith in God. For a while, this issue was very confusing for me. Now I understand that I can be a

Christian and a feminist. I believe this happened because of my exposure to a higher educational system in the United States that provided me with a global perspective. The opportunity to live and study in the pluralistic society of the United States introduced me to options and rights that I, as a middle-class Hispanic and former Catholic woman, would never have dreamed of. Once I was out of my home country, I saw things more objectively. I discovered numerous avenues to freely voice my feelings and thoughts. It was like waking up or being born again.

Education was key to my becoming a non-Catholic Christian feminist. I completed my elementary and secondary education in Panamanian public schools, then attended the University of Panama for three years. Later, I transferred to U.S. universities to earn a B.A., an M.A., and a Ph.D. in Spanish American studies. When I started working on my Ph.D. I spent a lot of time studying Marxist and non-Marxist feminist theory and critical literary feminists. It was then that I was able to make the distinction between "feminine" and "feminist." I realized that I had been a feminist my whole life; I just didn't know it. It is perfectly understandable, given my upbringing. I was brought up as the traditional Catholic girl wearing pink dresses, receiving the First Communion in a bridal dress, and taking home economics in high school. I can't blame my mother for this. She did what she was taught. For her, a woman was supposed to be passive, emotional, and submissive, destined to marry and have children. When I was younger, I didn't understand my mother's attitudes and behavior. Now I feel for my mother; I understand that she was another victim of the patriarchal system. She always wanted to become a teacher, but her parents never supported her because she was a woman. "Why educate girls?" they said. "It is wasted money. She is going to get married and her husband will provide for her."

Now I admire my mother's spirit of sacrifice. She always put us first. My sisters and I were luckier than our foremothers. Our parents were very supportive, and the three of us earned advanced degrees. Xenia, my oldest sister, is a nurse and has two boys. Xenia supports some traditional Catholic rules, such as condemning abortion and recognizing the Church as the pillar of society when it comes to morality and spirituality. She believes that "poverty is a social/universal problem and religion doesn't make it worse; on the contrary the Church tries to help the unfortunate ones by offering spiritual and moral support and special programs, such as courses for illiterate people, home economics, and arts and crafts workshops. The Church is against domestic violence." She seems to disagree with other traditional laws that won't allow women to become priests, especially now with the shortage of priests in the world. Like me, she supports feminism as long as the fight is for equal rights for women in education, religion, work, and politics. Her optimism is evident when she affirms, "Women's situation within the Church has changed a little bit—for example, now women can become sacristans."

Yova, my youngest sister, is a social worker. I am a professor. Yet Yova and I have been criticized for choosing not to have children. Yova sometimes declares, "I am a nonfeminist Catholic." Most of the time she doesn't really want to talk about religion. One thing is for sure, though—she believes in a divine power or a God. When we do talk about Catholicism, she claims to have had a relatively good experience. In her teen years, the Church was a spiritual refuge. For Yova, "Feminism is an extreme position like machismo. I am in the middle of these two movements. I think feminism is not arising inside the Catholic Church. What is happening is that we are starting to comply with God's commands that we are all equal." She believes that women "have to face some of the Church's patriarchal views and the problems of radical feminist views. Both Catholicism and feminism have to give up something in order to accomplish a reconciliation." My aunt Mely, a practicing Catholic, strongly believes that the role of women in the Church has changed. Women are allowed to participate more in positions inside the Church that have been traditionally reserved for men only. At her church, they can become ministers of the altar. They are in charge of giving the Communion, reading the Word of God, becoming active spiritual leaders in the community, and attending seminars.

But realistically, I have to admit that the traditional roles of Hispanic women living in any Latin American country have changed very little. Nuns and laywomen appear to have more freedom and responsibilities, but the law that keeps women from becoming priests still stands. Catholic authorities have condemned abortion, describing it as a criminal act, and they continue to reject any form of artificial contraception. Since the emergence of the feminist movement, the number of women supporting the right to abortion and to use artificial contraception has increased significantly. Yet abortion still creates tremendous tension in Church and in society. La Comisión para la Defensa de los Derechos Humanos en Centroamérica (CODEHUCA) reports that in Latin America "thousands of women die per year, because of the practice of illegal abortion and the violation of their physical integrity."[1] Poverty and illiteracy remain serious problems in Latin America. Especially in rural areas, women are trapped by primitive beliefs, taboos, and social appearances. As unbelievable as it may seem, there are cases of desperate women who quietly have an abortion to protect the family's honor and by doing so lose their life.

Granted, minor adjustments to the Catholic doctrines have occurred. The Roman Catholic Church has given women the right to become sacristans and even ministers of the altar. In the secular realm, we cannot deny that the average Latin American person is developing a global awareness. Nevertheless, I remain pessimistic regarding the possibility of radical transformations within the Catholic Church regarding women's issues. A true reconciliation between feminism and Catholicism would require transformation of the Church's institutional structure as well as many of its teachings. Given the long history of the Catholic tradition in the Hispanic culture, these transformations are unlikely to happen in Latin America.

NOTE

1. Consejo Directivo de la Comisión para la Defensa de los Derechos Humanos en Centroamérica (CODEHUCA), *Los derechos humanos de la mujer en Centroamérica* (Human rights of Central American women) (San Jose, Calif.: CODEHUCA, 1993), 15.

THIRTEEN

Reconciling the Places Where Memory Resides

Brad Peters

Place One: Feminisms

Julian of Norwich was a devout fourteenth-century English woman whose experience of mysticism resulted from an unusual prayer in which she asked to see Christ's Passion, to have a near-fatal illness, and to feel unending contrition for her sins—while also feeling endless compassion for others and longing for God. During her thirty-third year she fell deathly ill, and at the apparent end, when a crucifix was set before her, she saw it come alive and bleed. The crucifix spoke with her and gave her a series of sixteen revelations about God's love for humankind.

A twentieth-century feminist seeking reconciliation with Catholicism might hardly think that Julian's account of her visions would provide common ground for negotiations with the Church. Yet Julian's *Showings* has attracted the attention of many feminist scholars because it so readily invites personal interactions with Christian doctrine in general and with women's spiritual lives in specific.

This essay recounts three such personal interactions: my own, those of a graduate student with whom I worked, and those of a small-town parish in the Midwest. I will amplify three suggestions: (1) that *Showings* invites feminist readers to reclaim the meaning of spiritual experiences that may otherwise lie fragmented in the memory;

177

(2) that Julian's image of a feminine Christ offers a means for women to create a theology of integrity out of the memories of their own material suffering; and (3) that Julian's dialogical model of prayer opens up discursive spaces where women's voices and spiritual experiences can feminize collective memory, thereby transforming public dialogue in the Church. But first, I will provide some brief theoretical and historical context.

In defining feminism generally, Andrea Nye warns against two extreme approaches. The first invents a woman's language for women to write and speak to each other in order to build confidence, strengthen community, and form new concepts about their experiences. This approach does not directly engage or challenge the traditions of male logic as the universal method of reason in the discourses of law, programmed debate, theology, and science; it therefore renders women impotent in the arenas of public language.[1] Julian's language, on the other hand, engages and challenges the logic of the Pauline injunction against women who teach or preach. She says: "But for I am a woman, should I therefore believe that I should not tell you of the goodness of God, since that I saw in that same time that is his will, that it be known? . . . Forget me that am a wretch, and does so that I fail you not, and behold Jesus that is teacher of all."[2]

The second extreme approach accepts Plato's concession that women can enter the arenas of power if they master the "masculine" techniques of logic, where "there should be no answer possible" once a speaker has demonstrated his or her mastery of logical analysis over an opponent's logical weaknesses.[3] This approach puts women in the position of reifying hierarchical authority, silencing opposition, and eliding anyone who may be of a different cultural background or at a social/economic disadvantage. Julian, however, writes from a stance that levels unequal social relations, saying: "We be all one in love. . . . For if I look singularly to myself, I am right naught; but in general I am, I hope, in oneness with all my fellow Christians."[4] She tells her readers: "This book is begun by God's gift and his grace, but it is not yet performed, as to my sight."[5] Just so, she invites *all* of her readers to work prayerfully with God so that they may perform the message of her visions in their own lives.

Julian thus shows that an alternative language—the language of her memory—can differ markedly from the language of logic to identify, validate, supplement, complicate, challenge, and compensate for the gaps that logic (with its reductive representations of human reality) imposes on the mind. Yet her language of memory does not try to erase logic but seeks to work at a parallel with it. As such, Julian demonstrates how women may respond subtly to what Laurie Finke calls "the authoritative, monologic language of a powerful social institution," indicating what a reconciliation between feminism and Catholicism might entail and how a Catholic feminist might act.[6]

Although Cheryl Glenn warns that it would be anachronistic to call Julian a feminist or even a "protofeminist," she notes that Julian's "theology of inclusion . . . extends specifically to women; it includes all women in the worship of and dialogue with God, as well as including a feminine representation in the Trinity."[7] I hope the personal interactions that follow will indicate how Julian's *Showings* accordingly helps women *and men* develop "that steady subtle voice" that calls feminist readers in particular to reclaim our spiritual selves, to see our spiritual selves as we are, and to reveal our spiritual selves as participants in the community of Christian practice and belief.[8]

Place Two: Fragmentation

I identify myself as a Christian feminist reader because of my own experience of gender inequities in the Church. Shortly before I first read Julian's *Showings*, I was seeking to understand how my sexuality placed me in relation to the Church's teachings. A few years had passed since the Congregation for the Doctrine of the Faith had published its *Letter to the Bishops of the Catholic Church on the Pastoral Care of Homosexual Persons*. I struggled with the *Letter's* logic that gays and lesbians should expect increasing violence directed against them when they advocated publicly for civil legislation to protect their behavior.[9] To me, the *Letter* betrayed an un-Christ-like hatred at the center of the Church's teachings against homosexual behavior, which implicitly argues that gays and lesbians must convert their sexuality through prayer and group work.[10] I felt that this hatred paralleled attitudes toward women in the Church. Thus, I examined feminist responses to the *Letter,* many of which asserted that "an experiential approach to theological reflection is critical in areas pertaining to human sexuality."[11]

One evening, while trying to work through the debate, I saw a small speck of light appear before me, like a faint star. Simultaneously, I saw that I had somehow broken apart like a spectrum but that each band of light reflected back the white light of that star. These bands of light were the various fragments of my life: who I was as a teacher, a trainer of teachers, a brother, a son, a friend, a developing writer, a public speaker—and most surprising of all, who I was as a gay man. The distinct impression came to me that God was present and visible in *all* of these fragments and that God was the scintilla that brought them together. Was this a spiritual vision? Its intensity and clarity suggested as much. But I was tempted to discount it as a product of my overworked imagination. When I began reading Julian, however, I found a startling resemblance between my experience and one of hers, where she recalled seeing God "in a point . . . by which sight I saw that he is in all things . . . [and] that he does all that is done. I marveled in that sight with a soft dread, and thought: What is sin?"[12] As I read further, I came across her insight that "Christ has compassion on us because of sin . . . and to each person that he loves . . . he lays on him some thing that is no flaw in his sight, whereby they be brought low and despised in this world and cast out."[13] Would Julian include sexuality in that category of "some thing that is no flaw," I wondered? Julian then detailed her vision of a servant who fell into a gully in his eagerness to do his Lord's will and cultivate the earth. The servant's pain from the fall blinded him; he felt culpable, and in his culpability, he did not raise his eyes to see that *only he* blamed himself; his Lord loved, pitied, and held him blameless. After recounting this vision, Julian observed: "Thus has our good lord Jesus taken upon himself all our blame; and therefore our father may or will no more assign blame to us than to his dear worthy son."[14] She reasoned that Christ had fallen into Mary's womb, just as the servant had fallen into the earth.

Julian went on to explain: "And thus I saw that God rejoices that he is our father . . . that he is our mother . . . that he is our very spouse, and our soul his beloved wife. And Christ rejoices that he is our brother . . . that he is our savior. . . . And our savior is our very mother, in whom we be endlessly born and never shall come out of him. . . . And thus is Jesus our very mother in the nature of our first making, and he is our very mother in grace by taking on our created nature."[15] Here was how

Julian reconciled the Church's logic that sin must be punished, on the one hand, with a God who, on the other hand, "is that goodness that may not be wrathful, because God is naught but goodness."[16] She used techniques of memory that, according to Mary Carruthers, produced "a concentrated, 'brief' matter" of an image or phrase stored in her memory, "exfoliating it through the 'routes' of its associations," to demonstrate an entirely new perspective on retribution.[17] As such, I realized that Julian's text not only provided a narrative that challenged the rigid, harmful gender categories that the *Letter . . . on the Pastoral Care of Homosexual Persons* tried to enforce; it also provided a narrative beside which other feminist readers could compare and validate experiences they had had beyond the pale of logic, enabling them to make the connections that would help a deeply personal understanding of Christian doctrine to emerge.

I now draw on this initial realization to suggest that it points to one of the most significant contributions Julian can make in reconciling Catholicism and feminism. A Catholic feminism influenced by the *Showings* encourages extended contemplation of personal spiritual experiences whose origins logic cannot explain, yet whose meaning logic can lucidly and rigorously interpret, rather than repress. The reason that a Catholic feminism can so function is that it keeps God's unconditional, immutable love at the center of such contemplation, decentering the cultural biases that may sway the Church's teachings and its dogmatic stances in an un-Christ-like direction.

Place Three: Integration

When I once taught at a Church-sponsored university in the Southwest, a graduate student whom I will call Ana found out about my interest in Julian. Ana asked if we could do an independent study on medieval women mystics. She wanted to focus on Margery Kempe and Julian. And so we did. After an animated and enjoyable time reading Kempe and some useful secondary sources defining mysticism,[18] we moved on to Julian. We got to know each other well in a short time. Ana's candor was wonderful and often disarming.

Once we got to the *Showings,* Ana very quickly noted that Julian's tone and rhetorical stance revealed a woman who was canny and alert to those who might oppose her. She pointed to one of Julian's disclaimers: "I am not good because of the visions, but if I love God the better; and inasmuch as you love God the better, it is more to you than me. I say not this to the wise, for they know it well."[19] Ana mused that this was the tone she should have used while attending a conservative Catholic university as an undergraduate. Instead, she had taken a confrontational feminist approach. "The professors and administrators practically kicked me out, so I finished my undergrad work at a state school," she laughed. But Ana's keen interest in Christian women mystics revealed a profoundly enduring Catholic spirituality and an intense desire for reconciliation in theory, if not in practice.

Ana especially yearned to find evidence of a Catholic response to the material conditions of women's lives. Julian's representation of Christ's suffering on the cross disturbed Ana a great deal, for instance, but it opened inroads for her. When discussing Julian's extensive use of *colores*—"I beheld the body bleeding plenteously. . . . The fair skin was broken deeply into the tender flesh, with sharp blows all about the sweet body. . . . The sweet body was so discolored, so dry, so shriveled, so deathly, and so piteous that he seemed to have been . . . continually dying"[20]—Ana was moved to comment that the image reminded her of an abused woman and made her even more mindful of Christ's humanity. "I wonder if Julian is code-switching or signifying or using some other kind of medieval rhetorical device," she said, "because a woman who's experienced what I've been through can see that Julian's empathy for Christ might also be an empathy for women who have been knocked around." Ana told me about her former marriage to a violent man. She had met him after she had left the Catholic university and, rather symbolically, had gotten involved in the Sanctuary Movement. When they married, her husband abandoned the movement and turned to drug dealing. He changed into an utterly different, enraged person who turned that rage on her.

Accordingly, Ana was also attracted to Julian's image of a wrathless God. She liked Julian's reasoning in the brief passage: "Because he is God, he is good, he is truth, he is love, he is peace; and his might, his wisdom, his charity, and his unity suffers him not to be wrathful."[21] Wrath, she observed, had been a powerful force of disunity in her life. Her mother, whenever she had physically disciplined Ana, told her that

God turned his wrath on rebellious daughters. Ana became alienated from her mother as a result. Her university experience reinforced the idea, and she became alienated from the Catholic Church. Her husband continued the pattern, and she became alienated from him. Only after she became pregnant did she make an effort to distance herself from recurrences of wrath and alienation in her life. At that time, her husband committed a murder and was jailed. A period followed when Ana appeared before court every six months to testify that if her husband were paroled, he would attempt to murder her and his daughter as well. Eventually, she took her child and fled.

The most empowering passages that Ana found in the *Showings* had to do, predictably, with the motherhood similitude. She dwelt on the way Julian conjoined the suffering of the crucifixion with the suffering of childbearing: "Our true mother Jesus, he alone bears us to joy. . . . Thus he sustains us within him in love and travail, into the full time that he would suffer the sharpest thorns and most grievous pains. . . . Wherefore it behooves him to find us, for . . . our precious mother Jesus, he may feed us with himself . . . with the blessed sacrament. . . . The mother may suffer the child to fall sometimes and be distressed in diverse manners, for its profit, but she may never suffer that any manner of peril come to her child for love."[22]

Ana thought it was stunning that Julian perceived the crucified Jesus as a mother and thus sought to turn her readers' transformative, feminizing gaze on a dying male body. The motherhood similitude gave Ana a positive, life-giving image with which she identified. "A female Christ is a gestalt that encourages women to *become* Christ," she declared, "but not Christ the victim. I'm talking about a *resurrected* female Christ, so transformed by her suffering that no damn man could ever nail her down!"

On the basis of Ana's reactions to Julian's *Showings*—here only briefly sketched—it is obvious that a Catholic feminism must work toward a spiritual and *material* healing of the pain that a patriarchal world imposes on people. A Catholic feminist would thus have a material answer to the question of what the Church must provide when women find themselves in situations such as Ana's, and they would—as members of the body of Christ—help provide it: food, clothing, and shelter; child care; financial support; access to job training and education;

legal counsel; friendship. Julian underscores as much, saying: "I saw that two opposites ought not to be together in one place . . . the highest bliss and the deepest pain."[23] The highest bliss is the integrity that comes from living the life-giving ministry of Christ, and the deepest pain is anything that interferes with it. In a postmodern world that jubilantly proclaims the self to be as diverse as its different social functions, a Catholic feminist would therefore work toward a more foundational concept of the self, one that theologizes a feminine expression of God as the source of agency for women who struggle to pull together their lives as daughters, members of the Church, wives, students, activists, mothers, citizens, and professionals.

Place Four: Communion

This past year, a Lutheran pastor invited me to speak about Julian at a Wednesday night service during the season of Lent. For some time now, the Lutherans have been in dialogue about reconciling with other denominations, including the Episcopalians, the Presbyterians, and the Roman Catholics. Maybe that explains why over sixty parishioners came to learn about the *Showings*. I introduced Julian to them as a historical figure first, describing anchoritic life and reasons why certain women might choose to enclose themselves. I detailed these women's demanding schedules of daily prayer, meditation, reading, and consultation with troubled souls. I emphasized that mysticism grew out of the extraordinary claim that through grace, God engaged mystics in direct dialogue.

Women mystics in particular showed that dialogue was a crucial activity of spiritual life, not only in prayer but also in communion with others. In the *Showings,* Christ himself initiated the dialogue with Julian when he asked: "Are you well paid that I suffered for you?" and she responded, "Yes, good Lord . . . blessed might you be"—to which he replied, "If you are paid, I am paid. It is a joy, a bliss, an endless delight to me that ever I suffered the Passion for you; and if I might suffer more, I would."[24]

Nonetheless, I told my fellow Christians, Julian's dialogue with Christ grew increasingly challenging and difficult as she wondered about the anguish and tribulation in the world, about unsaved souls who had no occasion to learn of Christ, about devout Jews who held strongly to their own faith. She also feared for the souls of those who fell from Christianity, due to some great pain or loss in their lives and the despair it brought. Thus, Julian did not find complete comfort in Christ's assurances that "all shall be well, and all shall be well, and all manner of thing shall be well."[25] Paradoxically, I said, it was in this dialogue of doubt that her spiritual growth took root.

I then asked women volunteers to read short selections from Julian's text. A concatenation of women's voices—old women, young women, married women and single, career women, schoolgirls, grandmothers and mothers and daughters, sisters and aunts—brought Julian's message into the midst of that assembly, walking us through her visionary experience as if we were visiting the stations of the cross: *her prayer for illness* ("I desired that I might have suffered with him as others did that loved him"); *creation revealed* ("He showed me something no bigger than a hazelnut . . . it is everything which is made . . . everything has being through the love of God"); *the crucifixion* ("And in all this time I felt no pain but Christ's pains"); *Julian's question* ("Ah, good Lord, how might all be well for the great harm that is come by sin to your creatures?"); *the lord-servant vision* ("The servant was as good inwardly as he was when he stood before his lord"); *the motherhood similitude* ("Our savior is our true mother. . . . He feeds us and nurtures us as the high sovereign nature of motherhood wills"); *self-recrimination* ("When we be fallen . . . he wills us to see our wretchedness and meekly acknowledge it; but he does not will us . . . to over-occupy ourselves in self-accusation"); *Satan's attempted assault* ("With his paws he held me . . . but I trusted to be saved and kept by the mercy of God"); and *the meaning of her visions* ("Know it well, love was his meaning").[26]

The experience of women speaking and men listening gave way to a dialogue woven of questions rarely asked in organized religious settings. A man who announced he had been married thirty-five years asked, "Do women really experience God differently from men?" Others laughed when his wife patted his knee and said, "Why don't you ask me?" I pointed out that Julian had prayed for a vision that would place her among the women disciples of Christ, who indeed followed him faithfully to the foot of the cross, who later sought his tomb before all others, and to whom he first appeared in his resurrection. Then I mentioned that Julian's first vision revealed Mary as "more worthy and greater than all that God made. . . . For above her is nothing but the blessed humanity of Christ," and I suggested that these references foregrounded traits of a feminine spirituality, counteracting traditional stereotypes of women as passive, subservient, or undeserving.[27]

An older woman with an outspoken demeanor asked how the Church—and how individual parishioners—should react when they encountered a person who believed, as Julian, that God had spoken directly to her. I observed that Julian herself had expressed doubt about the divine nature of the visions but that on recovering from her illness she told a man of religion that she thought she'd seen the crucifix bleeding, and he "became very serious and marveled" and "he took it so soberly and with such great reverence, I grew greatly ashamed."[28] Maybe we've been trained by logic so thoroughly in a scientific age, I speculated, that we dismiss too readily what logic cannot explain, even though there are other ways of determining knowledge—especially spiritual knowledge. Might those other ways of knowing be women's ways, I asked?

Another man joked: "I've heard voices, too, but I never thought they came from God. Is mysticism genuine or a kind of hysteria?" Once again, I referred to the *Showings* and recounted the assurance Christ gave Julian in an after-vision: "Know it well, it was no hallucination which you saw today, but take and believe it and keep yourself therein, and trust it, and you will not be overcome."[29] Then I said the careful, methodical analysis Julian offered of her experience indicated such a formidable intellect and understanding of applied theology that we could not readily think of her as a hysteric.

A woman in her late fifties added warily that she had felt a strong call to ministry when she was younger, so she had gone beyond her four years in college to take classes in seminary at a time when the Lutheran church did not allow women to be ordained. She had read Julian during that period of her life, doubting herself and her irrational sense of vocation—above all, since she knew she would not be able to preach after she completed her studies. But Julian's theology had had an enduring effect on her decision because the words of the *Showings* had taught her how: "The bitterness of doubt be turned into the sweetness of kind love by grace."[30] This woman never did get ordained, she explained, but she often preached when the pastor went on vacation.

David Aers asserts that Julian develops a "theology that incorporates the feminine into what is more often described as a masculine zone of power."[31] Julian does so because "rather than establish terms that seek to contain—and inevitably delimit—the objects they signify, Julian creates a system [that] . . . collapses both fear and authority into love."[32] Although the conversation about Julian on that Lenten Wednesday night hardly overcame terms that contain and delimit, it marked the kind of exchange that nonetheless feminizes the public discourse of the Church by locating women's contributions in its history. Collective memory is reshaped by such conversations, so what is delimited by fear or authority changes, becomes redefined, invites negotiation and compromise rather than contention.

Place Five: Not Closure, but a Brief Disclosure

If historians such as Robert Connors are correct, the last time Catholicism markedly changed its rhetorical strategies was the Reformation, when the Roman Catholic Church adopted a language that was "agonistic, masculinist, Ciceronian, pragmatic, homiletic," to counter reformers such as Luther, Melanchthon, and others.[33] The results clearly did not serve women or marginalized others on either side very well. No doubt that is why the Church of our own time is so much overdue for another reformation. But if we want reconciliation rather than schism, we must use strategies that are significantly different. Julian's *Showings* imply what these strategies might be like: appropriative, feminine, nonforensic, materialist, and experiential. If Catholic feminists develop and engage in these strategies with enough persistence and numbers, they may compel Catholicism to respond in kind. And if Catholicism does so, it will have to open itself to a dialogue that positions the indwelling Christ at its core.

This indwelling Christ gives us the wisdom to choose revealed truth above tradition, material needs above dogma, and love above logic. She is the feminine aspect of the Triune God, and she can still transform the lives of all who follow her way.

NOTES

1. Andrea Nye, "Words of Power and the Power of Words," in *Rhetoric: Concepts, Definitions, Boundaries,* ed. William A. Covino and David A. Jolliffe (Boston: Allyn and Bacon, 1995), 450.

2. Julian of Norwich, *The Book of Showings to the Anchoress Julian of Norwich,* 2 vols., ed. Edmund Colledge and James Walsh (Toronto: Pontifical Institute of Medieval Studies, 1978), 1:222. My translations will preserve syntactical and semantic elements wherever possible, but I will also draw on Colledge and Walsh's translations where the modern meaning of medieval terms has changed; see Julian of Norwich, *Showings,* trans. Edmund Colledge and James Walsh (New York: Paulist Press, 1978). Scholars think Julian might have written her short account almost immediately after her experience, while she wrote the longer one after twenty years of meditation.

3. Nye, "Words of Power," 446.

4. Julian of Norwich, *Showings,* 2:321–22.

5. Julian of Norwich, *Book of Showings,* 2:731.

6. Laurie Finke, "Mystical Bodies and the Dialogics of Visions," in *Maps of Flesh and Light: The Religious Experience of Medieval Women Mystics,* ed. Ulrike Weithaus (Syracuse, N.Y.: Syracuse University Press, 1993), 29.

7. Cheryl Glenn, *Rhetoric Retold: Regendering the Tradition from Antiquity through the Renaissance* (Carbondale, Ill.: Southern Illinois University Press, 1997), 99.

8. See Nye, "Words of Power," 451.

9. Congregation for the Doctrine of the Faith, *Letter to the Bishops of the Catholic Church on the Pastoral Care of Homosexual Persons,* reprinted in *Building Bridges: Gay and Lesbian Reality and the Catholic Church,* ed. Robert Nugent and Jeannine Gramick (Mystic, Conn.: Twenty-Third Publications, 1992), 72.

10. See Leanne Payne, *The Broken Image* (Westchester, Ill.: Crossway Books, 1981); John Harvey, *The Homosexual Person* (San Francisco: Ignatius Press, 1987).

11. Mary Segers, "A Feminist Critique of the Vatican Letter," in *The Vatican and Homosexuality,* ed. Jeannine Gramick and Pat Furey (New York: Crossroad, 1988), 85.

12. Julian of Norwich, *Showings,* 2:336.

13. Ibid., 2:408–9.

14. Ibid., 2:535.

15. Ibid., 2:546, 580, 592.

16. Ibid., 2:493.

17. Mary Carruthers, *The Craft of Thought: Meditation, Rhetoric, and the Making of Images, 400–1200* (Cambridge: Cambridge University Press, 1998), 62.

18. E.g., Evelyn Underhill, *Mysticism* (New York: Meridian, 1974).

19. Julian of Norwich, *Showings,* 2:321.

20. Ibid., 2:342, 358.

21. Ibid., 2:493.

22. Ibid., 2:595–97, 604.

23. Ibid., 2:659.

24. Ibid., 2:382.

25. Ibid., 2:405.

26. Ibid., 1:201, 212–13, 234, 247; 2:516, 617, 705, 636, 733.

27. Ibid., 1:214.

28. Ibid., 2:633.

29. Ibid., 2:646.

30. Ibid., 2:673.

31. Lynn Staley and David Aers, *the Powers of the Holy: Religion, Politics, and Gender in Late Medieval English Culture* (University Park, Pa.: Penn State University Press, 1996), 96.

32. Ibid., 178.

33. Robert Connors, "Catholicism and Rhetoric," April 4, 2000, retrieved December 2002 from www.pre-text.com/ptlist/index.html. Scholarly Book Review List.

FOURTEEN

Journey from/to Catholicism

Jane Zeni

When I picture myself as a child—I could have been eight, or ten, or twelve—there is usually a knot of anxiety in my gut. Whether I was swimming at the pool, playing with a friend, copying the times tables at St. Anastasia's School, or riding a horse for a blissful hour earned with a week's chores, the fear lurked at the edge of my consciousness. By Wednesday of each week, I would start obsessing about Saturday's confession. Friday afternoon would bring the usual delight at the prospect of two free days but also a more intense gnawing of guilt.

What could I have done to generate such a conviction of sin? Part of the story must be the impact on a sensitive child of the "examination of conscience" exercise. Reading through the lists of possible sins, conveniently arranged according to the commandments, I would know immediately what I had or had not done. No, I had not murdered anybody, stolen anything, or destroyed anyone's reputation. Yes, I'd disobeyed my parents, but that was usually a little sin. But one item always caught me: "Bad Thoughts." What a vast space for the imagination! How was I to know that at some time during the week I hadn't consented to forbidden thoughts, usually about boys' and girls' bodies? Saturday afternoon's confession brought blessed relief, but by evening the tension began to grow again. Could I make it to Sunday morning's mass without committing another sin? And so I often fainted in church, just before Communion.

Yet forty other children sat with me under the tutelage of those nuns at St. Anastasia's, and many did not share my misery. From another perspective, the story must focus on my experience growing up in a troubled family, young peacemaker in my parents' volatile marriage. Both parents encouraged me to excel academically, never suggesting that because I was a girl I should set my sights anywhere but the top. I accept with gratitude this rather astonishing gift from a middle-class couple of the fifties. On the other hand, I believe that their pride in my achievements also led me to think I had the power to make them happy (an illusion fed by my father, who often insisted that if I "really tried" I could convince my mother to stop drinking so they could both be happy). But the evidence was clear: Mother drank, Dad raged, so I must be responsible. According to this perspective, the good nuns simply provided a name—mortal sin—for the guilt I was already feeling.

This story is important to me, but it seems to exonerate the Church a bit too quickly. If, as I believe, God cares about the suffering and the powerless, the god of my childhood only made my life more miserable. If that god were to appear today as a human being—threatening children with torture, playing on their fears, inflicting stomachaches and sleepless nights—he (or she?) could be charged with child abuse! While I've made my peace with the Catholic Church, I feel no nostalgia for the bad old days before Vatican II. The authority of the Church failed to protect children (or women, or Holocaust victims), and those failures need to be remembered. Today, when I hear friends romanticize their days with Father X and Sister Y (the stories are nostalgic and funny and oh, so sweet), I cannot be silent. "Well, that 1950s religious education wasn't so great for everybody. Lots of us got nightmares and felt awful!"

Vatican II promised to open the windows; in many cases, it blew us right out of the Church. I recall the excitement of entering Harvard in 1963, when all the old, sad, rigid constraints were being challenged in the Church as well as in society. An informal group of students met for daily mass with a Dutch priest who was doing graduate work in anthropology. At twenty, as I prepared to marry a man from that group, he and I talked through some issues. Should we use birth control? (It would be two years before I finished college. And Vatican II had just affirmed that Catholics really did have freedom of conscience in applying moral principles to specific life situations.) Our decision was typical of Catholic couples in the mid-sixties (and ever since): we would use birth control.

But what I remember most about that conversation was a second decision that seemed to flow naturally from the first. If we were going to take charge of our own fertility, then we would use the opportunity to adopt an interracial family. "We'll have one baby ourselves," I recall saying, "and then for the rest we'll choose kids who might not otherwise find permanent homes." Were we trying to atone for our projected sins by doing "good works" for social justice and world population?

In one of life's ironies, there was no pregnancy at all. However, a few years after that conversation, we adopted two boys whose ancestors included Hispanic, Navajo, and African people. Both children were baptized with ancient ceremonial rites; though the mass had long been said in English, I had joined a Gregorian chant choir. For awhile, it felt right in an exciting, eclectic sort of way. I can still picture my preschool children with their Star Wars figures as well as their small, plastic statues of Our Lady of Guadalupe and St. Martin de Porres. At times, when they joined together in strange, intergalactic adventures, I imagined the grim Lord of my childhood breaking into an indulgent laugh.

Yet during the decade after college, the Church played a steadily shrinking role in my life. There was no decisive break; I just attended less and less often, finding less and less meaning. Perhaps the same post-sixties depression that I felt in politics gradually soured my view of the Church. Perhaps I just slipped away, vacillating between a desire for faster change in teachings on such issues as the role of women and a paradoxical longing for the beauty of the old liturgy. Perhaps amid my deteriorating marriage and increasing dependence on alcohol, I didn't think much about God.

In the late seventies, I turned a corner in my personal life, beginning a course of recovery that would include twelve-step groups, a therapist, a spiritual director, reading, and journaling. Initially, while searching for a healthier spirituality, I thought it might be time for a clean break with Catholicism. I could certainly do better than this dinosaur of a male-dominated institution! Since I'd read Jung's psychological interpretations of myth and ritual, I considered the possibility of a female guide or higher power. Stories of Ishtar, Kali, and Spider Woman intrigued me, but they were not my stories. Protestant Christianity—even the churches with women clergy—held little attraction because the stress on sermon over symbol took away what I'd most loved in Catholicism. On the other hand, I came to recognize an earthier, life-affirming strand in my own tradition. For example, fourteenth-century mystic Julian of Norwich describes God in this way: "For as the body is clad in the cloth, and the flesh in the skin, and the bones in the flesh, and the heart in the whole, so are we, soul and body, clad in the Goodness of God and enclosed . . . for truly our Lover desireth that our soul cleave to Him with all its might, and that we be evermore cleaving to His Goodness."[1]

And so I drifted back to mass, attended some weekend retreats where I could hear a more contemporary Catholic message, and then formally rejoined the Church of my childhood. I found a very warm, diverse, progressive parish where I didn't feel myself saying "yes, but . . ." under my breath during the services.

Yet when it came time for my older son to attend the Sunday school (for children in public education), I balked. How could I expose my child, even for an hour a week, to those negative messages? I talked with the teacher who was preparing the children for Reconciliation (as confession was now called) and First Communion, only to discover that she expected parents to work through the lessons with their children. For me, this proved to be a healing experience, a chance to reconcile some issues from my own past as I saw the old teachings transformed with a focus more on love than on sin.

Five years later, when I filed for divorce, my parish loved and supported me through the process. My spiritual director, a sprightly, joyous nun, suggested I keep a daily journal and reread it often to discern where my life was leading (doing so, I grew convinced that I needed to leave my marriage). Parishioners also prayed for us to discern God's will—most of them without volunteering their own conclusions. They stressed that whatever happened, both my husband and I would continue to be welcome. After the divorce, I found that joint custody was beyond the grasp of our city and public school officials (when my younger son was suspended, the school notified his father, who happened to be out of town), but the secretary at church routinely sent notices to my children at both households. Amusing, I thought: the institution that didn't recognize divorce in theory dealt with it best in practice.

From time to time, reflecting on the way my life has unfolded, I ask the inevitable human question, "Why?" Maybe the best answer is suggested in the last scene of the film *Dogma,* when the Messiah figure asks God, "Why are we here?" She responds with a smile and affectionately tweaks the questioner's nose. I have come to believe that the power behind creation can be an active force in my life—when I am receptive—but that the nature of that power is and must be beyond my understanding. Perhaps the old nuns were trying to make the same point as *Dogma*'s Kevin Smith when, eyes skyward, they whispered, "It's a mystery . . ." in response to our questions! But this view of life is fundamentally positive. When Julian of Norwich asks Jesus why there is evil in the world, she receives the cryptic assurance that in spite of sin, "all shall be well, and all shall be well, and all manner of thing shall be well."[2]

As my children grew, I often shared with them my own search for an honest spirituality grounded in, but not limited to, the Catholic tradition. One day my son, then in his early teens, was discussing the racial attitudes in his (very diverse) circle of friends. Many of the African Americans expressed doubt and cynicism about the possibility of honest relationships across the races. My son disagreed on the basis of his own experience in an interracial family. As he explained to me, "It's sort of like that story about the kingdom of heaven—it's coming in the future but it's also within us today." We agreed that racism was still thriving in the United States and that we were a long way from achieving a just society. But we could choose to make our own lives an image of the world we hoped would come in the future, to celebrate diversity within our families and our friendships. I was impressed with my son's insight into religion and politics, as well as his awareness that a story can illuminate the everyday world with the perspectives of the spirit.

As Morton Kelsey says, "Myth and the rituals that spring from it provide the meeting ground in which the nonphysical half of reality makes contact with" human beings.[3] I value the awareness in Catholicism of natural symbols—the well, the bread, the late-winter tree whose dry branch tips are melting into a greenish haze—that suggest "nonphysical reality." In *Images of My Self: Meditation and Self Exploration through the Jungian Imagery of the Gospels,* Jean Gill invites women to weave together such symbols with the stories of Jesus and their own personal stories.[4] (Gill's imaging process draws on the techniques of Eastern meditation as well as the classic Spiritual Exercises taught by Ignatius of Loyola.) Instead of the dualist split between physical and spiritual, reality is viewed as sacramental, incarnational, whole.

This interpenetration of the physical and spiritual suggests another ancient Catholic concept—the "Communion of Saints." Past, present, and future are not simply lockstep units of linear time, as my son recognized in the stories of the kingdom of heaven. Instead, we as individuals are connected with our ancestors (personal and collective) as well as our church community. In practice, this means that we look to those who have gone before to find spiritual guides for our own journeys; we also pray for one another in the present. I have come to see this as an empowering message for women. We are not isolated, each working for her own salvation, but companions on a journey.

The history of the Judeo-Christian people, expressed in the Bible, continues to be recreated in the stories of their spiritual descendants. Although God is said not to change, our understanding of God must change in the course of our lives, growing in wisdom and maturity. (I had read Teilhard de Chardin in college, but his "evolutionary" concept of God[5] became real to me only as I experienced crisis and growth in my personal life.) The notions of a "faith journey" and of "telling one's story" are central to contemporary Catholicism. For example, the booklets supporting the nationwide Renew 2000 program list these "Faith Sharing Principles": "Each person is led by God in his/her spiritual journey. This happens in the context of the Christian community. . . . Faith sharing refers to the shared reflections on the action of God in one's life experience as related to Scripture and the faith of the Church."[6] Through Renew 2000, small faith-sharing groups meet in each parish to talk about their struggles and their evolving perspectives on God and the Church. The story I have told in the foregoing pages is of this kind.

As a college teacher, I've designed and taught a general education course in mythology that traces this journey in many religious traditions. My understanding of myth, whether the perspective is Jungian (*Hero with a Thousand Faces*[7]) or structuralist,[8] is that its very nature is transformation through many retellings. Today's sophomore must tell his or her own version of the tale in order to break open its meaning. After studying hero myths from diverse cultures, my students write an episode from their own lives as the journey of a hero facing inner and outer trials. After reading *Kiss Sleeping Beauty Good-Bye,*[9] students also explore how traditional tales reinforce stereotypical roles of the female—virgin, mother, temptress—instead of offering women an ideal of wholeness.

The mythic texts of Judeo-Christianity (like other world myths) reflect the patriarchal culture in which they grew. We can't sugarcoat the sexism in the Catholic tradition. Instead, I believe it is our job today, as women, to look closely at the problematic areas, asking if and how they can be transformed. By scraping off a few centuries of sentimentality, we can turn again to Mary and a host of spiritual guides diverse in gender, race, and class. Catholic women can learn from the Reform Jewish women who have designed a naming service for baby girls that parallels circumcision for boys. Our tradition takes rituals, symbols, myths, and the telling of personal stories seriously—but that need not mean rigidly or literally.

This stance reminds me of the theology expressed by Sylviana Martinez, a woman of the New Mexico pueblos, who for three years taught me the rudiments of her mother tongue, Tewa. I knew that she was a practicing Catholic, apparently devout; she was also one of the elders who organized the rituals and dances for the pueblo festivals. One day, over coffee and a lesson at her home, I asked, "Sylviana, do you feel any conflict between, let's say, what the Bible says about Creation and what the Tewa people say about the Emergence?" She looked at me, puzzled. "I am a Catholic and I know that what the priests say, and what is in the Bible, those things are true. But my grandma taught me about the people who emerged from under the lake, and I know that what my grandma says is true. How do I put these stories together?" She smiled and shrugged her shoulders. "I don't know, I'm just an old woman. But God knows, so it's all right!"

Sylviana's multilayered and nuanced view of knowledge has recently been echoed by Anya Dozier Enos, an academic woman whose roots are Pueblo and Catholic. While working on her Ph.D., she "began to see that what academics call 'emerging paradigms' mirror traditional Pueblo beliefs about the world and how one knows the world. . . . Pueblo people acknowledge that subjective ways of knowing are valuable (and that, in fact, human beings are not—and should not be—objective); that multiple, sometimes even contradictory, viewpoints are possible and what is true may vary from person to person, from culture to culture; that the stories people tell have multiple layers of meaning, and each time the stories are told new knowledge is gained."[10]

My own academic work reflects a similar paradigm. I do qualitative research in English education, often working collaboratively with teachers in K–12 schools. Instead of hiding ourselves behind a mask of objectivity, my co-researchers and I try to acknowledge and reflect on the personal, cultural, professional, and political experiences each of us brings to an inquiry. Principles of qualitative research[11] suggest that we deemphasize positivist notions of objective fact and seek multiple perspectives—from teachers, students, parents, administrators, others—to represent complex phenomena in an authentic way. Furthermore, principles of feminist inquiry[12] suggest that we articulate a personal standpoint—our gender, race, class, or institutional status. A perfunctory list of descriptors is not enough. Feminist researchers often approach an inquiry by first telling our own stories—acknowledging our subjectivity as a source of knowledge as well as of potential blind spots.

Feminist and qualitative inquiry has helped me make meaning for myself of Catholic statements on "women's issues"—quite simply because Church statements are still articulated exclusively by celibate males and must be limited by their perspectives. So, for the present, those of us who are not celibate males must take those limitations into account when considering birth control, abortion, divorce, homosexuality, and other matters about which our clergy cannot speak from their own, subjective experience.

All institutions are flawed. Whatever it means when we say that the basic principles are "infallible," even the popes acknowledge that historical policies and actions of the Church (from the banning of Galileo to the complicity with colonialism) may be deeply wrong. This sort of rethinking may be easier for us than for religious fundamentalists because Catholics believe in the dual authority of the Bible and "tradition." To Protestants, this concept of "tradition" seems merely a convenient excuse for ignoring the Bible, but in practice it allows for the Spirit moving in the community—not just in A.D. 100 but also today. The Church is also on a journey.

Today I remain active in a small, diverse parish where my views are not out of the mainstream. I'll describe my two "public" roles in the parish—as newsletter co-editor and lector coordinator—to illustrate what I have been saying about personal stories and multiple perspectives.

Five years ago, I was drafted by the pastor to help develop a newsletter that parishioners would want to read. My first reaction was a mixture of panic and embarrassment. Was I going to pen exciting reports of parish picnics and committees? Worse still, was I going to pen a monthly inspirational column? Then I grasped at an idea that just might work. The best feature of our small parish, I reasoned, was its diversity—in age, race, talents, and economic status. What if I invited a different parishioner each month for an interview at the local coffee shop? The profiles might strengthen the community as more people got to know each other; if nothing else, they would save me from fabricating the news.

Today, some forty profiles later, I realize how much I have learned from these monthly encounters and the writing they inspire. As an interviewer, I try to capture the mood, the eye contact, the spirit of each person. I look for the humor but maintain the respect. When interviewing young members, I try to present them as thoughtful people with complex lives; "cuteness" wears thin very fast. On the other hand, I like to show that our elders once were young, immersed in a range of experiences beyond bingo!

In my approach to interviewing, I draw on feminist research principles. For example, Gesa Kirsch warns us not to treat people as mere subjects or informants, listening with great interest for an hour and then disappearing. Rather they are "co-researchers" who have the right to co-interpretation and to "periodic re-negotiation of consent."[13] Since my interviewee and I will both continue as members of the parish, I take care to check my data and interpretations, typically by phone or e-mail. I also ask the interviewee to confirm any text that might cause embarrassment—stories may be shared in the intimacy of the coffee shop by a speaker momentarily forgetting the eventual audience of two hundred parishioners.

These interviews do reach a real audience. I have been astonished by the response from other parishioners, usually some variation on this theme: "I never realized that so-and-so had such an interesting life and accomplished so much!" I have consciously tried to tell the stories of people who didn't fit the typical Church mold. Several of my interviewees belong to interracial or interfaith families, and several have been divorced. The newsletter provides a space to celebrate the individual gifts of our diverse parishioners and the collective value of telling our stories.

My second official role in the parish is to coordinate the laywomen and laymen who read the scriptures at mass. Inevitably, one issue is the gender bias in even the most recent translation adopted by the American Church. Should we make the pronouns nonsexist when we read? My parish leaves this choice to the lectors, and I support that choice by sharing with each lector a published guide to nonsexist language. Eight of our lectors typically read the text as it stands, while three of us— two English professors and a retired nun—ordinarily use gender-neutral language.

At the same time, we don't whitewash the historical meaning of the text in its patriarchal context. "Wives be subject to your husbands." A few years ago, one of our lectors (male, incidentally) decided to substitute "be supportive," to the distress of the pastor. It sounds right to contemporary ears, but it is not what St. Paul said or meant. The next line is "Slaves, obey your masters." I fume when fundamentalist preachers choose to take the first verse as literal advice for present-day marriages but conveniently ignore the second verse (which, of course, was preached just as literally in churches before the Civil War). Instead, I see the whole text as an admonition to "bloom where you're planted." The kingdom of heaven is not limited to educated free males; Christianity is preached to those in any social position. This is a very progressive text—if we don't bowdlerize it. When such a passage is read at mass, I listen to see if the homily that follows explains the historical context. Today's society still oppresses and rejects many people, but the Church must affirm that it is open to all and welcomes their gifts.

Today the Catholic Church in the United States is faced with an aging population of priests and nuns, with few candidates volunteering to fill their ranks. As a consequence, noncelibate men and women are becoming the day-to-day parish leadership. A typical parish is run by an elected parish council, a married deacon, a parish administrator, and a director of religious education—as well as a priest, who may serve part-time in several parishes. In my own rather quirky view of "providence," I suspect that whenever the Church gets seriously out of touch, natural forces eventually pull it back to a healthier balance. The problem is not yet resolved—key decisions above the parish level are still made primarily by celibate males, and the diaconate is open to married men but not to women. Nevertheless, I see in the Catholic tradition signs of new growth beyond its patriarchal history.

This vision, if you will, helps me answer the question I've asked dozens of interviewees: "So what keeps you here?" For me there are two answers. If "here" is my parish, it is the warm, caring community of women and men who often amaze me with their openness about life—both spiritual and mundane. If "here" is the Catholic Church, it is the richness of that tradition that allows me to wander into a cathedral on the other side of the world and to resonate with the liturgies of home, "reading" multiple stories in the symbols, the statutes, the stained glass. "Here," in both contexts, my own story finds its place.

NOTES

1. Julian of Norwich, *Revelations of Divine Love,* comp. Roger L. Roberts (1393; Wilton, Conn.: Morehouse-Barlow, 1982), 19.

2. Ibid., 33.

3. Morton T. Kelsey, *Myth, History, and Faith: The Remythologizing of Christianity* (New York: Paulist Press, 1974), 180.

4. Jean Gill, *Images of My Self: Meditation and Self Exploration through the Jungian Imagery of the Gospels* (New York: Paulist Press, 1982), 12–19.

5. Pierre Teilhard de Chardin, *The Phenomenon of Man* (New York: Harper, 1959).

6. RENEW International, *RENEW 2000 Faith Sharing Booklet, Season III* (Mahwah, N.J.: Paulist Press, 1998), 4.

7. Joseph Campbell, *Hero with a Thousand Faces* (Princeton, N.J.: Bollingen, 1970).

8. Claude Levi-Strauss, "The Structural Study of Myth," in *Structural Anthropology,* vol. 1 (New York: Doubleday Anchor, 1967), 201–28.

9. Madonna Kolbenschlag, *Kiss Sleeping Beauty Good-Bye: Breaking the Spell of Feminine Myths and Models* (New York: Doubleday, 1979).

10. Anya Dozier Enos, "A Landscape with Multiple Views: Research in Pueblo Communities," in *Multiple and Intersecting Identities in Qualitative Research,* ed. Betty M. Marchant and Arlette Ingram Willis (Mahwah, N.J.: Lawrence Erlbaum, 2001), 83–84.

11. See, e.g., Jennifer Mason, *Qualitative Researching* (Thousand Oaks, Calif.: Sage, 1996).

12. E.g., Gesa Kirsch, *Ethical Dilemmas in Feminist Research: The Politics of Location, Interpretation, and Publication* (Albany: SUNY Press, 1999). See also Patti Lather, *Getting Smart: Feminist Research and Pedagogy with/in the Postmodern* (New York: Routledge, 1991).

13. Kirsch, *Ethical Dilemmas*, 40.

FIFTEEN

Catholicism and the Contraceptive Debate, 1914–1930

Kathleen A. Tobin

A new kind of feminism emerged in the United States after the turn of the century—one that embraced sexual freedom and reproductive choice. The women's rights movement already in place had laid the foundation for a myriad of demands designed to empower women, aside from that of suffrage. By 1914, control over one's own body for the simple purpose of healthily spacing children or for the more contemporarily outrageous end of female sexual pleasure without consequences brought the issue of contraception into the feminist debate. Contraceptives were viewed as a means to break traditional bonds and allow for "voluntary motherhood."[1]

The sale and distribution of contraceptives had become illegal in 1873, as the result of a Victorian moral crusade that defined contraceptive information as "obscene." By 1920, birth control activists throughout the United States were risking arrest by distributing illegal information and opening illegal clinics, arguing that women should have the right to control conception. As this had become a woman's issue, anyone who stood in the way would risk being declared "antiwoman." But while it is true that Margaret Sanger and others struggled to legalize contraceptives at least in part with the empowerment of women in mind, suggesting that they be allowed more control over their own reproductive systems, the movement was far more complex than that.[2]

In 1914, Margaret Sanger coined the term *birth control,* after having rejected other terms such as *voluntary parenthood, conscious genera-tion,* and *race control,* and began distributing contraceptive information and publicly challenging laws prohibiting such.[3] The public debate that ensued would naturally include religion, as it dealt with issues of mar-riage and family and the conception of human life itself. But the man-ner in which the debate began created an environment of animosity. Sanger, who took the lead in the battle to legalize contraceptives, made her antireligious feelings known, drawing criticism almost immediately from Church spokesmen. Her publication the *Woman Rebel,* a socialist monthly carrying the subtitle "NO GODS, NO MASTERS," served as an important vehicle for birth control activists during the early stages of the battle. In a tone common among socialists, the publication frequently attacked organized traditional religion, contending that the Church, in conjunction with the state and big business, had historically sustained an exploitative capitalist system that kept women in bondage.[4] She asserted that a high birthrate among the working class would serve to keep that class weak and prone to exploitation and that allowing working-class women access to contraceptive information—as was available discreetly to middle- and upper-class women from their personal physicians— would aid in their liberation. Though early on she did not always refer to the Catholic Church specifically, the Church became the object of most criticism as the debate over birth control evolved.

Several Catholic spokesmen, including William Cardinal O'Connell of Boston and James Cardinal Gibbons of Baltimore, condemned the women's rights movement and discouraged the participation of Catholic women, therefore providing fuel for Sanger in her birth control debates. Though virtually all denominations in the United States opposed birth control at this time, the foundation was being laid for a head-to-head battle with the Catholic Church. After World War I, when her move-ment grew less radical and more appealing to the mainstream, an anti-Catholic atmosphere in the nation as a whole contributed to a religious birth control debate, with battle lines drawn between Catholics and non-Catholics. In addition, the 1920s introduced confrontations from modernists, primarily liberal and mainline Protestants willing to accept changing roles for women and shift their teaching on contraception in order to alleviate some of society's ills—as had been promoted by birth control activists. Eventually it became clear that concerns for society would take precedence in the birth control debate, with the feminist cause taking a back seat. Just how the Catholic Church spoke to those concerns would help shape its position on birth control.

In addressing society in general and defining birth control as a social issue, Sanger blamed the system for masses of unhealthy children born to the working class. In 1914, she stated: "Women and men of the working class are so drained and exhausted in health and energy by their work, poor food and bad housing, that it is impossible for them to give birth to healthy offspring, thus making them unfit."[5] While others worked diligently to overhaul the system, the solution for Sanger lay in access to birth control for the working-class woman. According to Sanger: "If all the children could be gathered together from the orphanages, jails and reformatories, together with the crippled and feeble-minded, the child victims of the cotton and silk mills and the sweated home industries, this huge army of little victims would open the eyes of the working woman to the realization that she must take the matter into her own hands and decide whether she wants to add to this number of unfortunates."[6]

It is apparent in these early arguments that although Sanger may have been compassionate toward the working class, she also laid out a qualitative categorization of human life—a very common tendency among intellectuals and policy makers in those years. However, throughout the debate over legalizing contraceptives, the Catholic Church was in a unique position. First, a significant portion of the working class in the United States during this period was Catholic. When birth control advocates directed their efforts toward this segment of society, they were doing so toward Catholics, and Church leaders would react accordingly. Furthermore, when the religious discussion became centered on human life, the Catholic Church was less willing to distinguish among categories of human life based on quality. The need to address social ills reached every corner of American society in this "Progressive Era," and though at times comparatively radical, Sanger's intentions of improvement were more or less representative of a larger trend. Modernist thought suggested that scientific principles could be applied in administering reform policy designed to alleviate social ills[7] and eventually that controlling population was a necessary aspect of reform and might be carried out through modern contraceptive technology. Denominations embracing modernism began to see contraception in this light and to shift their positions by the early 1930s.

Though Sanger had begun her crusade with feminist intentions, her initial discussions of sexual freedom alienated the women's movement at large, which had centered on maternal virtue and chastity.[8] But she found an ally in the growing eugenics movement that warned Americans of social decay caused by recent population trends.[9] In examining her advocacy of birth control, it is important to note Sanger's observations related to *quality,* made apparent in her choice of words such as *unfit, crippled,* and *feeble-minded.* Proponents of birth control have often centered their arguments on *quantity,* particularly in their descriptions of resources and food supply. But inherent in birth control arguments of the Progressive Era were descriptions of quality. Neo-Malthusians of the period still based some of their arguments on numbers, with Charles Drysdale (one of the world's most prominent) noting that Charles Darwin had "shown beyond the possibility of dispute that over-reproduction leads to a constant struggle for existence. Animal life is one perpetual conflict, and man too has been in a constant state of war—the impelling force being really, although not always ostensibly the need for food."[10]

The outbreak of World War I offered neo-Malthusians proof of the consequences of population growth, and they went so far as to argue that birthrates should be addressed during the peace process. In June 1919, the Malthusian League proposed that "each nation desiring to enter into the League of Nations shall pledge itself to restrict its birth rate that its people shall be able to live in comfort in their own dominions without need for territorial expansion, and that it shall recognize that increase of population shall not justify a demand either for increase of territory or for the compulsion of other Nations to admit its emigrants."[11]

The proposal fell on deaf ears but shed light on the international nature of the debate and how migration concerns had become integral to the debate. But Malthusian population concerns did not stop with sheer numbers. Inherent in Malthusianism, which appealed to the upper classes, was the presumption that the poor were not equals with the privileged; indeed, Malthusians often voiced their concerns about breeding among the lower classes.[12]

Also fundamental to the birth control debate were developments in race theory. Conservatives embraced race theory as notions of inherent superiority and inferiority among the races that justified the social, economic, and political dominance of northern European white races in the world and of white Anglo-Saxon Protestants in the United States. Academics conducted extensive studies of the nature of race, providing what they considered scientific evidence of qualitative differences among the various peoples of the world. By the early twentieth century, to question race theory was to question science.[13] Race theorists warned that progress made by the enlightened superior races was threatened by race degeneration, caused by unmatched multiplication of the inferior races.[14] Such fears manifested themselves in the United States during this period in arguments over immigration that pointed to the questionable race origins of immigrants pouring into the country from southern and eastern Europe. Though the aim of many was to restrict immigration, apparent in the arguments were fears of family size among the immigrants. Prominent race theorist Madison Grant warned of the "dangerous foreign races" who, "in the insidious guise of beggars at our gates, [plead] for admittance to share our prosperity. If we continue to allow them to enter they will in time drive us out of our own land by mere force of breeding."[15]

The eugenics movement significantly influenced population theory and policy in the early years of the twentieth century. To many, progress had laid the groundwork for understanding who was fit or unfit to produce offspring and eventually led to the belief that contraception could aid in producing an improved race. Eugenicists warned of an imminent takeover by the "unfit," a situation they blamed on inefficient breeding. While the good stock had practiced family limitation, the inferior stock was breeding disproportionately.[16] The organization's secretary, Charles B. Davenport, in his 1911 article for *Popular Science Monthly,* illustrated the sentiment of the Eugenics Section of the American Breeders Association, which spearheaded the movement in the United States, when he wrote:

It does not seem right that there should always be about 3 per cent of our population on the sick list, that our alms houses should support over 80,000 paupers, not to mention the hundreds of thousands that receive outdoor relief or are barely able to earn a living; and that there should be 80,000 persons in prison. It ought not to be that the nation should have to support half a million insane, feeble-minded, deaf and blind and that a hundred million dollars should be spent annually by institutions in this country for the care of the sick, degenerate, defective and delinquent.[17]

Adding to the concerns of monetary expense was the notion that charity programs were in fact contributing to the problem of dependency. This point of contention increasingly drew Catholicism into the debate, as Catholics were viewed as overly sentimental and unrealistic in giving to the poor. In the early decades of the twentieth century, the idea of supporting the "well born" over the "dependent" had become prevalent among some British and American Protestants, who viewed Catholics as shortsighted and contributing to the degeneration of civilization through their relief efforts.[18]

Sanger argued that legalizing contraceptives provided a solution and tried to persuade the Eugenics Society to join her campaign, claiming that "birth control . . . is nothing more or less than the facilitation of the process of weeding out the unfit [and] of preventing the birth of defectives" and that "if we are to make racial progress, this development of womanhood must precede motherhood in every individual woman. Then and then only can the mother cease to be an incubator and be a mother indeed. Then only can she transmit to her sons and daughters the qualities which make strong individuals and, collectively, a strong race."[19] But eugenicists resisted joining the movement, arguing that legalizing contraceptives would be more destructive because availability might encourage parents of "worthy hereditary qualities" to limit their family size even more than they already had and because "defectives of the lower types do not greatly limit sex indulgence by the fear of having children, nor do they resort to artificial means to prevent conception."[20] However, there was eventually agreement that the upper classes were unwilling to increase their family size and that, with proper education and available contraceptives, the lower class might decrease theirs.

Monsignor John A. Ryan, head of the Social Action Department of the National Catholic Welfare Conference and professor of moral theology and industrial ethics at Catholic University, responded early in the debate with arguments rooted in natural law. In 1915 he wrote: "The so-called contraceptive devices are intrinsically immoral because they involve the unnatural use, the perversion of a human faculty,"[21] and though he maintained his natural law reasoning, he ultimately developed arguments directed at specific contemporary concerns over social ills. In his influential 1916 article "Family Limitation, Church and Birth Control," published in the *Ecclesiastical Review,* Ryan countered the claim that the quality of children should take precedence over the quantity, stating that both the quantity and quality of the human race would be adversely affected by contraceptive use and citing egotism, materialism, and self-indulgence as primary motives for limiting family size. He also responded to those who suggested that legalized contraceptives would alleviate social ills. Ryan recognized the eugenic ideals in the birth control movement, questioning their broad categorization of "defectives" and their concern for the "welfare of the race," which he contended meant the "welfare of the fortunate majority who do not desire the inconvenience of helping to support any considerable number of defectives." Regarding the need for social reform, Ryan suggested other methods, among them improvements in living and working conditions.[22]

Ryan acknowledged the prevalence of contraceptive practice among the middle and upper classes, maintaining that the underlying purpose of recent treatises had been "to make known and recommend to the poorer classes devices for the limitation of their families."[23] The Catholic Church represented much of the lower classes and was now speaking for them on the birth control issue. According to Monsignor William J. White, Diocesan Director of Charities in Brooklyn, "Today in the United States, the Catholic Church is the church of the workingman, the church of the common people, whom our Savior loved."[24] Although the position taken by the Catholic Church was essentially no different from official positions of any other denominations in 1916, it reacted to birth control advocates differently. Ryan called for improvements in the distribution of wealth, arguing that if workers were guaranteed a fair wage, they would not need to limit the size of their families. While some contended that poverty was the fault of parents who had more children than they could afford, Ryan called such statements shallow and inhuman. He described contraception, not as a woman's issue, but rather as an issue of economics at the family level, the corporate level, and the global level.[25]

One of Sanger's most ardent critics was New York's Archbishop Patrick J. Hayes, who wrote, in a pastoral letter to be read at masses the Sunday before Christmas in 1921: "The Christ-Child did not stay His own entrance into this mortal life because His mother was poor, roofless and without provision for the morrow. . . . He knew that the Heavenly Father who cared for the lilies of the fields and the birds of the air loved the children of men more than these. Children troop down from Heaven because God wills it. He alone has the right to stay their coming while he blesses at will some homes with many, others with but few or with none at all."[26] During the Depression, Hayes called for reformers to "re-order our economic and social structure as to make it possible for people to have children and to rear them in keeping with their needs."[27] And numerous members of the Catholic opposition quoted Leo XIII's encyclical *Rerum Novarum,* condemning maldistribution of wealth and calling for "less capitalistic control of the labor market, higher wages, better housing" to alleviate difficulties among the poor with large families.[28]

In a 1926 series of Lenten lectures given at Detroit's Sts. Peter and Paul Church, Jesuit John A. McClorey of the University of Detroit echoed this sentiment, calling for parents to "put their trust in that Heavenly Father who . . . will provide means, in some way or other, for their children."[29] In a lecture entitled "Wickedness of Birth Control," McClorey considered birth control "race suicide" and contrary to nature because it frustrated the natural effect of the marriage act. Nevertheless, he recognized that it would affect men and women in different ways, on the basis of his argument that men's and women's roles in general were inherently different. McClorey claimed that because the woman's responsibility lay in bearing and rearing children, contraceptives would give her too much sexual independence. He added that the Church was trying to protect her from mental and bodily harm that some doctors contended was caused by the use of contraceptive devices, and from sexual brutes, which was what husbands would become when they viewed her as a sexual object and not as a potential mother.[30] Sensitive to accusations that the Catholic Church was "antiwoman," Church spokesmen often argued that the Church was working in the best interests of women by opposing contraception. They maintained that the use of contraceptives would result in the degradation of both women and men as it robbed them of their dignity, making them instruments of sexual lust.[31] But like John Ryan, McClorey also saw birth control as an issue of class, as it was directed at the poorer classes for the benefit of the rich, who he said would be spared the blame for the "misery of the populace."[32]

The Church clearly saw discussions of birth control and family size as related to economics and society as a whole, but also as a question of moral law that applied equally and universally to all humans, not only Catholics. For this reason, Church spokesmen found it necessary and desirable to block efforts to legalize the distribution of contraceptives. Sanger took every opportunity to describe how Catholic women's organizations joined forces with Catholic men's organizations in taking the official Church stand in opposition to birth control, actively working to thwart her efforts by blocking legislation and preventing her from speaking.[33] But she also recounted endless stories of individual Catholic women contacting her—either in person or through the mail—pleading for help in obtaining contraceptive information. She wrote in her autobiography that she was forced to hire a staff of women to read and reply to these letters, many of whom "were constantly breaking down in health under the nervous depression these letters caused."[34] Sanger claimed that by the 1930s, Catholic women in general were "showing a gradual yet persistent spirit of independence"; despite Church doctrine, many of them were using contraceptives.[35] From the early years of her crusade, Sanger condemned the Catholic Church for holding onto antiquated superstitions that she considered more medieval than modern and for mixing in politics, infringing on her right to free speech, and attempting to impose its beliefs on all Americans.[36]

These kinds of comments helped to shape the debate over birth control into one divided between Catholics and non-Catholics. By the 1930s, Anglicans, Unitarians, Northern Baptists, Northern Presbyterians, and Reformed Jews, among others, had accepted the use of contraceptives, and U.S. courts ruled that physicians could not be prosecuted for possession or prescription of contraceptives for married couples. Although other denominations refused to change their positions, the Catholic

Church had become known as the enemy of birth control, a stance made clear in *Casti Connubii: On Christian Marriage,* the defining encyclical issued by Pope Pius XI on December 31, 1930. It expounded on *Acta Apostolicae Sedis,* 22: 560, which declared: "[A]ny use whatever of marriage, in the exercise of which the act by human effort is deprived of its natural power of procreating life, violates the law of God and nature, and those who do such a thing are stained by a grave and mortal flaw." *Casti Connubii* went on to admonish "priests who hear confessions and others who have the care of souls, in virtue of Our supreme authority and in Our solicitude for the salvation of souls, not to allow the faithful entrusted to them to err regarding this most grave law of God."[37]

Although the Church did not stand alone in its opposition, the religious/political atmosphere prevalent in the United States helped to shape such an image. In subsequent decades, reproductive control became more readily identified with abortion, a relationship that the original birth control activists never intended,[38] and the Church was drawn even more clearly into the role of enemy as it increased efforts to preserve human life. At the same time, reproductive choice became more deeply embedded in the women's rights movement of the 1960s and 1970s, thus setting the stage for further division between feminism and the Church. Only in revisiting the original debates over birth control can representatives of any side begin to see this as something more than a simple platform of the women's rights movement.

Brought into the public sphere cloaked in radicalism, calls for the legalization of contraceptives would naturally provoke response from various authority figures. Church authorities would speak to the issue not only as society's moral leaders but also as theologians addressing issues of human life. Clearly, the religious debate could not be isolated from history, as trends in immigration, race theory, eugenics, anti-Catholicism, and modernism influenced a shift among many prominent American denominations. Nevertheless, the Catholic Church maintained its original stand. Forced into a position of self-examination, the Church chose not to embrace early-twentieth-century notions that man could have ultimate control over the engineering of society, population, and human life. Once the history surrounding the Church's decision is properly understood, the debate may well take on a new dimension, addressing the issue in an entirely new context.

Catholic women who struggle with the Church's position on contraception while desiring to maintain satisfying sexual relations with their husbands and limit the number of their children can benefit from seeing the intensity of clerical pronouncements on the subject as originating largely in circumstances particular to the early twentieth century. Similarly, the Church can benefit by such recognition as well by developing a new leadership role in addressing the topic of contraception in coming years. The single common thread that is woven through so many of the Church's teachings today is the call to respect human life. It is this unceasing respect for human life that may provide the framework for new discussions on contraception.

The Church's positions on the death penalty and abortion demonstrate consistency in the protection of all human life; indeed, its recent support of global solidarity and human dignity worldwide provide further evidence of continued determination on this front. In turn, Catholic women have become increasingly active in embracing the ideals of universal human dignity through clerical and lay mission programs, often indirectly calling for women's rights in their demands for human rights. The topic of birth control cannot be isolated from this movement, as population control programs have become more international in scope than ever. The "problem" is no longer confined to the poorer classes in America; we now recognize that the need for population control pertains to the poorer classes around the globe.

It is important to recognize the racist and classist discrimination inherent in the early-twentieth-century movement to distribute contraceptives and to realize that those feelings persist. International birth control programs are funded by the most prosperous nations of the world and directed toward people who are often considered inferior in some way or another. Still, birth control continues to be seen by many as a panacea for the world's ills, such as poverty and hunger. But rather than blame the poor for their own poverty (by condemning them for having "more children than they can afford"), the Church and a growing number of activist Catholic women are calling for a global economy and social structures that are more fair and just—demands that echo those of Archbishop Hayes and Monsignor Ryan of the 1920s. By encouraging improved educational and employment opportunities for all, they are addressing the needs of women in particular, as women are denied equal access to education and to fair wages in far greater numbers than men. If overpopulation remains a primary concern, then critics must recognize that improved education and employment have consistently contributed to smaller family size, ultimately resulting in an improved standard of living. When women have better opportunities and the chance to live with greater dignity, they tend to have fewer children.

Equally important is the need to recognize that Catholic feminists can actively and openly embrace children, as well as women who choose to have children. While the feminist movement of the 1960s and 1970s alienated many with its demands for abortion rights and was thus viewed as antimother and antichild, feminists of the new millennium can expand their mission by actively demanding rights for mothers—by demanding better wages, family leave, and provisions for child care. In doing so, Catholic feminists would help to perpetuate the Church's call to respect human life.

NOTES

This essay was originally published in *The American Religious Debate over Birth Control, 1907–1937.* © 2001 by Kathleen A. Tobin. It is reprinted by permission of McFarland and Co., Inc., Jefferson, North Carolina.

1. Janet Farrell Brodie, *Contraception and Abortion in Nineteenth-Century America* (Ithaca, N.Y.: Cornell University Press, 1994), 253–66. Also see Carroll Smith-Rosenberg, *Disorderly Conduct: Visions of Gender in Victorian America* (New York: Oxford University Press, 1985), and David Pivar, *Purity Crusade: Sexual Morality and Social Control, 1868–1900* (Westport, Conn.: Greenwood Press, 1973).

2. Linda Gordon, "The Struggle for Reproductive Freedom: Three Stages of Feminism," in *Capitalist Patriarchy and the Case for Socialist Feminism,* ed. Zillah R. Eisenstein (New York: Monthly Review Press, 1979), 110–19 and Andrea Tone, *Controlling Reproduction: An American History* (Wilmington, Del.: Scholarly Resources, Inc., 1997), 147–55. Also see Linda Gordon, *Woman's Body, Woman's Right: Birth Control in America* (New York: Penguin, 1990), 93–113; Kathleen E. Powderly, "Contraceptive Policy and Ethics: Lessons from American History," in *Coerced Contraception? Moral and Policy Challenges of Long-Acting Birth Control,* ed. Ellen H. Moskowitz and Bruce Jennings (Washington, D.C.: Georgetown University Press, 1996), 24–25; and Mari Jo Buhle,

"Sexual Emancipation," in *Women and American Socialism, 1870–1920* (Chicago: University of Illinois Press, 1981), 246–87.

3. Margaret Sanger, *My Fight for Birth Control* (New York: Farrar and Rinehart, 1931), 83, cited in *Woman Rebel,* ed. Alex Baskin (New York: Archives of Social History, 1976), ix–x.

4. Emma Goldman, "Love and Marriage," *Woman Rebel* 1 (March 1914): 3, 5; Dorothy Kelly, "Prevention and the Law," *Woman Rebel* 1 (April 1914): 10, 16; Aegyptus, "The Pauline Ideas vs. Woman," *Woman Rebel* 1 (May 1914): 20; "Suppression," *Woman Rebel* 1 (June 1914): 25.

5. "The Unfit," *Woman Rebel* 1 (April 1914): 10.

6. Ibid., 12.

7. Robert Wiebe, *The Search for Order, 1877–1920* (New York: Hill and Wang, 1967), 137–45, 153–54. Also see Sean Dennis Cashman, *America in the Gilded Age: From the Death of Lincoln to the Rise of Theodore Roosevelt* (New York: NYU Press, 1988), 351–63; Richard Hofstadter, *The Age of Reform: From Bryan to FDR* (New York: Alfred A. Knopf, 1955), 216–23.

8. Carole R. McCann, *Birth Control Politics in the United States, 1916–1945* (Ithaca, N.Y.: Cornell University Press, 1994), 58.

9. Gordon, *Woman's Body, Woman's Right,* 114–32. Also see Steven Selden and Ashley Montagu, *Inheriting Shame: The Story of Eugenics and Racism in America* (New York: Teachers College Press, 1999); Daniel L. Kevles, *In the Name of Eugenics: Genetics and the Uses of Human Heredity* (Cambridge, Mass.: Harvard University Press, 1995); and Dorothy Roberts, *Killing the Black Body: Race, Reproduction, and the Meaning of Liberty* (New York: Pantheon, 1997).

10. C. V. Drysdale, *The Small Family System: Is It Injurious or Immoral?* (New York: B. W. Huebsch, 1917), 174. Also see Adelyne More, "Militarism and the Birth Rate," in *Uncontrolled Breeding; or Fecundity versus Civilization; A Contribution to the Study of Over-Population as the Cause of War and the Chief Obstacle to the Emancipation of Women* (New York: Critic and Guide, 1917), 64–71.

11. Margaret Sanger, *Woman and the New Race* (New York: Brentano's 1920), 162–63.

12. Eric B. Ross, *The Malthus Factor: Population, Poverty and Politics in Capitalist Development* (New York: Zed, 1998), 58–60; William Petersen, *Malthus: Founder of Modern Demography* (New Brunswick, N.J.: Transaction Publications, 1999), 197–201; David M. Kennedy, *Birth Control in America: The Career of Margaret Sanger* (New Haven, Conn.: Yale University Press, 1970), 21–22.

13. Kenan Malik, *The Meaning of Race: Race, History and Culture in Western Society* (Washington Square, N.Y.: NYU Press, 1996), 101.

14. Daniel Pick, *Faces of Degeneration: A European Disorder, c. 1848– c. 1918* (New York: Cambridge University Press, 1989), 11–15; Lothrop Stoddard, *The Revolt against Civilization: The Menace of the Under Man* (New York: Scribner's, 1923), 17–19.

15. See Madison Grant, *The Passing of the Great Race; or, The Racial Basis of European History* (New York: 1916), xx–xxi, quoted in John Higham, *Strangers in the Land: Patterns of American Nativism, 1860–1925* (New Brunswick, N.J.: Rutgers University Press, 1994), 155–57.

16. McCann, *Birth Control Politics*, 99–100.

17. C. B. Davenport, "Euthenics and Eugenics," *Popular Science Monthly*, January 1911, 16.

18. Marouf Arif Hasian, Jr., *The Rhetoric of Eugenics in Anglo-American Thought* (Athens: University of Georgia Press, 1996), 90–94.

19. McCann, *Birth Control Politics*, 99, 107.

20. Harry H. Laughlin, *The Scope of the Committee's Work: Report of the Committee to Study and to Report on the Best Practical Means of Cutting Off the Defective Germ-Plasm in the American Population*, Bulletin 10A (Cold Spring Harbor, N.Y.: Eugenics Records Office, 1914).

21. Quoted in Mary Alden Hopkins, "The Catholic Church and Birth Control," *Harper's Weekly*, June 26, 1915, 610.

22. John A. Ryan, "Family Limitation, Church and Birth Control," *American Ecclesiastical Review* 54 (June 1916): 687. Also see John A. Ryan's *Social Reform on Catholic Lines* (New York: Paulist Press, 1914) and *A Program of Social Reform by Legislation* (New York: Paulist Press, 1919).

23. Ryan, "Family Limitation," 687.

24. *Proceedings of the First Conference of Catholic Charities* (Washington, D.C.: Catholic University of America, 1910).

25. John A. Ryan, *Family Limitation; and, The Church on Birth Control* (New York: Paulist Press, [not before 1916]), 13–14, 22–23.

26. Quoted in "Archbishop Hayes on Birth Control," *New York Times*, December 18, 1921, 16.

27. Quoted in "Cardinal in Pulpit Scores New Moves for Birth Control," *New York Times*, December 9, 1935, 5.

28. "Report of an Interview with Mr. P. J. Ward of the National Catholic Welfare Council," March 2, 1926, and John LaFarge, S.J., "Deceit, Fraud and Trickery in Birth Control Propaganda," *America*, April 5, 1941, 708–9, quoted in Kennedy, *Birth Control in America*, 147.

29. John A. McClorey, *The Republic and the Church: A Series of Lenten Lectures Mainly on Divorce and Birth Control* (St. Louis, Mo.: B. Herder, 1929), 138–39.

30. Ibid., 118, 124, 137–41.

31. Dominic Pruemmer, O.P., *Birth Control* (New York: Paulist Press, 1933), 9; Bertrand L. Conway, *The Church and Eugenics* (New York: Paulist Press, n.d.), 4–5.

32. McClorey, *The Republic and the Church,* 142–43.

33. Sanger, *My Fight for Birth Control,* 200–207. For more on Catholic efforts to block legislation, see Kennedy, *Birth Control in America,* 148–52.

34. Ibid., 206.

35. Margaret Sanger, *An Autobiography* (1938; New York: Dover Publications, 1971), 411–12.

36. Sanger, *My Fight for Birth Control,* 224, 227 (for more on politics, see the chapter "Arrogance in Power," 226–37); Sanger, *An Autobiography,* 411–15.

37. Pope Pius XI, *Casti Connubii,* December 31, 1930; Norman St. John-Stevas, *The Agonising Choice: Birth Control, Religion and the Law* (Bloomington: Indiana University Press, 1971), 83–84.

38. Margaret Sanger, "Prevention or Abortion—Which? Letters Showing the Dilemma Faced by Many Mothers," *Birth Control Review,* July 1923, 181–82, cited in Tone, *Controlling Reproduction,* 156–59.

SIXTEEN

Politics and Paradox in Nineteenth-Century Irish American Society: Mary Anne Sadlier and the Catholic Woman's Role

Mary Jo T. Marcellus

As the first of many nineteenth-century Catholic woman writers, Mary Anne (Madden) Sadlier broke new ground in American Catholic literature. Instead of writing strictly catechismic books and religious texts like priests and religious before her, this laywoman wove tales based in America and Ireland that pertained to her contemporary brethren. Sadlier's most popular stories, and the work that commenced the Catholic novel trend, consisted of characters who encountered and addressed Catholic issues and problems in the Old and New Worlds of the nineteenth century. It was Sadlier, a woman writer, who made American Catholic literature an industry and who quickly became the most influential force in Catholic letters.

Born in Ireland in 1820, Sadlier was the first Irish Catholic woman to establish herself as a popular American writer. Few people at this time were capable of producing didactic novels in such an acceptable manner. Simultaneously moralistic and entertaining, Sadlier's writing brought her acclaim in what was traditionally a man's field, yet her novels did not condone a self-reliant, business-oriented attitude. Rather, she encouraged her Irish sisters to pursue the opposite lifestyle—to stay in the home and care for their husbands and children. These dual messages reflect the paradox that she lived and the issues for which she fought.

The Early Years: A Woman Writer in a Male-Dominated Society

Mary Anne Sadlier established herself as a writer while she was still a teenager in Cootehill, County Cavan. On her father's suggestion, she submitted some of her poetry to the London-based magazine *La Belle Assemblee*. When her father died suddenly following business setbacks, Sadlier decided, at age twenty-four, to leave home. As a member of the Famine Generation, she knew that Ireland held few opportunities for single women. With only money enough for her passage, she sailed off to the New World.

As a matter of survival in nineteenth-century America, immigrants such as Sadlier sought jobs immediately upon arrival to sustain themselves and often their families overseas. Women found occupations in service, needle trades, textiles, clerical work, sales, and teaching; however, the vast majority of all Irish women who came to the United States before 1900 entered domestic service.[1] Not Sadlier. Drawing on the memory of her father's support as well as her publication success, Sadlier continued writing when she arrived in Montreal in 1844. During her first months in Canada, she published articles in two Montreal papers, the *Literary Garland* and the *True Witness*. Less than a year after her arrival, she published her first novel, *Tales of the Olden Times: A Collection of European Traditions,* serialized in the *Garland*. By age twenty-five, Sadlier had established herself as a writer in the small Irish Catholic community around Montreal.

In the mid-1800s, men and women were confined to separate spheres. Women did not hold public jobs or enter into the public arena, for that was the male domain. A woman's place was in the home, but Sadlier wanted more. She composed verses and books to earn money but also because she loved her craft. Wanting to be well reviewed and published, yet cognizant of the attitudes regarding a woman's role, she penned the following inscription to *Olden Times* when it was first serialized in the *Garland:* "[H]ad it been my fate to contribute to that fortunate class which is happily exempt from the necessity of working, I should, in all probability, never have presented myself before you; . . . authorship is a perilous craft . . . seeing that there are so many masters to be pleased. It is foreign to a woman's nature, moreover, to 'move in the uncongenial glare of public fame'—hers are, or should be, the quiet shades of retirement, and woe to her who steps beyond their boundary, with the hope—of finding happiness."[2] Little did she realize when penning these lines that doors in the literary world would be significantly opened the day she met James Sadlier.

At a time when Irish girls were marrying later in life due largely to their positions as household servants, Mary Anne Sadlier married her husband James only two years after leaving Ireland. James Sadlier owned a thriving publishing house in New York. Whether Mary Anne's literary talents and reputation precipitated their meeting is not clear, but when she and James Sadlier, an immigrant from County Tipperary, Ireland, met during a business trip to his Montreal office, they fell in love. With this union, they established the strongest Catholic publishing force in North America.

Impressed with his wife's talents, James Sadlier soon viewed her as a fundamental component of his company's success. While he advised, edited, and encouraged her, Mary Anne wrote, published, and brought in revenue and publicity for the D&J Sadlier Publishing House. The company rapidly became an essential part of the growing Catholic American culture by printing inexpensive copies of books such as *Lives of the Saints,* Catholic Bibles, devotionals, school texts, and pious literature.[3] As a partnership, their marriage aided both careers in the literary world. Mary Anne Sadlier published numerous articles and stories in her husband's weekly Catholic newsletter, the *Tablet,* as well as in Patrick Donahoe's *Pilot,* while they lived in Montreal. Between bearing six children, maintaining her household, and aiding her husband in the publishing house, Sadlier wrote. Late at night, while her babies slept, she turned bedtime tales into full-length stories published in serial form within the newsletters and later collected and published as books. In her lifetime, Sadlier edited and wrote poetry, short fiction, children's stories, translations from the French, plays, religious catechisms, magazine pieces, and Irish- and Irish American–based novels—altogether nearly sixty volumes of work. When she left Canada for America with her family in 1860, her reputation was well established.

The Life of an Irish American Woman: Sadlier's Contradiction

Sadlier's popularity was due in part to her belief in the preservation of Old World values. At a time when women had little or no say regarding political issues in society, this woman writer had plenty to offer to a growing Irish population that chose to listen to her. With the support of prominent Catholic figures in the burgeoning New World, Sadlier emerged as a prolific woman writer and ultimately the voice of Catholics everywhere.

At the beginning of the twentieth century, few women could equal Sadlier's literary success. Her method of dispersing her views to a large audience was characteristic of a masculine agenda, with its adamant, intellectual, and God-fearing delivery. Yet she never considered herself a feminist, for ultimately her messages remained conservative: cling to the Catholic faith and traditional family values. Indeed, Sadlier's role in the public spotlight as a writer was generally accepted because of these stringent religious and didactic messages. The Church itself supported her work while still promoting "the idea that a woman's place was in the home."[4] Sadlier's work clearly altered the traditional view of women because she reached out to the public, but her novels promoting female domestic Catholicism signify a paradox. Were her dual messages regarding the role of women—one in writing, the other in life—a conscious decision on her part? Was she aware of her own contradictions? If so, did her written message excuse her actions as a female political voice? Given her boundaries as a nineteenth-century woman as well as the attention she received due to her public role in promoting a traditional ideology, could Sadlier be considered a precursor to the twentieth-century Catholic feminist?

Unlike the modest, secluded women in her novels who found joy in keeping a clean house and raising children, Sadlier knew she would not be content if she remained silent in that conservative sphere. She wanted her opinions on the welfare of children, the Irish, and Catholicism to be heard. In this, Sadlier clearly did not follow the advice she proffered her readers concerning the role of the traditional Irish woman. Her success as a writer and her marriage to a publisher allowed her more freedom to pursue her dreams of writing and influencing people's opinions. Empowered by such a connection, Sadlier aspired to move beyond the feminine sphere of domesticity. She pursued her own economic and matrimonial successes, yet she equally rejected the ideology of feminism. In this, she reflected the beliefs of her fellow Irish Catholic immigrants. The Irish believed that women and men had their own roles in society, and they were anxious to uphold that tradition in America. "The division of the sexes into rigidly discrete categories, each with its own locus, each with its own tasks, made the world rational and orderly, while the feminist cause demanded that separate spheres for men and women be obliterated."[5]

Despite the inherent contradiction, many Catholic fiction writers such as Sadlier depicted the ideal role of "the good Catholic woman" who renounced all personal ambition at the altar. But Sadlier herself was different. Ambition was a trait she evidently possessed and did not surrender, considering the amount of writing she produced and published in her lifetime. In this exceptional case, the Sadliers' marriage, based on Catholic values, did not mean that James automatically governed the household. Because of her career and social status, the Sadliers achieved a relationship that broke down the traditional domestic patriarchal order. Sadlier was considered pious and devout in her faith in all regards; however, America had some influence on her. Women around her fell in line with the women's rights movement, and though she would not go that far, the public life beckoned to her, and Sadlier answered the call.

Politics, Feminism, and Religion: A Catholic Woman's Voice

In 1862, Sadlier published *Old and New; or Taste versus Fashion,* in which she gives a full rendering of her conservative social values. Madam Von Weigel, an Irish Catholic married to a German Catholic, speaks for Sadlier when she declares: "I belong to a Church that teaches unlimited submission to the Divine Word, and holds with St. Paul that women should obey their husbands, and moreover, keep silent in public assemblies." The domestic life, she continues, is a "wise provision of the Divine Ruler for the wants of the human family."[6] Catholic culture in the nineteenth century viewed suffrage and the women's rights movement as deviant, for they challenged Church tradition. As a pious and devout churchgoer, Sadlier agreed, though she did not stay silent. In

Old and New, Sadlier made it clear to her audience that she would not be a part of such a revolution. She wanted her fellow Irish to retain the Church's teachings. According to many Christians, male and female spheres should be kept apart, "for usurpation by either sex of activities belonging to the other was unnatural. . . . Catholic journals, newspapers, and spokesmen, lay as well as clerical, assailed this alleged reform for endangering social stability and, more important, woman's redemptive mission."[7] As a laywoman writer who contributed to Catholic journals and newspapers, Sadlier belonged to this group of antisuffragists and opponents of "woman's rights." But while she condoned separate spheres, Sadlier embraced the "masculine" role of public voice and writer to do so.

Sadlier broke the mandates for Catholic women in her society: "As early as the eighteenth century, Catholic girls were taught that ladies should possess [certain] virtues and were warned that public affairs and public persons were not fit subjects for conversation." Such precepts had been "repeatedly confirmed during the nineteenth century" as "Christian tradition" and were said to be "ordained by God, exemplified by the Virgin Mary, revealed by scripture and the natural law, and reinforced by biological differences."[8] Sadlier's strong Irish nationalism and Catholicity, however, made it impossible for her to follow suit. Though she oscillated between traditionally feminine and outwardly masculine roles, the greater good of reaching her people made others who noticed overlook society's limitations on her as a woman and listen to her messages.

Most women who advocated women's rights in the nineteenth century came from Protestant families. Motivated by strong public figures such as Elizabeth Cady Stanton and Susan B. Anthony, many Protestant women saw suffrage as their escape from domesticity and their path to equality with men. Irish women, however, viewed suffrage differently. While Protestants gave up strict domestic rules of the nineteenth century, Irish Catholics refused to part with the virtues that defined them as a people. Sadlier and her Irish brethren had good reasons not to conform.

The Protestants who advocated equal rights were the same people who "at best patronized the Hibernian newcomers and more frequently vilified them, discriminated against them, and sought to hamper them in every way possible."[9] As a result, feminists appeared to Sadlier and others as anti-Irish and anti-Catholic. "A strongly worded anti-Irish, anti-Catholic message ran through much of the nineteenth-century women's rights campaign. . . . Suffrage newspapers, for example, indulged in the same stereotyping and labeling of Irish men and women as did the general American press, commenting in a variety of ways on their ignorance, lack of common sense, volatile tempers, and total submission to ecclesiastical authority."[10] It is no wonder that Sadlier rejected such a movement, for it openly condemned the very ideas of Irish nationalism and religion that she promoted. Such direct contrasts of ideas in the crusade for women's rights confirmed the animosity already established between Protestants and Catholics.

Sadlier's opposition came through her literature. Her novels show-case Protestant characters such as the Reverend Julietta Fireproof, B.A. (Bachelor of Arts), and Dorothea Mary Wolstoncroft Brown, both of whom appear in *Old and New*. The latter character is a direct allusion to the eighteenth-century women's champion Mary Wollstonecraft, au-thor of *The Vindication of the Rights of Woman* (1792). By depicting caricatures of Protestant women who flaunt their educational degrees and who represent past influential feminist figures in a ridiculous manner, Sadlier succeeds in sending her own message: the best type of woman stays at home with her family. She, and the majority of her beloved Irish, believed that "while Protestant homes might be rich in material posses-sions, in actuality their family life contains an inner poverty. From Sad-lier's perspective, the women's rights movement consists of confused and silly females who have no understanding of true womanhood—just as they have no idea of true religion."[11] In appearances and through cer-tain outlets of expression, the push for the rights of women became just another means of rejecting the Irish and their values.

Sadlier saw this movement as an upheaval in the fight to restore and bolster Catholic values. Servant girls like Bridget and Sally who lost their faith in *Bessy Conway; or, the Irish Girl in America* (1861) would be the ones to follow in Susan B. Anthony's and Elizabeth Cady Stan-ton's footsteps. To them, religion took a distant second place to indi-vidual rights. The Catholics, as a group, venerated the family over self, with God at the center, holding the unit together. "Family life provided dignity, peace, and security for the mother and exercised an ennobling and steadying influence on the father. For both parents, it awakened and developed a sense of responsibility while fostering their growth in self-lessness, sacrifice, and patience."[12] Sadlier believed that such concepts were void or unimportant to female activists. To her, the women's rights crusade based itself on anti-family and anti-Catholic sentiments. Most Irish saw suffrage, not as liberating, but rather as destructive to home and married life. It unsettled Sadlier to watch women follow a movement she believed a major contributor to the breakdown of family values.

Catholic America and Sadlier's Life, Fiction, and Paradox

Sadlier left behind a body of work that challenges the status quo, en-courages Irish Catholic culture, and rejects all opposition to her cause. While she strove for the traditions equated with gender separation in her literature, she never passively followed male authority.

The paradox between Sadlier's life and fiction was most likely a conscious decision. The Irish knew that "the average Protestant Ameri-can of the 1850's had been trained from birth to hate Catholicism; his juvenile literature and school books had breathed a spirit of intoler-ance."[13] From childhood, Protestant Americans were inculcated with a strong resentment against Catholics that stemmed from religious and cultural differences. Why, then, would Sadlier want to ally herself with an ideology that aspersed her beliefs, her heritage, her culture, and her traditions? How could she, and those of Irish descent, relinquish the values and customs that constituted their ethnic and religious identity? "The writers and editors of the Irish press inevitably linked feminist ide-ology with sexual license, polygamy, abortion, birth control, divorce, and the like—all being supported by 'demoralized females, who have outraged every instinct of womanly decency, and every truth of Chris-tianity.'"[14]

Each issue that contradicted Catholic dogma seemed to be accepted by, and linked to, the women's movement. Because the ideology of the feminist cause contradicted historical Catholic teachings, many writers and readers of Catholic papers were outraged. Furthermore, "accord-ing to the Irish-American male world view, the convergence of feminism and sexual vice flowed naturally from the fact that the vast majority of activists in the women's movement were native-born Protestant women of Anglo-Saxon stock who subscribed to a religious ideology allowing divorce and greater sexual freedom than did that of Catholic Ireland."[15] Irish Catholic men and women were raised with different beliefs that established them as a community and identified them as Irish. To relinquish those values that constituted their education, their faith, and their history would be to deny their identities altogether. Essentially, the Irish would have to become new creatures to follow and promote a cause so completely alien to the beliefs in which they were raised and educated.

Many aspects of nineteenth-century society discouraged and disheartened the Irish immigrants. They were discriminated against for being Catholic, Irish, and poor. They faced Protestant bigotry on the streets, in the schools, and at the market. When Protestant women fell in league with the feminist crusade, they sought others to join their efforts. Leaving the home to attend rallies, marches, and to join clubs was viewed by many Catholics as an abandonment of home and family values. Suffrage, along with other rights and freedoms for women in the public realm, contrasted with the notion of domestic Catholic virtue. Though some Catholic women joined the movement, many others saw it as deviating from their religion and continued to endorse separate roles for men and women in the public and private realms. "A much larger group of Irish women [such as Sadlier] emphatically went on record against the ideas of the 'new women' or remained totally uninterested in issues raised by the organized suffrage campaign."[16] Catholics were taught to uphold the patriarchy and traditions of Church and society; therefore, they felt the feminist movement cast these notions to the winds. When an Irish woman opted not to align herself with this crusade, she reaffirmed her Catholic allegiance and traditional values.

Sadlier clearly discouraged Catholic involvement with the women's rights coalition. She showed in her novels how Protestant women attempted to rob the Irish of their religion and values by using persuasive tactics to entice them with their cause. "Mary Anne Sadlier, perhaps more than any other Catholic woman writer, clearly told her female readers not to be bullied into accepting Protestantism," or in other words, not to abandon Catholic values and become feminists.[17] Even though her occupation as a female writer defied the opinion of the patriarchy, her own desire to be in the male-dominated sphere of the work force was not sufficient to overcome her aversion to feminism.

The question still remains, however, about how much Sadlier's private and public interests actually collided. She was indeed a popular American writer with her conservative messages. But is it possible that she wrote to appease an audience that might object to a woman's writing, by extolling autonomy within marriage? Did she pen her didactic messages laced with Old World conservatism in order to satisfy her desire for individual expression? As some writers today write popular fiction to turn a profit, is it possible that Sadlier consciously fought feminist notions and wrote conservative literature to fulfill those yearnings for independence? It is a confounding thought that further complicates the paradox of Sadlier's life, but it is a definite possibility. On the basis of the history of her writing, as well as the obviously male-dominated informal review board of the nineteenth century, Sadlier could have produced her works for a very different reason.

Recall Sadlier's introduction in the *Literary Garland* in which she apologizes for stepping into the public arena. Since the seventeenth century, women writers have been "apologizing," and Sadlier naturally joined a long line of apologizing predecessors. Sadlier did, in fact, gain an inordinate amount of "public fame" outside the "shades of retirement"; however, in this passage this young, ambitious woman plays down her talents and placates her audience by telling them that she has been forced to write in order to make a living. The "masters," as she calls them, are men who will undoubtedly judge her work and who need appeasing, apparently, for her to be successful. As a young woman, Sadlier acknowledged her disadvantages as a female writer. Consequently, it is more than possible that she wrote to appease others more than once.

Not only did Sadlier write for a large Irish readership that would knowingly embrace her conservative messages, but she was able to do so because she married young. Other Irish girls married later in life because their wages were needed to support families back home during a time of famine and unemployment. With such a weighty responsibility, it is no wonder they worked so hard for several years without considering marriage. Sadlier's situation, however, differed. She had no family to support, and she married after less than two years in the New World. Is it a coincidence that she married a book publisher? James, and his brother Denis Sadlier, owned a thriving publishing house at that time, and it makes one wonder if Mary Anne used her womanly ways to marry into a publishing family. She was utterly driven to succeed in her dream of achieving a literary career, as evidenced by her "apology" and the numerous works she produced in her lifetime. But because of the mystery surrounding this woman, one has to ask if her marriage to the founder of the Sadlier Publishing Company, the man who edited and promoted her work, was an act of divine intervention or of a cunning woman using her feminine wiles to reach her goals. Did Mary Anne Sadlier have a hidden agenda, or was she true to her traditional messages despite her public role as a writer?

Though there is room for questions, the majority of evidence accumulated on Sadlier points to a conservative woman with her people's best interests at heart. She felt that to forsake home and family, the foundations of good Catholic virtues, and join women's auxiliaries, marches, and demonstrations would be wrong. She knew that embracing feminism, despite the opportunities it might provide working women, would mean denying her ethnicity and her religion. The obstacles she overcame as a woman in a man's world justify her reputation as an independent female prototype for future generations of Catholics. Overall, Sadlier represents the values and concerns of a people during a period in Irish American history who held a firm commitment to Catholic heritage, but she also represents the type of woman who refused to stand by without speaking her mind and fulfilling her desires. Sadlier embodies the type of woman the twentieth century would more willingly accept. The patriarchies of household, Church, and society failed to confine her as a woman and a Catholic. She lived during a difficult time of religious ignorance and oppression, but she emerged as a successful working woman. Her literature reflects a strong woman who remained constant to her convictions. Mary Anne Sadlier's vision was clear, and her dual messages were illustrative of her time.

NOTES

1. Janet A. Nolan, *Ourselves Alone: Women's Emigration from Ireland, 1885–1920* (Lexington: University Press of Kentucky, 1989).

2. Mary Anne Sadlier, "Our Table," *Literary Garland*, 1845, 576, citing the "Preface" to *Tales of the Olden Times*.

3. Colleen McDannell, "'The Devil Was the First Protestant': Gender and Intolerance in Irish Catholic Fiction," *U.S. Catholic Historian* 8 (1989): 53.

4. Nolan, *Ourselves Alone*, 36.

5. Hasia R. Diner, *Erin's Daughters in America: Irish Immigrant Women in the Nineteenth Century* (Baltimore: Johns Hopkins University Press, 1983), 140.

6. Mary Anne Sadlier, *Old and New; or Taste versus Fashion* (New York: Sadlier, 1862), 130.

7. James J. Kenneally, "A Question of Equality," in *American Catholic Women: A Historical Exploration,* ed. Karen Kennelly, C.S.J. (New York: Macmillan, 1989), 126.

8. Ibid., 125.

9. Diner, *Erin's Daughters*, 147.

10. Ibid.

11. McDannell, "The Devil," 63.

12. Colleen McDannell, "Catholic Domesticity, 1860–1960," in *American Catholic Women: A Historical Exploration,* ed. Karen Kennelly, C.S.J. (New York: Macmillan, 1989), 52.

13. Ray Allen Billington, *The Protestant Crusade: 1800–1860* (New York: Macmillan, 1938), 345.

14. Diner, *Erin's Daughters*, 145.

15. Ibid., 145–46.

16. Ibid., 151.

17. Colleen McDannell, "Catholic Women Fiction Writers, 1840–1920," *Women's Studies* 19 (1991): 398.

Looking Ahead:
Feminism and Catholicism
in the Next Generation

SEVENTEEN

Conversations between Mothers and Daughters in the Father's House

Lorraine Liscio and Jeanne Noonan-Eckholdt

I found the opening and conclusion of this essay already written on a disk in my computer. Like messages lingering in the unconscious, the text was hiding in my memory within some proximity to an earlier version of this essay, waiting for another chance—a repetition—to surface and remind me of the words I had wanted to speak but had repressed or censored in the interest of linearity, direction, logic. The original, bound for a collection of essays on how literature changes lives, focused not on my narrative but on that of my former student, Jeanne Noonan, with whom I wrote it. In it I introduced and framed her account of how my course, "Introduction to Feminisms," had changed her life. What I left out of the printed version, but what was called up on the screen, were my remarks about how it changed mine too.

In this symbolic mother-daughter relationship, I became a silent mother/object to which the daughter responded and against which she established self-identity in the world. In keeping with this deficient model, I denied my own status as a speaking subject. This effacement recalls patterns common to mothers and daughters used to living as ambiguous allies in the father's house.

As a second generation Italian American raised in the Catholic Church and educated in Catholic schools, I'm used to living in the father's house, and my current campus

231

is one in a long series of such domiciles, a historically male (now coed) Catholic university. At times in the past (I no longer am a Catholic), this version of paternal authority seemed to have served me in good stead: I remember the impact in college of an essay by Daniel Berrigan that put Central America's poor on the map for me, and of Teilhard de Chardin's writings, which led me to imagine a glorious omega point of convergence for believers and nonbelievers alike. My memory of these Jesuit fathers, themselves on the margin, undoubtedly influenced my later decision to do doctoral work at the college where I now remain as lecturer in English and women's studies, in some ways still a daughter in a father's house.

I had my first symbolic mother-daughter or sisterly conversations during my doctoral studies while working with Judith Wilt, who in 1980 introduced me to some of the cornerstone works of feminist literary theory and criticism. Despite my guardedness in approaching these readings, it was a jolting experience that I recall each time my own women's studies students try to regain their equilibrium in the wake of assigned readings like Woolf's *A Room of One's Own* and Mary Daly's *Beyond God the Father*. For a majority of students coming from strong Catholic backgrounds, a room of their own where they might imagine themselves as autonomous agents who can go beyond the father produces great anxiety. To add to the dilemma, real fathers at times refuse to pay for this course while mothers often quietly (but sometimes vociferously) urge them to enroll.

Parental prohibitions conflate easily with Catholic attitudes and beliefs to make one feel like a disobedient daughter even for teaching women's studies. My first experience of what felt like a paternal reprimand came from the dean in the spring of 1990. It was an "it-has-come-to-my-attention" letter from an angry mother complaining about the "adverse" effects of a text (assigned in my "Introduction to Feminisms" class) on her daughter's friend. Her motive, I deduced, was the fear that her own daughter's thinking might be similarly "contaminated." The text in question was Mary Daly's *Beyond God the Father*, which critiques, among other things, the Catholic Church's doctrine of the Immaculate Conception (that Mary was born without sin in order to bear Christ, the redeemer). According to this mother's report, the student was so upset by Daly's analyses that she "tore off" her Mary medal, planning not to wear it again. While this bathetic account of the student's gesture may not seem worthy of mention, we know that her action and the mother's distress both point to its symbolic import: the student's shift vis-à-vis the tenets of a religion that may have shaped her identity and vision of the world. In other words, the stakes are high. And they are high because the father is threatened with usurpation of his place. Heavily invested in the father, this mother never feels the need, as Woolf does before she addresses women, to verify that he's not indeed hiding somewhere in the room.

Reflection about this incident prompted me to invite a former student, Jeanne Noonan, to chronicle her journey with me and other women students and student teachers (each playing the roles of mother or daughter) through the texts and contexts of "Introduction to Feminisms," a women's studies core course at our institution. We decided to use selected excerpts from Jeanne's weekly journals to see what happened when mothers spoke to daughters in the father's house.

"Introduction to Feminisms" is an interdisciplinary course that combines weekly seminars led by student teachers (who have already taken the course) and periodic large group lectures by women's studies faculty. Students write weekly journals (40 percent of their grade), participate in weekly discussion (40 percent of their grade), and write a final paper (20 percent of their grade). The student teachers are enrolled in my "Seminar in College Teaching" course, where we prepare the readings for "Introduction to Feminisms" together and attend to the mechanics of their responsibilities in the seminar groups. In an ongoing dialogue with their students, they read the journals, responding to and challenging students' ideas and reactions to readings in their marginal notes.

I met Jeanne in my "Prose Writing" course during the spring of 1988. As a third-year student wanting to improve her writing, she was a strong and articulate presence in our small group, but she would never have identified herself as a feminist. In fact, an incident occurred in which Jeanne first missed and then denied the significance of a gender-related problem raised by another woman in the class. The student had written an essay about her disappointment when a priest, an admired professor with whom she had been friendly, ignored her completely when she was in the company of her boyfriend, whom the priest addressed. Her point was that when a male was present, she became invisible.

Jeanne agreed with other members of the class that the student was imagining this neglect. I cite this incident to establish a baseline attitude against which to consider changes brought about by her experience in "Introduction to Feminisms." While I never discussed these attitudes with Jeanne, I see from my recent reading of her first journal (I had never read these journals before), in a response to Susan Brownmiller's *Femininity,* that I had provided an entree into her reflection on gender: "I never knew much about feminism last semester when I took Prose Writing. My teacher, Lorraine Liscio, would frequently correct the usage of certain words such as mankind and chairman. Slowly, I realized she was a feminist and I became interested. I have never considered myself a feminist but I am not a submissive female either" (Journal I).

My casual (and yet not so casual) remarks set in motion a process of rumination about a subject that no other instructor had broached. As an English major, Jeanne had by that time—spring semester of junior year—jumped through the hoops of required literature courses in which neither text nor class context jarred hegemonic approaches to the subject matter. Our encounter would lead Jeanne to a new selection of readings (woman centered) and a new context (collaborative learning) in "Introduction to Feminisms."

However, other women in "Prose Writing" were not similarly piqued. Clearly my remarks fell on fertile ground in Jeanne's case, enriched by her background. As the journals show, in her father's house the Catholic system of beliefs did little to hamper what she perceived as a fluid and positive model of gender relations and self-identity: "My father is not a male chauvinist and has set a good example of the male sex for me. He thoroughly enjoys a woman's company as much as a man's and does a great deal of contributing to the domestic duties that come with raising a family. My mother has worked full-time since I was in third grade, which has also added to my liberated beliefs" (Journal I).

However, the following week's readings, which focused on the economic and working conditions of women, led her to see her own familial (American, Catholic) expectations for mothers and fathers: "She [Jeanne's mother] wants to go back to school, but has to wait until money is more available after I graduate from college. She is far too intelligent for the positions she has held, but knows that the second income is needed to raise a family. This example of my mother seems relevant to Feminist Frameworks. My mother sacrificed her thirst for knowledge so that my sister and I would obtain a good college education. Women seem to always be the ones to make such a sacrifice in this sort of situation" (Journal II).

From the outset, Jeanne anticipates the potential effect of probing why women make such sacrifices: "I have a feeling this class is going to enlighten me on a great number of topics that affect me tremendously" (Journal I). The following week's readings in history—speeches of Sojourner Truth, Elizabeth Cady Stanton, and others—stir up reflection about past injustices against women and political action: "Reading about Susan B. Anthony's trial after she wished to vote but was not permitted to because she was a woman made me realize how much I take for granted. I am not even registered to vote for November's election. I will do so, but Susan B. Anthony had to go to jail simply because she wanted to exercise her democratic freedom as a citizen" (Journal II).

During my subsequent meeting with the teachers, they reported on the anger and wonder expressed by students at the heroic feats of such maternal ancestors whom conventional historical accounts had ignored or silenced. As the teachers noted, students wanted to know why they had been denied this knowledge.

In the wake of such passionate analyses, Jeanne's journal two weeks later on Woolf's *A Room of One's Own* comes as no surprise:

A woman not being taken seriously or being looked upon as inferior is a major theme throughout Woolf's book. I found myself writing different comments in the margins of every single page that I could relate to my own experience. . . . The part of the book which really made me think was Woolf's hypothetical imagination of Shakespeare's sister. It is inconceivable how little regard is shown for women writers, even today. An example of this: I was coming home from Martha's Vineyard this summer, waiting for the ferry. I noticed a woman with a lap-top computer. She was, as I found out, writing a novel about an Irish woman. The concept of the novel was to express her own personal philosophy through the use of a fictional character. I asked her for the title of the book as well as her name. She told me the name and her name but said my pen name is (masculine). When I asked her why she did not use her real name, she said she wanted to be accepted as a serious novelist and she wanted her philosophy to be taken seriously. (Journal IV).

Woolf's text recalls this incident and explains the history and rationale for the use of male pseudonyms. Judith Shakespeare's story structures for Jeanne a way of thinking about the dilemma of the woman writer. Woolf's detailed analysis of women and fiction benefits her in other ways, too, by helping her navigate the problem of "correct" feminist views (a variety of which she encounters in her weekly meetings): "Another aspect of Woolf's writing which I could relate to was her statement that 'Art is useless to ask such questions [about certain male/female occupations], for nobody can answer them.' I find myself since I have begun this class often confused when I read different feminist views and ideas. They all make sense to me, but I can't pinpoint if they are right or wrong and if I believe whole-heartedly in their views. Woolf's statement that there really are no answers alleviated a great deal of my confusion."

After Woolf introduces the topic of women and fiction, the students read Harriet Jacob's (Linda Brent's) slave narrative, followed by poems and short stories by women. The former elicits in Jeanne a visceral response to the institution of slavery. The bitterness provoked by circumstances Jeanne (and few of her colleagues in the seminar group) will never have to face—racial discrimination—gives way to more conflicted and unresolved feelings when she reads Gwendolyn Brooks's poem "The Mother":

This poem struck me so much because I felt sadness for not just this particular woman, but all women who are forced to endure the tragedy of abortion. While abortion is considered a freedom and an expression of woman's rights, it seems like a double-edged sword because it is both horrible and is supposedly a battle won in the fight for equality. Personally, I believe in pro-choice, however, I don't think I could ever go through with such a tragic operation. While I do not look down on those women who chose to have abortions, my own personal feelings would be to accept the mistake I and my partner have made and assume the responsibility.

In the case of "The Mother," the abortions seem to have been out of desperation and could not be prevented. The sadness this woman feels is expressed so vividly in her poetry. I could picture a little child being killed. As awful as that may sound, all I envisioned as I read was the useless slaughtering of a baby. It seems so unfair that this woman, who emits a loving attitude towards those children, for whatever reason, should be in such a desperate situation. She wanted those babies but was forced to terminate their existence. All she is left with is the confusion and bewilderment of what they might have one day become. As I read this poem, I also thought of stories I have heard about girls who have gotten pregnant and had abortions. I never felt sorry for these girls because I was angered by the fact that they would allow themselves to get into such a situation as to have to destroy a human life. I still don't feel sorry for these girls. I do, however, feel so sorry for this woman in the poem. *I can't figure out the discrepancy.* I think maybe it is because these girls have never seemed desolate or depressed after I had found out about their abortions. This woman genuinely expressed sorrow and I felt for her a great deal. (Journal VIII)

"The Mother" forces Jeanne to acknowledge contradictory feelings: empathy for the fictitious woman and "all women who are forced to endure the tragedy of abortion" but anger at the "girls" who allow themselves to be vulnerable to an unwanted pregnancy. The speaker in the poem unlocks a whole range of emotions that Jeanne has never observed in young women ("girls"). Perhaps the new knowledge of the complexities involved and her apparent closeness in age to these young women chafe at her own strong sense of self-control and responsibility for her actions expressed in the first and last paragraphs. As feminist critic Marianne Hirsch states, speaking of feminism's "discomfort" with the unpredictability of the female body: "Nothing entangles women more firmly in their bodies than pregnancy, birth, lactation, miscarriage, or the inability to conceive."[1]

Jeanne's unresolved feelings suggest this discomfort. The small group discussion will do little to help her with clear-cut solutions, since the majority of other students grapple with similar uncertainties: How do I reconcile a Catholic upbringing with new claims of self-determination?

How do I integrate responsibility to self with responsibility to others? What about the morality of abortion? Although there are no easy answers here for Jeanne, the group discussion allows for a processing of questions usually overlooked in other classroom contexts.

Her feelings of discomfort continue to intensify as the semester draws to a close with Mary Daly's *Beyond God the Father*. Given the Catholic background of the majority of students at our university, her struggle is not unusual. Jeanne writes:

> A great deal of what she [Mary Daly] said made so much sense to me. As I have said before though, it is hard to admit or come to the realization that a religion which I have been brought up with may have negative implications for me and other women. . . . She states something that I agreed with completely which is: "Part of the problem with this moral ideology is that it became accepted not by men but by women, who hardly have been helped by an ethic which reinforces their abject situation." So often I think that women perpetuate the problem of inequality by not facing or dealing with it. They accept it because it's easier that way. They fear change or they fear being outspoken or radical. They are acting precisely the way men want them to—submissive and accepting of their "position" in society.
>
> Another aspect of Mary Daly's writing which disturbed me greatly was: "Typically, Thomas Aquinas argued that women should be subject to men because 'in man the discretion of reason predominates.'" If respected theologians denounce women's capabilities, it is going to be acknowledged and accepted by society as fact. What a scary thing, how an ignorant man can have such an impact on our world. He is so respected and that statement completely sickens me. . . . One more topic which affected me is the topic of abortion: "One hundred percent of the bishops who oppose the repeal of anti-abortion laws are men and one hundred percent of the people who have abortions are women." It is obvious the decision makers are of the wrong sex.

Jeanne's remarks register the inner turbulence this text provokes among the students. During the seminar meeting some claim to be completely at sea, hanging on to the life raft of religious beliefs nurtured by their family and former teachers. Others, because of an emotional readiness, fearlessly follow Daly's radically new track. Falling into the latter group, Jeanne at one point in her journal addresses Karen, her teacher/ mother, observing the inspirational effect of Mary Daly's teaching on Karen (she had studied with Mary Daly the previous semester) and wishing that her own ideas were as solidified.

During the following semester, this did happen for Jeanne when she in turn became one of the teachers. As I supervised their work, I watched her deepen her analyses of the texts in preparation for the group discussions. In this context, unlike that of prose writing, where she understood the young woman who felt wronged by the priest, she struck me as a very powerful instrument for effecting change in the lives of other women. A summary of her own theory and practice of feminism, written at the end of the semester, traces the distance she traveled in three semesters:

> Feminism was a distant, rarely contemplated subject to me prior to entering college. It has become, however, a large part of my life. The initial spark which set me on the feminist trail, so to speak, was precisely that, education. The course, "Introduction to Feminisms," exposed me to the atrocities of women's existence. . . . Education and knowledge of the atrocious state of women shatters [the] myths which have socialized us. My initial exposure to these myths evoked a great deal of anger and frustration in me. Questions such as "Why haven't I been told this?" and "Who is responsible for this?" plagued me. I had to find out why it was happening. . . . By teaching students who are for the most part ignorant of feminism, I learned that anger was not the solution to the problem. I witnessed a profound change in many of Andrea['s] [the other student teacher] and my students. I learned that in order to accomplish anything, I had to be receptive to other ideas. . . . I know that I cannot change the world singlehandedly, but I also know that I am not going to ignore what is going on around me either.

My ongoing work relationship with Jeanne, who graduated almost two years ago, approaches a new kind of alliance between mothers and daughters, one that conventional pedagogy and male-centered subject matter preclude. Our partnership in "Introduction to Feminisms" paired Jeanne's perspicacity and intelligence with my experience and knowledge in women's studies, allowing each of us to take the lead at different times, each to learn from the other—always within the context of a community of women.

But—for there always is a but—as I round off the last sentence, its utopian ring gives me pause because as one used to teaching and learning in the father's house, I am also used to his rules. Consequently, I can recite a litany of problems that wouldn't arise under "normal" classroom conditions: Collaborative learning can make me uneasy because of the reduced control I have over the way material is presented. At times I am called upon to mediate disagreements among students. Never had I imagined a seminar in which I would be faced with the pain of five students' disclosures of the trauma of having been raped. Some of my radical feminist students claim that I am more the mother of sons than the mother of daughters. Finally, my part-time position among women's studies faculty at the university makes me simultaneously an insider in women's studies, an outsider with regard to the privileges of rank, and a disobedient daughter in the eyes of the Catholic father.

On the plus side, I reap untold benefits as both mother and daughter in a supportive women's studies environment that raises questions considered to be nonquestions elsewhere and that contributes significantly to releasing the untapped power of texts and ourselves. At the same time, I am less tied to the father, since his commitment to me is less binding than to others.

The history of the relationship of Catholic mothers, daughters, and fathers is a long and complicated one. As historian Regine Pernoud explains in *La femme au temps des cathedrales*,[2] the Catholic Church initially served as a liberating force for women who during the first three centuries in Western Europe were among its first beneficiaries (it granted them personhood in a state where the father had the absolute power to deny them life itself) and its most influential proselytizers (Clothilde, for the Franks; Theodelinde, in Northern Italy; Theodosia, in Spain; Berthe de Kent, in England). But—again but—many early Catholic women paid a high price—martyrdom or denial of their sexuality—for their exalted place.

Teaching women's studies on our campus is in some ways similar to the upturns and downdrafts of women's position in the history of the Church. It is an ongoing challenge, with delights and disappointments. For as I remind my Intro students, we are never completely "finished" with either the mother or the father.

NOTES

1. Marianne Hirsch, *The Mother/Daughter Plot* (Bloomington: Indiana University Press, 1989), 166.
2. R. Pernoud, *La femme au temps des cathedrales* (Paris: Edition's Stock, 1980), 18.

EIGHTEEN

Race, Sex, and Spirit: Chicana Negotiations of Catholicism

Theresa Delgadillo

Classroom Scene #1

"Is it a contradiction to be a Chicana feminist lesbian Catholic?" I ask the class. We are reading Cherríe Moraga's *Loving in the War Years,* a narrative that proclaims her faith as well as her lesbianism, feminism, and commitment to Chicana/o movement politics.[1] The hands shoot up.

"Not at all," an African American student responds passionately. "You don't have to go along with everything the Church says to be Christian or to believe in God. I have many gay friends who also belong to church communities. They have a right," she continues. "They have a relationship to God."

"Many people do not go along with everything the Church says, with 'Church rules,'" adds another young woman, a Chicana. "But that doesn't mean that they don't have faith. For example, the Church says that we're not supposed to have sex before marriage, but most people don't follow that. Because I wear a cross around my neck doesn't mean that I do what the Church tells me. And because I do not 'follow all the rules' does not make me less of a Catholic. I can decide what is right for me but I am also a religious person."

Other students nod in agreement.

Classroom Scene #2

We are discussing Ana Castillo's *So Far from God*.[2] Charmed by the narrator and characters, inspired by the activism it describes, touched and angered by the tough lives of the women it portrays, students are, nonetheless, initially hesitant to discuss religion. I present a reading of the funeral scene and some discussion of the character of Doña Felicia.[3]

"I like how this novel shows characters participating in their faith," says a young Chicana student.

A young Asian American student comments on the traditional healing practices described in the novel and notes that forms of these are common to many cultures. He likes that both non-Western and Christian practices appear in the novel. A young Anglo man observes that homeopathic medicine is now widely practiced. Both a Chicana and an Anglo female student address the novel's feminist critique of gender norms. We are off to a great discussion.

I leave the classroom feeling elated about the quality of our discussion. In the hallway, a Chicana student stops me to talk.

"I'm glad we're reading this novel," she tells me, "because it includes all kinds of things that go into the spiritual and it shows many aspects of religion. I'm religious, but that doesn't mean just one thing."

My students' comments suggest that their initial hesitation to speak was caution—either not wanting to be misperceived and, therefore, exoticized or dismissed once again, or feeling strange about discussing religion in the classroom.

Classroom Scene #3

I am a student in a Catholic elementary school. Because we are preparing for confirmation, the parish pastor has come over from the rectory for our catechism lesson. He talks about venial sins and mortal sins. The rules. Several of my classmates either ask a silly question or try to pose clever conundrums to the rules. The pastor sometimes looks exasperated. The discussion gets derailed. We were never a particularly reverent bunch. Years later when I hear George Carlin's comedic routine about just such a scene I laugh in recognition. The rules.

Growing up Chicana, Feminist, and Catholic

I am not entirely surprised by my students' responses to Chicana narratives that deal with feminism, sexuality, and Catholicism. Their readings suggest a more complex relationship to Catholicism than is perhaps commonly assumed, an ongoing negotiation rather than blind obedience.

A passing comment made almost fifteen years ago by a Marxist acquaintance reverberates in my memory. He had just returned from Mexico City, where, on a brief jaunt through some popular tourist sites, he stopped at the shrine of Our Lady of Guadalupe. "Those cunning Spaniards." His remark, rather humorously he thought, suggests that Guadalupe worship is nothing more than a massive fraud perpetrated by the Catholic Church on the Mexican population. "Those cunning Spaniards." In a few words, he had dismissed the faith and practice of an enormous population and of a nation and cultures very much associated with the figure of Guadalupe. He had rendered all of us simply pawns in someone else's history.

His was a glib comment; one that could just as easily have been made by a sophisticated Protestant or a Chicana/o intellectual. Recognition of the hegemonic power of religious institutions, unease or suspicion about the passion of religious faith, and regard for the sober reasoning process of rational thought are common currency in intellectual circles. Unfortunately, they sometimes lead to a sense of intellectual superiority in relation to religion.

When I heard his comment I saw him there in my mind's eye—among fervent brown people. I also saw my mother's room—her print of Guadalupe over the dresser, a rosary hanging from a wall-mounted votive candle nearby. I remembered the moment during my older sister's wedding ceremony when she and her new husband stood before the altar to Guadalupe and offered her flowers. I remembered countless Sunday masses with my parents at Our Lady of Guadalupe Church and the deep sense of satisfaction that hearing the mass in Spanish always gave me.

Although my friend and I shared many of the same goals and ideals and were committed to the same causes, his comment revealed a gap between our respective experiences of nation, race, gender, and spirituality. The question that arose in my mind was similar to that which

Richard Rodriguez asks in *Days of Obligation:* "Why do we assume Spain made up the story?"[4]

That my encounter with the import of religion and spirituality in the lives of Chicana/os and Mexicana/os in the United States began in a Catholic childhood, grew through activism for social justice and contact with liberation theology in the Nicaraguan revolution, and has now become the focus of my scholarship speaks to the possibility for spiritual discourse to register in multiple valences, each inflected with particular meaning. Chicana/o engagement with the spiritual is complicated. For me, even, to represent the issue as one between the white socialist and the Chicana socialist doesn't adequately capture the whole picture because I also remember my Mexican father's suspicion of Church authority, his deep-rooted Mexican anticlericalism.

Yet we belonged to a community who gathered together each Sunday for the mass in Spanish at Holy Trinity–Our Lady of Guadalupe Church in Milwaukee. This church was both a spiritual and a social center for a Mexicana/o and Chicana/o working-class community drawn to that cold, northern locale by the city's industrial economy. While some succeeded in securing unionized employment, many, my father included, labored in the city's many nonunion industries. My father worked fourteen-hour days at a tannery until he retired. My mother raised and kept house for eight children while also working thirty-hour weeks as a seamstress or janitor. I recall Sundays with much fondness, perhaps because, given my parents' work schedules, it was one of the few times we had together. We went to the mass in Spanish; afterwards my parents often conversed with friends and acquaintances on the steps of the church. On the way home we stopped first at the Mexican store for carnitas and tortillas and second at the Mexican bakery for pan dulce. At home, we ate and rested. Those Sundays felt like moments of grace in our lives. Although Our Lady of Guadalupe was no longer our official parish—we had moved two miles away—in many ways, it remained our spiritual home.

The Chicana/o movement came into Guadalupe Church. One year I participated in the performance of an Aztec-inspired dance procession for the offering of gifts at Christmas mass. Our dance group was also invited to perform the procession at the cathedral. I can remember how it felt to be there but was unable to see much of the interior of the cathedral—Sister Carol had insisted that I dance without my eyeglasses because they were not Aztec. This was not the first, or last, of my encounters with the issue of the authentic. In contrast to Holy Trinity–Our Lady of Guadalupe, with its deep brown wooden pews, altars, and moldings—the cathedral felt bright and light. Unfamiliar space and unfamiliar parishioners. I felt like I was on display.

In those years, the church also provided some support for the United Farm Workers representatives who came to Milwaukee seeking to expand the lettuce boycott. One of my older brothers invited me to participate in the picketing of local stores, and, for one summer, I went as often as I could. My ongoing link to Catholicism owes much to the mission of living the faith that my church, in those years, conveyed. Sunday homilies were vibrant, thought provoking, and sometimes, if my parents' reactions were any indication, controversial. Our young, progressive priest's sermons often addressed issues of social justice.

My introduction to feminist activism, however, was not through the Church. The women's movement of the late 1960s and early 1970s had succeeded in altering the terms of the discussion. A nationwide movement in support of the Equal Rights Amendment had emerged, as had activism to support and expand a woman's right to choice in reproductive decisions. Affirmative action programs allowed women to enter professions and occupations from which they had been previously excluded. And women's studies programs and departments began to take shape on campuses across the country. Feminism was a growing movement, and although Catholics and the Church had been a force in critical reevaluation and activism on other issues of social justice, I found debates, discussion, and activism on women's questions outside the Church.

When the Nicaraguan revolution and the Salvadoran liberation struggle broke out in 1979, I became involved in the movement in solidarity with these struggles. Over the next ten years, I met many clergy and religious individuals who participated in the solidarity movement as an expression of their religious convictions. They gave time, space, and funds to people in struggle at a critical moment. They sought to end U.S. support for war in Central America. In Central America, liberation theology was a motivating force in the effort to build a society fueled, not by capitalist market relations, but instead by social, economic, and political equality for all. While the Catholic Church did not speak with one voice on this question, a discussion did open up in the Church, perhaps more widespread than on previous issues of social justice, that revealed a divide between hierarchical and participatory conceptions of religious activity. Once again, both the power and the potential of religious communities to engage in important social change became evident.

Contemporary Dialogues

No community is ideal. Yet I came away from the experience of the solidarity movement with a better sense of the struggles within communities that attempt to live up to their ideals as well as the existence of multiple communities within the Catholic Church. I think I came to understand and intuit how my family's religious choices and practices shaped a faith both responsive to them and in which they were participants: my sister's decision to change her parish, my mother's private devotion to Guadalupe, my family's enduring connection to Our Lady of Guadalupe parish.

This did not make it any easier to deal with the sight of a Latino man wielding a banner of Our Lady of Guadalupe against the human barricade in which I stood, defending the right of women to receive an abortion. It was 1991, and Operation Rescue had arrived in Milwaukee to try to shut down the city's reproductive rights clinics. The Catholic district attorney seemed slow to act against Operation Rescue and lenient when he did. The women of my family were divided on this issue, but we respected each other's right to make an individual choice. When I saw that man, I felt angry. At first, I wanted him to go away. Then I wanted to tell him that he had no right to invoke Guadalupe in his cause. I wanted him to know that his version of Guadalupe was not mine.[5] And then I realized that his understanding was *not* mine. Despite the Christian right's attempt to lay sole claim to the power of religious discourse in recent years, and to wield that power in the service of a right-wing agenda, religious experience and belief in the United States are much more heterogeneous than the right represents, particularly for communities of color.

In text, in practice, and in belief, Chicana/o religious and spiritual matters, as well as manners, are inseparable from questions of national/

ethnic/racial identity. Cherríe Moraga writes: "I had closed my heart to the passionate pull of such faith that promised no end to the pain. I grew white. Fought to free myself from my culture's claim on me. It seemed I had to step outside my familia to see what we as a people were doing and suffering. This is my politics. This is my writing."[6]

Her "growing white" in this passage suggests her anger and frustration with a racialized identity in which Chicana/o, Catholic, and suffering are conflated. "Growing white" is also her flight from that particular understanding of identity in the act of passing—made possible by her light skin color. Yet she reveals passing to have been both subtly beneath the surface of her consciousness and voicelessly conveyed to her by racial hierarchies among Chicana/os.

To understand both the ways in which that suffering is imposed and the ways in which it remains unchallenged within Chicana/o communities, Moraga explores her fear, her racial identity, her sexual identity, and her own sense of faith and spirituality. In doing so she separates what has been conflated while also recognizing how faith, politics, and art are intertwined. Moraga tells us that her willingness to engage in that task sets her apart from other Chicana/os, has made her the "outsider" that many "fear."[7]

Although Moraga articulates an affinity with Catholicism in *Loving in the War Years,* especially in the figure of Our Lady of Guadalupe, fourteen years later as she writes *Waiting in the Wings,* she wonders if she has betrayed her infant son by baptizing him in the Catholic Church: "One year ago, I relinquished Rafaelito to his godparents at the baptismal fount of a humble East Los Angeles church. It is the church of the poor, and the presiding priest, a pastor of the poor. Still, when they return Rafaelito's newly christened self back into my arms, I feel I have betrayed him. I hold him tight against the breast of an unanswered prayer. I want to protect my son from deceit, from the failure of male gods and god-fearing males."[8]

Moraga's 1983 articulation of a racial and sexual identity involves her recuperation of the figure of Our Lady of Guadalupe and her reevaluation of her own mother's strength and survival skills. In 1997, however, as she describes the unease, rejection, and hostility that she and her partner repeatedly encounter in the process of becoming co-mothers to a premature boy whose early fragile state inspired fear and worry, her increasing sense of alienation from Catholicism finds expression.[9]

Moraga is not alone. Lara Medina also writes of her sense of distance and exclusion from the Catholic Church in "Los Espíritus Siguen Hablando: Chicana Spiritualities."[10] Medina decided to leave "the patriarchal Eurocentrism of the church, as the contradictions were too great to reconcile."[11] For many years, I attended mass only when I visited my family, a shared experience I still cherish, or joined in commemorating the important life events of family, friends, and acquaintances—baptisms, quinceñeras, weddings. Catholicism still pulls me. I have witnessed individuals and communities define its meaning for themselves, particularly women—often through popular religious practices. I value the way that spiritual communities bring people together to act for the better. Yet I have also seen many women leave the Church to join or form other spiritual communities. While women, young and old, can now serve in the mass, we are still excluded from ordination. While many parishes have lesbian and gay ministries, the Church will not sanction the union of gay couples. Thinking back on my students' comments, I am struck by their optimism as well as their individualism. Will they succeed in making Catholicism more inclusive and feminist? Or will they continue to live their faith in contrast to official Church proclamations? These are the negotiations that Chicanas still face.

NOTES

1. Cherríe Moraga, *Loving in the War Years: Lo que nunca pasó por sus labios* (Boston: South End Press, 1983).

2. Ana Castillo, *So Far from God* (New York: Plume, 1994).

3. For further discussion of *So Far from God*, see Theresa Delgadillo, "Forms of Chicana Feminist Resistance: Hybrid Spirituality in Ana Castillo's *So Far from God*," *Modern Fiction Studies* 44 (1998): 888–916.

4. Richard Rodriguez, *Days of Obligation: An Argument with My Mexican Father* (New York: Viking, 1992), 19.

5. For further discussion of Guadalupe's meaning in Chicana/o and Latina/o lives, see Ana Castillo, ed., *Goddess of the Americas: Writings on the Virgin of Guadalupe* (New York: Riverhead, 1996).

6. Moraga, *Loving in the War Years,* ii.

7. Ibid., iii.

8. Cherríe Moraga, *Waiting in the Wings: Portrait of a Queer Mother-hood* (Ithaca, N.Y.: Firebrand Books, 1997), 108.

9. My work-in-progress analyzes the shifts in consciousness regarding religion, politics, and feminism in contemporary Chicana/o literature, film, and drama more fully.

10. Lara Medina, "Los Espíritus Siguen Hablando: Chicana Spiritualities," in *Living Chicana Theory,* ed. Carla Trujillo (Berkeley: Third Woman Press, 1998), 189–213.

11. Ibid., 190.

NINETEEN

A Most Noble City of Ladies: University Students Explore Their Catholic Identity through Literature by French Women

Henrik Borgstrom

Last year I found myself in the rather peculiar position of being asked to step in as chairperson of my university's women's studies program while the regular director took a temporary leave of absence. I call it peculiar partly because as a white male I am always already inscribed in that traditional patriarchal paradigm which most women's studies curricula mean to deconstruct. However, what made the situation even more interesting was the fact that my university is affiliated with an order of the Roman Catholic Church, the presence of which is highly visible on campus. It was this that prompted a fellow colleague from a state university to ask me with unsubtle astonishment, "How is it possible to run a women's studies program at a Catholic university? Don't the two cancel each other out?" Little did I realize then that my colleague's facetious question would launch a quandary that was to loom over me for an entire academic year.

It was during my brief tenure as chair of said program that I taught for the first time an undergraduate survey course with the rather sweeping title "Literature by French Women through the Ages." This constituted one of a handful of elective courses with equally sweeping titles that together made up the recently devised women's studies program at my institution. As my primary concern with this course remained my own paradoxical position as a male, I entered my classroom on the first day aptly armed with an artillery of poststructuralist disclaimers, ready to validate myself in the eyes of my twelve female students. I quickly came to realize, however, that these young women had little to no interest at all in an academic discussion about maleness, mine or anyone else's. To my intrigued surprise, the recurrent topic of class discussions was not women's identity with regard to men per se, but women's identity with respect to the Catholic Church. In retrospect this should not have been altogether unexpected, since the majority of women writers that we were studying wrote in a francophone society strongly dominated by Catholicism. Subsequently, within the first few weeks of the semester, my students transformed this somewhat superficially titled survey course into an ongoing personal examination of women and women's literature in the shadow of the Catholic Church.

The focus of the course was a series of ten texts written by women in the French language over nine centuries. As we averaged one writer and one century for every ten days of the semester, there remained necessarily several historical gaps in our literary survey; nonetheless, the Catholic Church seemed to leave its trace in all but a couple of texts. Consequently, the fiction proved to be an opportune portal to a serious examination of the ecclesiastical status of women. Whether the texts praised, denounced, or conspicuously ignored the Church, students could explore their own notions and struggles with Catholicism through various perspectives provided to them by women in a number of different social and historical contexts. What I shall present in this essay are some of the more poignant issues raised by my students over the course of the semester. Although I cannot claim that this course resolved the fundamental conflicts between feminism and Catholicism, the texts seemed to provide many of my students with their first opportunity to examine and discuss their faith from a feminist perspective.

The majority of the female students in the class had, by their own admission, grown up in the traditions of the Catholic Church, and all students in the class, whether or not they had chosen to remain with the

Church, were consistently exposed to it by virtue of their daily life on campus, where liturgical invocations begin most public meetings and a portion of the students' required courses are taught by priests. Nearly all the students were in their third or fourth year of study and had thus completed their three-course religious studies requirement before entering my class. As a result, the majority of young women in my course had a good knowledge of Christianity and the Catholic Church, and most had probably given some serious thought to their own role in the Catholic tradition. I shall focus in particular on discussions that emerged in our treatment of two specific authors, writing on two different continents about six hundred years apart, whose works provided a kind of dialectic frame for the course itself: Christine de Pizan, whose writings date from the beginning of the fifteenth century in France, and Denise Boucher, a twentieth-century dramatist and television writer from Montreal. The first upholds in her works the glories of the Catholic faith, the sanctity of marriage, and the supreme importance of feminine virtue; the latter writes against the patriarchy of the Church, condemning its institution for closing the door to women's liberty and power of expression. However different in style and content, the two texts allowed my students to consider a traditionally male-dominated faith system through a feminist lens.

Although Christine de Pizan is not the first documented woman writer in French literary history, she is the first one to have left behind a relatively comprehensive collection of historical material concerning her life, her education, and her political and literary opinions. Christine professed consistently her singular faith in God as she carved out in her fiction a privileged place for women within the structure of the Catholic tradition.[1] In her allegorical work the *Book of the City of Ladies (Livre de la Cité des Dames)*, completed in 1405, Christine recounts in first person how she is visited by three divine creatures calling themselves the daughters of God.[2] Embodying the noble ideals of Reason, Rectitude, and Justice, the three Ladies commission Christine to build a holy city for the glorification and defense of women throughout history. Over the city will govern the sovereign paragon of female virtue, the Virgin Mary. Despite certain obscure allusions, my students seemed immediately drawn in by Christine's straightforward literary style and her blunt criticism of such seemingly modern issues as sexual violence, spousal abuse, and socially sanctioned misogyny.

Nowhere in the *Book of the City of Ladies* does Christine condemn the Catholic Church. In fact, in each of the three segments of this work, the author stresses the importance of feminine virtue and respect for the Christian sacraments. She does, however, dispel any popular or canonical assertions that women hold a lesser place in earthly or heavenly realms. Christine also does not condemn men in general, and aside from a few ironic jabs at the more misogynist texts of the popular literary canon of her day, the tenor of the entire text is optimistic. She focuses less on the unfairness of the patriarchal system than on the individual historic accomplishments of women. Indeed, my students seemed to appreciate the positive tone of this work, created in an era when women's freedom of expression was negligible. In the first segment of the book, Christine insists that God created men and women as perfect spiritual equals, both modeled upon God's own divinity. She then sets out to prove that women are indeed capable of excelling in matters of virtue, strength, intelligence, courage, and faith. At a time when the Church acknowledged far more male than female saints, and when the pope did not allow much visibility for women in its institutions, Christine set out, through literature, to construct her own holy institution, a divine kingdom built in the spirit of reason and justice, conceived specifically and exclusively for women. Although the Church of the twenty-first century is considerably more welcoming to women, none of the female students in my class had ever seen a woman presiding or even serving at the university's baccalaureate mass, nor had they ever seen a woman acting as their university president. The proposal in the *Book of the City of Ladies* to create a feminine space within the context of the Catholic system therefore did not seem irrelevant to my students, despite its having been written almost six hundred years before they were born.

Refuting traditional notions of class hierarchy that served as the primary basis for social relationships in the fifteenth century, Christine opens the gates of her poetic city to all women willing to realize their feminine potential. For Christine, true nobility resides in the soul; therefore, all persons, regardless of their social caste, may through their own actions attain a state of grace. As E. J. Richards points out in the introduction to his English translation, "[Christine] transposes the dignity afforded to noble women in the late medieval French class structure to women who have proven their worthiness through their achievements, whether military, political, cultural, or religious."[3] This insistence on personal achievement over innate worthiness seemed to strike a chord with several of the young women in my class, for whom individual freedoms seemed limited by their Catholic environment. Two students, whom I shall call Allison and Erika, were particularly vocal in their reactions to Christine's work.

Allison's interest was primarily philosophical. In the final stages of completing her undergraduate honors thesis on Sartrean existentialism, she had previously admitted to me that she was often troubled by Sartre's preoccupation with the absence of God but was simultaneously drawn to his notion that all persons are individually responsible for creating their identity through their own actions. Without proposing that Christine de Pizan was some kind of premodern precursor to existentialism, Allison saw the *Book of the City of Ladies* as suggesting a possible reconciliation of two ideals that, at that particular time in her life, seemed mutually exclusive.

I concede that the convocation of Christine de Pizan with Jean-Paul Sartre may be contrived and somewhat simplistic, yet the question that Sartre seems to have posed for Allison was fundamental: How might a woman define herself through her accomplishments against an institution that had already established certain limits in terms of her vocation, personal choices, and ecclesiastical role? Any student of existentialism would no doubt reply that she would not be able to do so without compromising her existential freedom of choice and would therefore always act in what Sartre described as *bad faith*. For Sartre, organized religion and existential freedom are incompatible. Christine's City of Ladies, however, exists to celebrate in Christian glory the personal accomplishments of all women. In fact, Christine does not limit herself to those women who have been officially sanctified by the Church. Alongside the traditionally acknowledged saints of the Catholic canon, she includes such controversial figures as Semiramis, the warrior queen of Babylonia, and Thamiris, the mythological ruler of the Amazons, neither of whom was Christian or even particularly scrupulous. Christine seems to suggest in her work that a woman of any age and background enjoys the individual freedom to act to a limitless potential and that God will celebrate her for her achievements.

Early in the *Book of the City of Ladies,* Christine reinterprets the traditional Catholic paradigm of sin and redemption by placing it within a positive and specifically feminine framework. As Allison pointed out in a general class discussion about the role women have played within the Christian tradition, most negative attitudes surrounding the female sex play themselves out around the scriptural arch-mother of humankind, Eve. Allison was quick to note that each time our culture wishes to emphasize the shamefulness of the original sin, most of the blame seems to fall on Eve, the temptress, the seductress, the fundamentally weak link. On the other hand, whenever the Christian tradition introduces the possibility of salvation through Jesus, attention usually shifts to the tragic father figure, Adam. As Saint Paul writes to the young churches of the Roman Empire, whereas all die through Adam, all find eternal life in Christ. Since the beginning of the Christian tradition, the fundamental balance of sin and redemption has been governed by male figures.

Christine refines this paradigm by casting it in the persons of Eve and Mary. Divine Reason tells the narrator at the beginning of the first segment, "Man [. . .] gained more through Mary than he lost through Eve when humanity was conjoined to the Godhead, which would never have taken place if Eve's misdeed had not occurred."[4] Although Christine was not the first nor the last writer to depict the Christian cycle in terms of Eve and Mary, this was the first time that most of my students had ever considered the founding principle of their faith within a feminine framework. Christine underscores the idea that beyond God, it was two women who initiated the Christian phenomena of sin and salvation. This concept seemed to resonate with almost every one of my students, most of whom had visualized their Christian tradition only through its male representatives. It was as if many of them felt for the first time included in a Christian tradition for which they had always been spectators and not positive actors.

If Eve's action is understood as an archetypal expression of free will—the first recorded instance of existential choice—Christine de Pizan valorizes it by emphasizing the subsequent possibility of redemption offered through Mary. My students unanimously agreed with the theological hypothesis that God created human beings free to choose between good and evil. They subsequently concluded that Eve's original misdeed did not in fact damn humankind forever but rather allowed successive generations of humans to choose rightly and thereby join themselves to the glory of God. Christine's interpretation of this legendary first choice graces Eve with a sense of independent agency rarely acknowledged in Scripture. Likewise, the women that Christine immortalized in her text were chosen, not on the basis on some universal feminine essence of virtue, but rather because of specific deeds that singled them out as exemplary. My students seemed struck by Christine's apparent juxtaposition of feminist independence with the Christian canon. Her text suggests that a woman's spiritual capacities need not be limited by a canonical structure arbitrated by men. Indeed, it proposes a feminine universe based on individual women's choices that remains nonetheless compatible with the Catholic tradition. In response to Allison's dilemma, then, Christine's text seems to suggest that, despite the earthly patriarchy, a woman's individual accomplishments are not bound by man-made institutions, as God will ultimately recognize, protect, and glorify all women who realize their full potential.

Whereas Allison's interest related to an abstract reconciliation between her understanding of existential freedom and the Catholic faith system she did not wish to abandon, her classmate Erika's comments revealed a concern with more practical issues. Freely admitting that her personal views did not always conform with those of the Vatican, she looked upon the pope somewhat as a benign grandfather whom she continued to love and respect, despite what she referred to as "irritatingly outdated" views on abortion, sexuality, and the ordination of women. Like any number of Catholic women in the United States, Erika had resigned herself to the kind of theological equivocation that seems to perplex so many non-Catholics. A dedicated participant in the campus ministry programs, she considered the Catholic Church her spiritual home; yet faced with certain irreconcilable discrepancies between the Church's stance and her own, she would simply shrug her shoulders, as if to suppress certain guilt under the hope that one day, as she told her classmates, the holy fathers would wake up and join the twenty-first century. Needless to say, Christine de Pizan's text does not touch in the least on canonical questions concerning abortion and sexuality. It does, however, acknowledge the underlying uncertainties of the position of women within the Catholic Church. By validating a feminine space within an otherwise masculine system, the *Book of the City of Ladies* seemed to provide Erika with a sense of feminist solidarity that allowed her to dialogue with her peers, not to mention with the antiestablishment views of a fifteenth-century career writer, regarding the contradictory nature of her relationship with her faith and her church. This dialogue may not have resolved her inner conflict, but she did later mention to me that it made her feel less like a "bad Catholic."

In many ways, the *Book of the City of Ladies* was quite a safe text for my students, in that it allowed them to explore the possibility of creating a feminine space within the already established Christian structure. Christine sought, not to break down the existing tradition, but rather to construct a feminine realm that could peacefully coexist with it. After this text, the class examined a series of other works that equally left the Church more or less intact; from Marguerite de Navarre's *Heptameron,* with its bawdy attacks on dissolute monks intermixed with a neo-Platonic discourse on Christian love; to the inimitable heroines of Mesdames de Lafayette, de Duras, and de Graffigny, who end their days in chaste seclusion; to various short texts by Colette, Marguerite Duras, and others that barely mention the Church at all. The final text of the semester, however, Denise Boucher's 1978 play *When Faeries Thirst (Les fées ont soif),* not only mentions the Catholic Church but makes a concerted effort to break down certain foundational beliefs of the Christian tradition.[5]

Like the *Book of the City of Ladies,* Boucher's play is an allegorical foray into the struggles women face in finding their identity in a world dominated by patriarchy and the Catholic tradition. Contrary to Christine, however, Boucher shows little restraint in her criticism of the Church. The piece caused quite a stir when it opened at the Théâtre du Nouveau Monde in Montreal in an era when the feminist movement was just beginning to take root in Quebec. Boucher's controversial portrayal of the Virgin Mary as a whitewashed prison for Christian women everywhere prompted the Archbishop of Montreal to call for a general boycott of the production. Predictably, the scandal only served to heighten the popularity of the play, which subsequently ran for two months to standing ovations. *When Faeries Thirst* is composed rather like a vaudeville variety act, where two archetypal women—Mary, the sexless housewife/mother, and Magdalen, the "fallen woman"/whore—play out generalized feminine anxieties in short dramatic scenes, intimate monologues, and songs that are often humorous and biting. On a raised platform above these two stands a third actress who speaks her lines from within a large painted plaster cast of the Virgin Mary, the likes of which can be seen in churches and garden shrines all over Quebec. As Judith Miller states in her commentary on the play, "In the case of either of these two archetypes, virgin or whore, women are set up for the benefit of men and male-dominated institutions. . . . The Virgin Mary is the key representational figure of this oppression, the major cultural sign of male domination."[6] Like Christine's holy city, Boucher's text and performance are exclusively female, countering the established patriarchy by allowing visibility solely to women. Nevertheless, despite several unsympathetic critiques to the contrary, the work does not reject men categorically; rather, it calls out to men to behold, perhaps even participate in, the creation of a new feminine universe, as the three women on stage systematically reject the symbolic chains that hold them to their traditional roles within the established social order.

The scene sparking the liveliest discussion in class was doubtless the one that lay at the heart of the social controversy surrounding the initial production of the play. Approximately two-thirds into the text, the three women collectively perform a ritualized rape, as the enormous shadow of a bird descends over the one of them who is being victimized. Boucher's stage directions insist on the significance of the Christian symbolism in this image, as if to show Mary being forcibly overcome in order to conceive and bear the savior of Man. Contrary to the reaction I was expecting from my students (and no doubt another indication of the generation gap existing between me and them), the young women in my class were only minimally shocked by this image, which most of them found rather heavy-handed and silly. Instead, their attention turned once again to the question of personal freedom. If one is to understand Boucher's assertion that the only feminine participant in the Christian holy family is primally a glorified rape victim forced by God to conceive, how might modern women negotiate their personal independence in the face of their Catholic faith? Although reactions to this sweeping rhetorical question were numerous and varied, I shall limit my focus to those of one of my more outspoken students, a third-year undergraduate whom I shall call Mona.

Mona related to the class that as a child she and her friends had all shared a schoolgirl fantasy to join a convent and become nuns. Several of the other students in the class admitted a similar childhood dream. For Mona, however, as for most of her peers, fantasies of the monastic life dissipated at puberty, when the ideals of self-denial no longer seemed feasible nor desirable. Nonetheless, the sexless image of Mary, paradoxically both virgin and mother, is held up as an ideal for young Catholic girls from an early age. Like the housewife in Boucher's play, Mona expressed the serious frustration she had felt repeatedly in her life in trying to come to terms with this impossible and, as Boucher writes, "bleached-out" ideal.[7] As the Statue tells Mary a few minutes into the performance, "You've seen too many pictures and statues of me. Too much blackmail, too many threats, too many promises have stuck you with my image."[8] For a young Catholic woman, it can be rather exasperating when the feminine paragons of the Church are fundamentally impossible to live up to. Mona identified with the characters in Boucher's play because they represent women who, like her, are trying to come to terms with their own personal strengths against the backdrop of a male-dictated iconography of femininity.

In the final sequence of the play, the actress playing the Statue crawls out of the cast's abdominal cavity and joins the other two women in a neutral space at the front of the stage. The plaster statue is then raised slowly into the flies. With the plastic icon of an unrealizable ideal out of the picture, the women collectively represent the rebirth of a modern woman. The three women have abandoned the metaphorical male-imposed markers of society's expectations of them and now stand poised on the threshold of a new, heretofore unshaped, feminine identity. Together they address the audience, asking us simply to *imagine*— that is, to bring to life—a new female being. On the surface, Boucher seems to suggest that only by shedding the rigid emblems of the Church and society can a woman attain any sense of personal freedom. As our class discussion revealed, however, this liberating gesture need not necessitate a violent rejection of Christian faith.

Although in a later version of Boucher's collectively written text, the Statue of the Virgin explodes at the end of the play, the 1997 translation we used in class, which is based on the original 1978 manuscript, leaves the Statue very much intact. Moreover, the Statue's departure from the stage is not violent but quite gentle and therefore, as my students suggested, reminiscent of the Assumption, when Mary's body is lifted to heaven to be forever joined with God. Consequently, what is left on the stage is the material human being, faced with the reality of creating a new self beyond the limitations of an inimitable ideal. Also, with the actress playing the Statue standing at the front of the stage in the final tableau, one might say that a vital essence of Mary, having emerged from her artificially imposed persona, plays a critical and visible role in the collective creation of the newly born woman. Figuratively born of the Virgin and presumably conceived by the Holy Spirit, this woman can be seen as the daughter of God in human form. It is this feminine messianic figure who will lead humanity toward a new world order where women are free to "exult in living."[9] As the class discovered in their collective analysis of the text's stage directions, despite the iconoclastic tone of Boucher's text, the Christian framework is not utterly evacuated from the play's ultimate rite of feminine re-creation. As in Christine's *Book of the City of Ladies,* the supreme Christian woman figure is integrated, albeit indirectly, into the feminist utopia.

At the end of fifteen weeks, we were probably no closer than we had been at the beginning of the course to reconciling the essential contradictoriness of feminism and Catholicism. That was not, after all, our primary objective. However, for several weeks in an academic and literary setting, a small group of women had the opportunity to engage in open discussions about the choices and questions they often face when imagining their identity in the context of the Church. As agnostic as our society and our academic institutions tend to be, it is quite revealing to hear young people debating fundamental questions of their belief systems. Now that my interim period as chair of our women's studies program is drawing to a close, I reflect upon my colleague's ironic query about the plausibility of such a curriculum at a Catholic university, and I am immediately struck by the obviousness of the answer. Not only is it possible and important to teach women's studies at a Catholic institution, one might even say that it is advantageous because, in all likelihood, the majority of female students in a highly visible Catholic academic setting are already dialoguing with issues of their role and identity with respect to the Church. The easiest response in a nonreligious setting would perhaps be to simply reject the religious structure and to call for a feminine identity conceived in the absence of the Church. It is a proposition much more challenging, however, to consider an individual feminine identity that can coexist with, although not necessarily conform to, the established Catholic tradition. So, as my students continue to negotiate their identity as women and as Catholics beyond the classroom walls, I remind them of Christine's final exhortation to the ladies of her fortified city, "Rejoice and act well."[10]

NOTES

1. For more information on the biography and literary production of Christine de Pizan, I suggest Charity Cannon Willard, *Christine de Pizan: Her Life and Works* (New York: Persea Books, 1984).

2. Christine de Pizan, *Book of the City of Ladies,* trans. Earl Jeffrey Richards (New York: Persea Books, 1998).

3. Earl Jeffrey Richards, introduction to ibid., xxxiv.

4. Pizan, *City of Ladies,* 24.

5. Denise Boucher, *When Faeries Thirst,* trans. Judith Graves Miller, in *Plays by French and Francophone Women: A Critical Anthology,* ed. Christiane P. Makward and Judith G. Miller (Ann Arbor: University of Michigan Press, 1997). For more complete biographical information on Boucher, as well as details of the 1978 and 1989 productions of this play, see Lise Gauvin's introduction to *Les fées ont soif* (Montreal: Hexagone, 1989).

6. Judith Miller, introduction to Boucher, *When Faeries Thirst,* 127.

7. Boucher, *When Faeries Thirst,* 134.

8. Ibid., 138.

9. Ibid., 166.

10. Pizan, *City of Ladies,* 257.

TWENTY

Evolving Feminisms

Sally Barr Ebest

I grew up believing I was Scotch-Irish—half Scotch and half Irish. I retained this belief until I met my husband, who explained that this was merely a euphemism used by Protestant immigrants from Northern Ireland to avoid being stereotyped as Irish Catholic. Although I no longer attended the Presbyterian church, I strongly embraced my Irishness. Part of this acceptance was due to my husband, Ron, who is half Irish, completing a doctorate in Irish studies, and knowledgeable about both Irish history and Catholicism. The other part was due to his religion, for he was raised in the Roman Catholic Church.

What impressed me about the Catholic Church—and differentiated it from my conception of Protestantism—was the Church's emphasis on forgiveness. As an outsider, I saw this element as symbolized by the confessional. In my eyes, Catholics did not have to bear the brunt of their so-called original (or continual) sin; they had the comfort of confession and forgiveness, which they could receive every week, if not every month (although I couldn't imagine confessing some of my sins to a male priest!). I saw this sacrament embodied in the Catholic family I married into, and so I came to respect the Church.

Eventually, these interests began to filter into my teaching and research. After years of teaching seminars on feminist pedagogy and contemporary American women writers, I began adding Irish American women to the readings. When I felt sufficiently educated on the subject, I developed an undergraduate seminar on Irish American women writers. As Ron and I discussed what books and authors should comprise the course, we also considered supplementary readings, for I wanted to explore the intersection of feminism and Catholicism. After much research we determined that no single book would meet our needs and thus began plans to develop our own. Out of this emerged *Reconciling Catholicism and Feminism?*

While I was teaching the course, the essays started rolling in. Reading them was extremely beneficial, for they helped deepen my understanding of the Church and provided answers, insights, and focal points for class discussions. This was an interactive process, for as I taught the course I was tracing my students' growing understanding of feminism and correlating it with their much greater knowledge of Catholicism, with the intent—which I shared with them—that I would center this final chapter on our mutually (re)conceived definitions of both feminism and Catholicism gleaned from our discussions and from the daily response journals we wrote and exchanged.[1]

I grouped the novels chronologically and, within certain time frames, by focus. Mary McCarthy's *The Group*, Maureen Howard's *Bridgeport Bus,* and Mary Gordon's *Final Payments* focus primarily on individual women struggling to define themselves, whereas Elizabeth Cullinan's *House of Gold,* Joyce Carol Oates's *We Were the Mulvaneys,* Alice McDermott's *Charming Billy,* and Anna Quindlen's *One True Thing* examine the changing roles and relationships of wives, mothers, and daughters within the family unit. My purpose in offering this course was to introduce undergraduates to the novels of Irish American women, to discuss the definitions of feminism illustrated by these writers, and to explore the influence of Catholicism on these definitions. My purpose in writing this chapter is to trace my students' evolving understanding of feminism and how they reconciled it with their Catholic beliefs.

The Search for Self in *The Group, Bridgeport Bus,* and *Final Payments*

"Irish-American Women Writers" attracted six young women ranging in age from eighteen to thirty. All had traces of Irish ancestry and four of the six were Catholic. On the first day, after establishing our common backgrounds, I asked how they defined *feminism*. Through the students' responses, we discovered that the class members represented a variety of understandings and beliefs. Rebecca and Stephanie stated outright that although they were Catholic, their feminist beliefs could best be expressed by the fact that they were pro-choice. Fawn, a Southern Baptist, Charlotte, an agnostic who had once considered converting to Catholicism, and Julie, a Catholic, defined *feminism* as the belief that women should be paid and treated equally. Such self-descriptors placed these young women among what Whelehan terms "liberal feminists"— those who readily "support women's equality in the workplace and in law" but avoid calling themselves feminists, dissociate themselves "from any hint of 'extremism' and have confidence that, if most of women's demands have not already been met, . . . they will be achieved by lobbying and reason."[2] Easily the most conservative and traditional Catholic of the group was Heather, who admitted that she was not a feminist and that she had never considered what the term meant to her.

Mary McCarthy's 1963 novel, *The Group,* provided a good starting point for defining feminism. In exploring the aspirations of seven female graduates of the Vassar class of '31, McCarthy juxtaposes what Janet Kalven terms "prefeminist" desires for a meaningful career and a happy marriage with the mores and realities of American society in the 1930s. In the process, McCarthy introduces the reader to formerly taboo subjects such as birth control, women's sexual pleasure, adultery, impotence, mental illness, homosexuality, spouse abuse, and the ubiquitous double standard. Among the postfeminist generation, the existence of these issues has been taken for granted. Consequently, encountering them within the context of a novel helped to raise the students' awareness of the rights they had inherited as well as the necessity for continued vigilance.

When McCarthy's antagonist, Norinne, visits a doctor to seek advice about her husband's impotence, she reports that the doctor asked "whether I wanted to have children. . . . When I said no, I didn't, he practically booted me out of the office. He told me I should consider myself lucky that my husband didn't want intercourse. Sex wasn't necessary for a woman, he said."[3] Stephanie was irritated by this stance. "If women are not supposed to enjoy sex," she wrote, "then they are merely instruments to be used for the pleasure of men, and in return are viewed as objects rather than humans with feelings and emotions of their own. Also, it would then mean that the only reason a woman should engage in sex is for the purpose of procreation, while men are allowed to have sex for physical pleasure alone."

On the subject of sex, my twenty-first-century students were otherwise conservative, believing it should be postponed until marriage. Heather found McCarthy's description of Dottie's first sexual encounter shocking. "I never expected to read anything like that," she wrote. "The scene sounded very romantic even though I can't quite understand Dottie's reasoning behind losing her virginity [with a man she barely knew]. Why did she even want to do it?" Despite condemnation by the Church, these students believed in the right and necessity of the use of artificial birth control by married couples. Thus, they were intrigued by McCarthy's treatment of the subject. Fawn noted that when birth control is mentioned by one of the male characters, he attributes its use only to "adulteresses, mistresses, prostitutes, and the like," as opposed to respectable married women. Similarly, Julie was surprised when McCarthy's protagonist, Kay, declares that "birth control . . . was for those who know how to use it and value it—the educated classes."[4] In her response journal, Julie retorted: "This seems ridiculous to me and probably to most people in my generation because people in the U.S. are huge advocates of birth control, especially for the lower class." Needless to say, the students were appalled when I pointed out that birth control had been illegal in this country until the 1930s and, worse, that (as Kathleen Tobin explains in chapter 15 of this book) Catholics had been demonized during arguments for legalization.

This generation was particularly cognizant of the disparity between the Group's liberal theories versus the reality of their marriages. Charlotte found it interesting that the book begins with the characters maintaining they "want to marry who they want and don't want to be treated as anyone's property" but that once they marry, independence disappears. In a journal assignment analyzing the relationship of Kay and Harald, whose marriage opens the novel, Rebecca pointed out: "At the beginning of the novel when the two are being married, it seemed to me that Kay was a strong-willed, independent woman—and perhaps she was a bit like that—but as the story progresses she becomes more and more helpless and miserable. . . . Soon the reader finds her tip-toeing around Harald, eager to please him and dreadfully afraid of upsetting him."

Through such discussions, the students ultimately concluded that although Mary McCarthy might be considered an early feminist for writing such a daring novel, her characters did not achieve a similar level of self-confidence. Julie felt they showed "small threads of feminism in them. . . . The problem is that they think one thing and do another. When it comes down to it, they seem to feel that they live in a man's world and that they should follow his rules without much question."[5] Nevertheless, McCarthy's characters did represent the seeds of change. Fawn summarized these changes: "I think that these women are the next step up from their mothers and so their daughters will be that much closer to independent women." Heather agreed, writing, "It seems that they all know what they want but they need an extra push to go out and get it. But in the world they live in, this kind of change is hard and takes a long time." Stephanie best expressed her peers' evolving conception of feminism when she wrote that "most of them still had to struggle with the patriarchal control that tried to suppress them."

Analyzing the characters in *The Group* introduced choices still dictated by the Church—premarital sex, birth control, and divorce—while it simultaneously provided the students with a strong base from which to dissect Mary Agnes, the main character in Maureen Howard's *Bridgeport Bus,* and Isabel, the protagonist in Mary Gordon's *Final Payments.* These novels complement each other nicely, for their basic plots are similar: grown women who have devoted their lives to caring for a widowed parent leave home in their thirties to begin experiencing life and discovering who they are. In terms of maturity, they are thirty-year-old teenagers; consequently, the novels revolve around the characters' loss of sexual innocence.

These journeys begin conventionally enough. Mary Agnes (or "Ag," as her mother calls her) moves to New York City, where she finds an apartment and a job and begins a relationship with her co-worker, Stanley. Perhaps because he is the first man she has slept with, she believes she has fallen in love. However, she panics when it's time to meet Stanley's mother and so impulsively has sex with a young artist. After meeting Stan's family and seeing his paintings—both of which reflect the lower-middle-class background she's trying to escape—Ag begins to withdraw from this relationship. After subsequent encounters with the young artist, Ag finds herself pregnant, so she breaks off with Stanley (even though he obviously loves her), moves home, grows increasingly out of touch with reality, kills her mother, and apparently wills herself to die in childbirth.

Isabel's journey begins when her father dies, after which she is given a job by John Ryan, husband of her best friend. She then moves upstate, finds an apartment, begins the job, willingly has sex with Ryan, and continues the affair, reasoning that she can't turn him down because he's her boss and that she deserves this treatment since she initially consented. However, after meeting Hugh, another married man, Isabel begins an affair and falls madly in love, only to break it off after his wife publicly exposes them. At that point Isabel, like Ag, renounces her lover and her new-found life, atones for her sins by becoming the caretaker for a woman she hates, and sinks into depression manifested by deep sleep, cutting off her hair, and compulsive eating. But whereas Mary Agnes descends into madness, Isabel transcends her troubles. *Final Payments* ends with Isabel returning to New York with her friends, vowing to lose weight, and then (and only then) resuming her relationship with Hugh, who has left his wife.

In discussing these novels, my students' evolving feminist consciousness began to factor religion into the equation. Charlotte wrote that Isabel was a stronger character than Mary Agnes because "in the end, she seemed to wake up. She seemed to realize that [in becoming a caretaker] . . . she was wasting her life again. I enjoyed how the author compared Isabel's views on life with the life of Christ [when Isabel states,] 'Christ had died, but it was not death I wanted. It was life, and the body, which had been given to me for my pleasure, and the love of those whom loving was a pleasure.'"[6] To Charlotte, this realization was preferable to Ag's, who declares, "Here I will say to my child, your mother burst forth upon the whole dry world and knew . . . and knew she had triumphed, that it was no great sin to be, at last, alone."[7] Put off by Howard's rendering of Ag's madness (and apparently appalled at the notion of a single lifestyle), no one recognized Ag's closing lines as a strong feminist statement. Rather, Rebecca argued that in Isabel, Mary Gordon had reconciled feminism with Catholicism. "Although Isabel fell away and 'lost her faith,' . . . she still rose in the end to put away those old school Catholic beliefs of sacrifice and suffering on earth. She decided to contribute to society in more useful and productive ways, to work for the government rather than drown in her own sorrow and self pity. She was triumphant in the end, while still holding on to her desire and intent to 'be a good person,' to be a good Christian and do right in the eyes of God." In this, Heather agreed, writing that whereas "Isabel lived with her friend Eleanor until she lost weight and got her life back together again, . . . Mary Agnes just did not have the will power and determination to make her life the best it could be."

For most of the class, "getting one's life together" was equated with losing weight, which would in turn lead to Isabel's getting a job and resuming her relationship with Hugh—a stance that reflects what Naomi Wolf terms the "beauty myth"—the late-twentieth-century, antifeminist belief that physical perfection is essential to happiness and success.[8] But not everyone agreed. Julie argued that Isabel "doesn't seem to be on the right track with John or with Hugh, but eventually she seems to gain perspective on the situation, and realizes that her actions have consequences." For both characters, religion was the problem, not the solution. "Since they're out on their own, they want to do what they want to do and since it was forced for all those years, the first thing they do is rebel against their religion. These authors seem to be sending the same message: If a parent forces religion on his/her child then the result may be that some day their child will withdraw from the religion all together." Ultimately, we decided that one difference between the characters was that Mary Agnes associated religion with her hypocritical mother and rejected it, whereas Isabel's rejection was more an act of "teenage" rebellion that faded as she began to mourn her father and find solace in their shared faith.

These varying opinions led us to reexamine feminism in light of the twenty-first-century's mores. Heather found it difficult to label either character or novel as feminist because for the most part, the women's actions could no longer be considered acts of independence. She and her peers were attending college because they planned to pursue careers; in their eyes, getting jobs and finding apartments, as Isabel and Ag did, were neither feminist nor exceptional. They were merely facts of life. Whelehan's *Modern Feminist Thought* would label such an analysis postfeminist because it undermines and trivializes the women's move-ment.[9] Luckily, I didn't have to make this distinction because Heather's peers were able to move beyond this conception. Julie argued that both novels qualified as feminist because they portrayed "a woman's struggle to fit into a man's world." The fact that Mary Agnes failed did not make *Bridgeport Bus* "any less of a feminist statement." Stephanie agreed, summarizing the problem when she wrote that "both women needed to engage in healthy relationships that would build up their self-esteem in a positive way, meaning not through sex. They both needed to find out who they were and that they were worthy of love, life, and indepen-dence. . . . Isabel eventually came to realize that life is uncertain and that is the beauty of it. She wanted life and loss. In my opinion, she came to realize that it was better to love and to lose than to never have loved at all. I think this shows she was ready to take a stand, accept who she was, and to be an independent individual." Similarly, Mary Agnes "dis-covered who she was, and was therefore able to realize that her rela-tionship with Stanley would not work out because they had nothing in common. She was strong enough to give up a relationship that she knew would not work out. In this way, I think that she also became inde-pendent by the end of the novel."

Mothers, Wives, and Daughters: The Changing Roles of Women in *House of Gold, We Were the Mulvaneys, Charming Billy,* and *One True Thing*

As we moved into the second half of the semester, the readings described female characters within the context of their families. These novels rep-resented a clear departure from those of the nineteenth century, when family life paralleled that described by Mary Jo Marcellus in chapter 16 of this book: led by strong matriarchs, families were idealized as strong, loving, loyal and fiercely religious. Elizabeth Cullinan's (1970) *House of Gold* was the first to turn that notion on its head. As Charles Fanning describes it, "Mrs. Devlin imposes a rule of duty, controls her family by withholding love, and dominates her children into sharing her distorted vision of the world."[10] At first glance, Joyce Carol Oates's *We Were the Mulvaneys,* published almost three decades later, appears to revive the traditional family; however, the reader soon realizes that the Devlins and the Mulvaneys are two sides of the same coin. Whereas Mrs. Devlin is so focused on her children that her husband fades into the background, Corinne Mulvaney disregards her sacred obligation of motherhood in order to "save" her husband from shame and incipient alcoholism. In both cases, the children pay the price of their mother's tunnel vision.

My reading of the book led me to despise Mrs. Devlin, but my students found it difficult to fault her. As they discussed her death, they recalled the passing of their grandparents and the gathering of the family sympathetically. Fawn pointed out that Mrs. Devlin's children "didn't seem to mind the way they were raised [and] four of them took up the religious life." Julie felt Mrs. Devlin had had a hard life and deserved praise for surviving her children's deaths and raising the others; similarly, Rebecca decided the character was "very proud of her children and loved them all, as equally as she knew how, and that she was fiercely proud of her motherhood." Nevertheless, Rebecca cited her "overbearing possessiveness" as a sign that "she was a very dominating woman, despite her loving nature."

Heather also noted these traits but conflated them with feminism: in her eyes, Mrs. Devlin was "very feminist rather than the meek Catholic female," as exemplified by her dominance and her belief that children should never "see your doubts" or "know your feelings."[11] Such comments, coming at mid-semester, reflected Heather's (admittedly) lingering confusion over the definition of feminism. Only Stephanie and Charlotte were initially able to move beyond the Devlin family's facade. Stephanie maintained that Mrs. Devlin was "very possessive of her children and seemed to have control over them even into their adult lives. One of the ways she established this control is through guilt." As a result, the "family life seems to be all surface and no depth." Charlotte, herself a mother, agreed: "She was a fake and she demanded too much from everyone around her. . . . Not only was she a religious fake, she was a bad mother. . . . [A] good loving mother doesn't make her children feel guilty for living and showing their feelings."

Such discussions helped to expand the students' definition of feminism within the context of motherhood; consequently, by the end of the novel, the others had begun to gain insight into Mrs. Devlin's impact on her children. Julie found it odd that none of the characters cried when their mother died. Heather was surprised that there was no talking or reminiscing, and Fawn noted irony in the survivors' self-centeredness and lack of familial concerns. Stephanie summarized the family's problems when she wrote that "one of the main lessons to be learned . . . is that keeping your feelings inside and living your life as if it was a fairy tale will end up destroying your life and the lives around you." Indeed, Julie concluded that the family's problems "always seem to point back to the mother. I think Cullinan sums it up when she writes: 'What she'd done was something considerable—created a myth for them to inhabit, made them legendary characters to themselves. That was the trouble. Inside the legend they had both safety and happiness, but outside of it the two things didn't go together or stay together, anyway.'"[12]

These students' criticism of the mother echoed critiques leveled at Joyce Carol Oates's previous novels, which tend to chastise women for submerging themselves in motherhood,[13] but this was not the case in *We Were the Mulvaneys*. Instead, Corinne Mulvaney, mother of four, casts out her daughter, Marianne, after she is raped so as to spare the feelings of the girl's father, Michael, who has reacted with rage, feelings of impotence, and heavy drinking. Thus, when Michael confesses, "God help me, I can't bear to look at her," Corinne decides to send their daughter away and "save" her husband.[14] These reactions infuriated my students. They were contemptuous of Corinne, disgusted with Michael, and—to my surprise—angry with Marianne for refusing to seek legal action, failing to defend herself to the gossip mongers, and meekly acquiescing to her parents' wishes. But none of those who disliked this character had ever been raped.

These feelings were challenged by one of their classmates who, tragically, had firsthand knowledge. Marianne "seems very lost at this point," she wrote. "I can relate. She has cut off all of her hair, dropped out of school, and is pretty much going nowhere. . . . The shame she feels and the need for compassion and love are so true. I know what it is like being shunned from a small town. Feeling worthless or actually most of the time feeling nothing, just skin and bones as she felt, so have I. Cutting off her hair, dressing rather unusual, are all things that I also did. . . . The way [Oates] tells only bits and pieces because it is the way Marianne remembers things is so realistic. In all actuality it is too realistic for me." In addition to offering insight into Marianne's actions, this student also helped us to understand Marianne's father. Regarding his inability even to look at his daughter, she wrote, "The message that I received is that the victim is so full of shame that the person doesn't see the shame others feel. It did help me understand a few people in my life. I thank the author for this."

These admissions, coupled with subsequent discussions, helped the students gain a better understanding of the issues. Whereas Julie had initially disliked Marianne for being "a wimp," she now felt she had "an awful lot of strength." Although Stephanie agreed that Marianne's response was somewhat weak, she believed the character was also "somewhat strong, because of her deep faith. She still stuck by her faith after the terrible tragedy." Heather, always considering both sides of the issue, agreed that Marianne might appear strong because of her faith; nevertheless, she said, "I would have pictured a feminist standing up for herself a little more than she did. Yes I understand that she wants to just forget it happened, but as a feminist, don't you think that you would want to stop that guy from harming another girl?" Such questions, despite Heather's claims of confusion, suggested a burgeoning consciousness of the political ramifications of feminism. So did her comment that although she initially considered Corinne a feminist because she "seemed to be more opinionated and sticking up for herself and others," the character's preference for her husband over her daughter revealed her weakness. Similarly, Julie noted that Corinne did not "seem to have any confidence in herself as a woman," and Stephanie similarly wrote that Corinne "depends too much on her husband for a sense of identification. . . . She is too afraid of upsetting her husband and driving him away." Equally important was Julie's recognition that Oates was definitely spotlighting a major feminist issue: "the double standard between men and women when issues concerning things like rape are considered. It shows how men get a pat on the back . . . and women get a slap in the face."[15]

This novel proved to be a watershed in the students' acceptance and internalization of feminism. When I distributed a description of women's studies courses offered the next semester, everyone jotted down course numbers that interested them. When we discussed possible research topics, Heather told us she planned to explore "feminism and the Church," and Charlotte excitedly announced that these discussions had convinced her to change her major from accounting to English. Most important, as we closed our discussion of Oates's work, the student who had been raped said this novel had been instrumental in helping her to face and resolve many of the issues she had struggled with in the three years since it occurred.

Just when they thought they had begun to understand feminism, the students had to reexamine it in light of the behavior of the women in Alice McDermott's *Charming Billy* and Anna Quindlen's *One True Thing*. McDermott's Maeve, who remains married and faithful to her husband Billy as he descends into alcoholism, provides a foil for Quindlen's Kate, a Martha Stewart type who happily and apparently blithely provides the perfect home for her unappreciative children and philandering husband. When they began reading *Charming Billy*, the students could find little to respect in Maeve. "[S]he never worried about herself, but instead she dedicated her life to taking care of her husband," wrote Stephanie. "[S]he has always been passive in her life. She does not seem to be an independent individual." Rebecca lamented Maeve's labors in hunting down Billy and dragging him to bed rather than letting him sleep on the floor and termed her an enabler, while Charlotte called her codependent. Even after Billy dies, some questioned Maeve's eventual remarriage, suggesting that a real feminist would not want to become "entrapped" again.

Although I disagreed with the latter opinion, I too had found Maeve uncomfortably passive; nevertheless, she had remained faithful to her husband and carried on her life. Could this behavior, clearly sanctioned by the Church, be construed as feminist? Could there be a Catholic version of feminism? After introducing this notion into our discussions, the students' opinions began to shift. They noted that after Billy's death, Maeve held a job and lived alone, which suggested "that she could stand on her own after all." Julie said that for her, "feminism is a woman sticking up for herself and her beliefs no matter what the circumstances. While Maeve's choices aren't the way that I would have gone . . . it's possible to say that Maeve wants it this way. She's taken care of her father when he was drunk and dying [so maybe] she thinks it's the right thing to do based on how she was raised."

This discussion helped pave the way for the students' understanding of Quindlen's Kate Gulden, who is dying of cancer. Whereas I (like her daughter Ellen) had initially perceived Kate as a mindless housewife, my students immediately believed in her strength, not only because she is for the most part stoic and uncomplaining but also because she had lived her life purposefully, as she wanted. Granted, she had never worked outside the home and had devoted herself to making it a perfect haven; however, the students regarded this as a vocation, as her own career. "How ironic," wrote Rebecca, "that of all the mothers from our novels, Kate would be both the most domestic and the most feminist."

Kate Gulden is easy to understand because the growing relationship between her and Ellen, her daughter, provides the book's focus. Ellen is clearly the most feminist of all the characters we had encountered—independent, outspoken, goal oriented, and angry at being guilted into caring for her mother—so I wondered if the students would dislike her. But to my surprise, they immediately related to her. In this character, they perceived that feminism could be multifaceted, that it encompassed not only career and independence but also a strong voice and a capacity for love. In this character, they saw themselves—and thus the inequity of Ellen's position. For Stephanie, this was best illustrated when Ellen angrily tells her unsupportive boyfriend, "Whenever one of you guys says people deal with bad stuff in their own way, it means you don't deal with it at all. You just wait for it to go away. You don't help. You don't listen. You don't call. You don't write. WE deal with it in our own way. WE deal with it. We girls. We make the meals and clean up the messes and take the crap and listen to you talk about how you're dealing with it in your own way. What way? No way!"[16] For Heather, it was dramatized when Ellen's father refuses to call on his sons to help with their mother's care. "What about the brothers?" she asked. "Why can't they help out? It is just the girl's job?" For Rebecca, it was the father's selfishness: "I know he is suffering inside over her dying, but yet again, it isn't about *her*. It's still about him*self*: . . . His main concern is not in her dying but in how her death will affect *him*." And more than one cited Kate's admonition to Ellen—"It's a mistake to base your life on one man's approval"[17]—as the key to Ellen's problems.

This latter statement suggests the distance these students had traveled since midterm, when they praised the vow of Mary Gordon's

Isabel to lose weight before reuniting with Hugh. By the end of the semester, the students had developed a working definition of feminism that allowed for some expansion beyond the traditional stereotypes. They now had a broader view, best summarized by Heather: "I've realized that hairy armpits are not the one true sign of a feminist. There are different orders of feminists as there are with any other group of people. It's a broader category because I can see even some males as feminists." Could these beliefs be reconciled with the teachings of the Church? Again, all agreed. According to Rebecca, "Just because I'm Catholic doesn't mean I can't be pro-choice and use birth control. These issues are so far from what it means to be a good Catholic—philanthropy, following Christ, prayer, tolerance and acceptance, to name just a small part." Julie concurred, writing, "The main focus of the Catholic religion is a strong belief in God and good morals. Of course, they have differing opinions on some things, but who doesn't? It's all in the interpretation of the two and I feel that I am both [feminist and Catholic] after all we've done this semester."

Reconciling Feminism and Catholicism

Over the course of a single semester, my undergraduate honors students moved beyond stereotypes to an understanding that feminism, like Catholicism, is not a monolithic structure. Through our readings and discussions, they began to perceive that beneath the rubric of feminism, numerous factions, theories, and theorists exist within a system that tends to sway with, if not reflect, sociocultural, economic, and political trends. In this, their views came to parallel those of Whelehan, who argues that "the strength of modern feminist thought is its interdisciplinarity, its resistance to easy categorization."[18] Yet for those unfamiliar with feminism, categorization comes easily. The first wave, which culminated in women's enfranchisement, is generally overlooked. The second wave of feminism, which emerged in the late 1960s when women realized that voting rights did not ensure equality, led to a wide range of feminist activism designed to challenge traditional conceptions of femininity and reinterpret the status quo. Unfortunately, those activities were crystallized by the media into images of man-hating bra-burners.[19]

Second-wave feminism is more accurately represented by the phrase "The personal is political."[20] The truth of this statement can best be demonstrated not by tracing the history of feminist theory but by re-examining the stories and understandings expressed by the women in this chapter—and throughout this volume. Remembering these stories, and those who told them, is essential if we are to resist the temptation to revert to stereotypes or, conversely, to dismiss feminism as passé.

If we agree that "the personal is political," then it follows that this slogan has broader applications. As the essays in the collection reveal, the human stories—of young girls' lives stunted in the convent; recollections of feisty, independent nuns; telling one's parents of a failed marriage; love overpowering the vows of celibacy; weekly fainting spells in fear of confession—convey political messages about the Church. The fact that they are narratives in no way lessens their import. In her discussion of Irish American women writers, Maureen Howard reminds us, "It is in the telling of our stories that we reveal how bound we are to rituals of family life, yet how we strain against them."[21] The same could be said of the essays in this volume: in the telling of their stories, these writers have revealed how bound they are to rituals of the Church and how they have strained against them. Those writers who reconciled feminism with their Catholic beliefs were able to do so because they chose to focus on what the Church meant to them personally rather than rejecting the institution as a whole. Those who could not felt no choice but to leave the Church because its rulings were too personal to overlook.

My point is this: neither feminism nor Catholicism is a perfect entity. Although one was designed by women and the other by men, both bear traces of the times in which they were conceived. Precisely because of their origins and beliefs, both continue to evolve. Given its relative youth and smaller scope, feminism's changes will be considerably less glacial than those of the Church. But change is both imminent and unavoidable in the Church; indeed, as McMillin demonstrates, change is imperative if the Church hopes to continue its mission through the clergy.

So I close this volume by coming full circle. Just recently, I learned that the sacrament of confession that so attracted me to the Church has been renamed the sacrament of reconciliation. Perhaps the reconciliation

278 | SALLY BARR EBEST

of feminism and Catholicism may be achieved if both sides can move beyond the political arguments and embrace the personal—the people—for they represent the future.

NOTES

1. All of the quotations and comments attributed to my students were taken from their daily response journals. The students granted me written permission to use their given names when quoting and paraphrasing their comments. They also read drafts of this essay and provided valuable feedback. I thank them for their insights and their honesty.

2. Imelda Whelehan, *Modern Feminist Thought: From the Second Wave to "Post-Feminism"* (New York: NYU Press, 1992), 42.

3. Mary McCarthy, *The Group* (San Diego, Calif.: Harcourt Brace, 1963), 165.

4. Ibid., 75.

5. As Carol Brightman's biography, *Writing Dangerously: Mary McCarthy and Her World* (San Diego, Calif.: Harcourt Brace, 1992) illustrates, this stance reflects McCarthy's own actions and beliefs.

6. Mary Gordon, *Final Payments* (New York: Ballantine Books, 1978), 303–4.

7. Maureen Howard, *Bridgeport Bus* (New York: Penguin Books, 1961), 309.

8. Naomi Wolf, *The Beauty Myth* (London: Chatto and Windus, 1990).

9. Whelehan, *Modern Feminist Thought,* 43.

10. Charles Fanning, "These Traits Endure," in *The Irish Voice in America* (Lexington: University of Kentucky Press, 1990), 335.

11. Elizabeth Cullinan, *House of Gold* (Boston: Houghton Mifflin, 1970), 108.

12. Ibid., 293.

13. See, e.g., Mary Lou Morrison Parrot, *"Subversive Conformity: Feminism and Motherhood in Joyce Carol Oates"* (Ph.D. diss., University of Michigan, 1984).

14. Joyce Carol Oates, *We Were the Mulvaneys* (New York: Penguin Putnam, 1996), 185.

15. This stance echoes the arguments expressed by Marilyn French in *The War against Women* (London: Hamish Hamilton, 1992).

16. Anna Quindlen, *One True Thing* (New York: Dell, 1994), 122.

17. Ibid., 59.

18. Whelehan, *Modern Feminist Thought*, 3.

19. Whelehan details this history—as well as the fact that no bras were ever burned—quite convincingly.

20. Whelehan, *Modern Feminist Thought*, 13.

21. Maureen Howard, introduction to *Cabbage and Bones*, ed. Caledonia Kearns (New York: Henry Holt, 1997), xii.

CONTRIBUTORS

FLAVIA ALAYA was the "wife" of New York diocesan priest and historian Henry J. (Harry) Browne from 1958 until his death in 1980 and is the mother of their three children. Her memoir, *Under the Rose: A Confession* (Feminist Press, 1999), is fruit of a long struggle to express the power of this life-defining relationship. A writer and teaching scholar, founder in 1971 of Ramapo College's pioneering School of Intercultural Studies, she remains professor emerita there and continues her lifelong activism in urban historic preservation and community development from her home in Paterson, New Jersey.

MADELEINE BLAIS is a Pulitzer Prize–winning journalist and Full Professor at the University of Massachusetts. She is the author of *The Heart Is an Instrument: Portraits in Journalism, In These Girls, Hope Is a Muscle* (a finalist for the National Book Critics Circle Award in nonfiction), and the memoir *Uphill Walkers.*

HENRIK BORGSTROM is Assistant Professor of French in the Department of Modern and Classical Languages at Niagara University. He received his doctorate with a specialization in modern French theater from the University of Wisconsin–Madison in 1998. He has authored articles on a range of topics in francophone drama and performance studies.

THERESA DELGADILLO is an Assistant Professor of Women's Studies/Chicana Studies at the University of Arizona. She received her Ph.D. in English from the University of California, Los Angeles. She has previously published on both Chicana/o and Native American literature and is currently working on a manuscript on hybrid spiritualities in Chicana/o literature, film, and drama.

SALLY BARR EBEST is an Associate Professor of English at the University of Missouri–St. Louis, where she teaches courses in contemporary American writers, Irish American women writers, composition and feminist theory, and pedagogy for the English Department and the Institute for Women's and Gender Studies. Her publications include *Writing from A to Z* and *Writing With: Collaborative Teaching, Learning, and Research*.

RON EBEST is a journalist and writer who has authored several articles on Irish American and Jewish American literature. He is currently at work on a literary/social history of Irish America between 1900 and 1935.

SANDRA M. GILBERT is a Professor of English at the University of California, Davis. Her works include six collections of poetry, two anthologies, a memoir, and a critical study of the poems of D. H. Lawrence. With Susan Gubar, she has coauthored *The Madwoman in the Attic: The Woman Writer and the 19th-Century Literary Imagination* and *No Man's Land: The Place of the Woman Writer in the 20th Century*. At present, she is working on a book tentatively titled *Death's Door: Mourning, Modernity, and the Poetics of Memory*.

KATHLEEN M. JOYCE is an Assistant Professor in the Department of Religion at Duke University. She received her M.A. (1992) and Ph.D. (1995) in religion from Princeton University, and an M.Div. (1990) degree from Princeton Theological Seminary. Her current research focuses on the moral issues raised by prenatal genetic testing.

JANET KALVEN is a feminist educator, author, and activist with a long-term commitment to the empowerment of women. Since 1942 she has worked in the Grail movement, helping to establish Grailville in Loveland, Ohio, as a center of alternative education for women. She is contributor to a number of books, including *Your Daughters Shall Prophesy: Feminist Alternatives in Theological Education; Women's Spirit Bonding;* and *With Both Eyes Open: Seeing beyond Gender.* Her most recent book (SUNY Press, 1999) is *Women Breaking Boundaries: A Grail Journey, 1940–1995,* an insider's story of fast women in a slow church, pioneering on many fronts, from feminist spirituality to sustainable lifestyles on threatened Planet Earth.

MARY KENNY is an Irish-born writer and journalist, well established on both sides of the Irish Sea, publishing in the media in both Dublin and London. She is an experienced columnist and commentator on a range of social issues, from the history of feminism and the family to Catholicism and Ireland. She has published in over twenty Irish and British newspapers and magazines and has authored five books, the most recent being *Goodbye to Catholic Ireland,* a social history of Ireland from the 1890s to 2000. She is married to the writer Richard West, and they have two sons in their twenties. She lives both in London and Dublin.

VICTORIA KILL holds a Ph.D. in English from the University of Washington. She teaches English and women's studies at Seattle University, is a peace activist with Women's International League for Peace and Freedom, and works in solidarity with Cuban women to end the United States's blockade of Cuba. Her research and writing interests include ethnographic narratives, global feminisms, and diversity literacy.

NILSA LASSO-VON LANG was born in Panama, Republic of Panama. She became an American citizen in 1992. She studied international relations for three years at the University of Panama and received her B.A. and M.A. in Spanish from the University of Northern Iowa. From 1994 to 1998, she attended the University of Arizona, where she earned a Ph.D. in Spanish American literature. Currently, she is an Assistant Professor of Spanish at Southwest Missouri State University.

LORRAINE LISCIO has taught in the English Department at Boston College, where she also directed women's studies. Her most recent writing projects are on Paris and on medieval manuscript illumination.

JEAN McGARRY is the author of five books of fiction, *Airs of Providence, The Very Rich Hours, The Courage of Girls, Home at Last, Gallagher's Travels,* and *Dream Date.* She has published stories in *Yale Review,* the *New Yorker, Southern Review, Boulevard, North American Review,* and other journals. McGarry is professor and chair of the Writing Seminars at Johns Hopkins University.

LINDA A. McMILLIN is an Associate Professor and Head of the History Department at Susquehanna University. She is a medieval historian and author of a number of studies on religious women in twelfth- and thirteenth-century Barcelona. She is currently coediting a collection of essays on the tenth-century canoness and playwright Hrotsvit of Gandersheim.

NANCY MAIRS, Ph.D., is a Research Associate with the Southwest Institute for Research on Women and also serves on the boards of the Arizona Center for Disability Law and the Amazon Foundation. A poet, essayist, and memoirist, she has won a National Endowment for the Arts Fellowship and the Western States Book Award in Poetry. Among her various works are a book of poetry, *In All the Rooms of the Yellow House;* a memoir, *Remembering the Bone House;* a spiritual autobiography, *Ordinary Time: Cycles in Marriage, Faith, and Renewal;* and several collections of essays. Her current project, *Life's Worth: Rethinking How We Live and Die,* is supported by a fellowship from the Project on Death in America of the Soros Foundation's Open Society Institute.

MARY JO T. MARCELLUS is a native of Rochester, New York. She received her B.A. from John Carroll University in Cleveland, Ohio, and her M.A. from Kansas State University in Manhattan, Kansas. Ms. Marcellus is currently teaching English at Solon High School in Solon, Ohio. She has received awards for both creative writing and teaching and is currently at work on a novel.

JEAN MOLESKY-POZ, Ph.D., is Assistant Professor of Latin American and Theology/Religious Studies at the University of San Francisco. She received her doctoral degree from the Graduate Theological Union, Berkeley, researching the public emergence of Maya spirituality in the Guatemalan highlands.

JEANNE NOONAN-ECKHOLDT currently resides in New York City, where she works in publishing.

BRAD PETERS is Associate Professor and Coordinator of the Writing-across-the-Curriculum Program at Northern Illinois University. He teaches rhetorical theory and writing. He publishes on critical pedagogy, feminist methodologies, and issues of teacher training. He also writes about the rhetoric of medieval mysticism.

ROSEMARY RADFORD RUETHER was the Georgia Harkness Professor of Applied Theology at Garrett-Evangelical Theological Seminary in Evanston, Illinois, from 1976 to 2002. She is currently the Carpenter Professor of Feminist Theology at the Graduate Theological Union in Berkeley, California. She is author or editor of thirty-five books and numerous articles on feminist theology and social justice issues in the Church and society.

KATHLEEN A. TOBIN received her Ph.D. in history from the University of Chicago. Her article on Chicago Catholics as outsiders in the birth control issue was published by the *U.S. Catholic Historian* in the spring of 1997, and McFarland released her book on religion and the birth control debate, 1907–1937, in the autumn of 2001. She continues to do research on church/state and population issues.

JANE ZENI is Professor of English Education at the University of Missouri–St. Louis, where she works with preservice and inservice teachers. Previously, she taught diverse K–12 students in Philadelphia and in northern New Mexico. Her books and articles have focused on computers and writing and on culturally sensitive teaching. In 2001, she edited *Ethical Issues in Practitioner Research* (Teachers College Press).

INDEX